ON THIS DAY

ON THIS DAY

LANDMARKS OF OUR TIME

Sandra Kimberley Hall

NEW
HOLLAND

Dedicated to my parents Owen and Raie Kimberley
for raising me on a diet of curiosity, history, travel, humour…and memories.

First published in Australia in 2005 by
New Holland Publishers (Australia) Pty Ltd
Sydney • Auckland • London • Cape Town

14 Aquatic Drive Frenchs Forest NSW 2086 Australia
218 Lake Road Northcote Auckland New Zealand
86 Edgware Road London W2 2EA United Kingdom
80 McKenzie Street Cape Town 8001 South Africa

10 9 8 7 6 5 4 3 2 1

National Library of Australia Cataloguing-in-Publication Data:

Hall, Sandra K.
On this day: moments in time

Includes index.
ISBN 1 74110 295 2.

1. Chronology, Historical. I. Title.

909

Publisher: Fiona Schultz
Project Editor: Michael McGrath
Designer: Karl Roper
Picture Researcher: Michael McGrath, Getty Images
Printer: C&C Offset Printing Company, China

INTRODUCTION

What is a day? What is time? I can recall as a small child singing the hymn with the line, 'time (is) like a never-ending stream'. I was captivated to know that the days of my golden, apparently never-ending, youth would become part of a stream, which would become part of the larger river that we call history.

In *On This Day*, I have devoted a page to each day of the year, from January 1 to December 31. The subjects for the short articles and timeline events on each page were chosen for their interest, their power to inspire, or to show the quirky side of humanity.

Some people I have written about may be well-known to you, others may be strangers. I have tried to achieve a balance between the living and the dead, the young and the old, men and women, and to explore many ethnicities and nationalities.

In researching *On This Day*, I was fascinated how some days seem more monumental than others. Just as amber apparently randomly captures some insects, and not others, so too does history remember some people and events and forgets others. Why do people in certain professions, such as scientists, actors or artists, often share the same birth date, decades or centuries apart? What are the odds that a person like William Shakespeare would die on his birthday? What are the odds that two framers of the American Declaration of Independence, John Adams and Thomas Jefferson would die not only on the same day, but on the very day that honours that Declaration, July 4?

I hope that as you browse through *On This Day* looking for the special days that have meaning for you personally, the day you were born, the day you fell in love the day you married, the day you won a prize, those days that are the fibre of the tapestry of your life, that you will be fascinated by who else and what else shares it with you. I also hope that for those other days which do not have such personal meaning, you will discover events and profiles that rekindle some sparks in the far-reaches of your memory, and a sense of what we fellow travellers all have in common: time.

JANUARY 1

1 JANUARY

2000: Y2K

For centuries New Year's Day, the first day of the Western calendar, has been celebrated with rituals ranging from eating special foods such as black-eyed peas or sashimi, to sweeping the house, making resolutions or going to church.

Not just the start of a new year, a new decade, a new century, this New Year was the start of a new millennium. From tiny pinpricks on the map to villages, towns and the world's greatest cities—no matter where you lived—a huge proportion of the world's population turned out to party. They helped set a record for the biggest party in the planet's history. The record will probably not be broken for another thousand years.

The planet was the stage as the drama unfolded. Time, the leading character, took centre stage. For once nothing else mattered but time. The party-goers—the audience—wore attire according to their location. In the Northern Hemisphere, people partied in layers of snug winter clothes. In the Southern Hemisphere, swimsuits and one layer were adequate.

On New Year's Eve, sunlight faded into night, first on the tiny Chatham Islands, 800 km east of New Zealand, population 750, with one pub and countless representatives of the world's media. The new millennium was officially proclaimed from Chatham Islands. Soon the New Year was greeted in New Zealand, then Australia. In Sydney, fireworks mesmerised party-goers. Water-borne fire sculptures floated on the Harbour and bungee jumpers performed a choreographed dance on the Opera House sails. In Paris, pyrotechnics lit up the Eiffel Tower. In Gaza, Egypt, the Pyramids were lit by a thousand giant candles, lasers and searchlights.

Millions of people partied in the streets with their arms around loved ones or strangers, singing and dancing; and billions more watched the 24-hour party highlights on television. In the words of the prophetic Canadian sage Marshall McLuhan, we were truly a 'global village'.

Australians welcome in the new millenium with a massive fireworks display on Sydney Harbour.

1449 Lorenzo de Medici, aka 'The Magnificent' was born. The enlightened Renaissance statesman of Florence, Italy was patron to artists such as Michelangelo.

1484 Ulrich Zwingli, the influential Swiss theologian and reformer, was born at St Gall, Switzerland. He was ordained a Catholic, but converted to Protestantism.

1785 *The Daily Universal Register,* a broadsheet newspaper, was launched in London. In 1788 it became *The Times.* Now a Murdoch-owned tabloid, it has wielded enormous influence in world history.

1892 Fifteen-year-old Annie Moore, from Ireland, was the first of the more than 12 million destitute immigrants who passed through the Ellis Island Immigration Station in New Jersey, in search of hope and a new life in America.

1905 The first train on the Trans-Siberian Railway, begun by Tsar Alexander III in 1886, set off on its 9000 km maiden journey. The world's longest continuous railroad, it links the Pacific Ocean port of Vladivostok with Moscow in European Russia.

2 JANUARY

1904: Sally Rand

Sally Rand, the ostrich-plumed exotic dancer who became an enduring cult figure, was born on this day. She resented being called a fan dancer or a striptease artist. People still debate whether she wore a flesh-coloured outfit or her birthday suit.

1920: Isaac Asimov

The Russian–American author and biochemist was born. An extraordinarily prolific writer, he wrote or edited over 500 books. He often worked on several books simultaneously. Asimov, who died in 1992, wrote at least one book in every category of the Dewey Decimal System, except philosophy! Besides non-fiction, he published science fiction, fantasy, children's books and 'naughty limericks'. He was afraid to fly and only ever did so twice. Asimov once said, 'If my doctor told me I had only six minutes to live, I wouldn't brood. I'd type a little faster.' Asimov's *Foundation Series* and *I Robot* are regarded as masterpieces of science fiction.

1969: Rupert Murdoch

The proprietor of News Limited, Murdoch outbid rivals to buy the British *News of the World* newspaper group. The Australian media magnate now had a foot in the door with this Fleet Street, London purchase. Later he became the owner of major US media holdings, including *Fox Television*.

1993: Bosnia

Two events happened on this day in the Bosnian Civil War. In 1993, at the Dayton, Ohio peace talks, the three leaders of the warring Muslim, Croat and Serbian factions reached an agreement and signed off on the Dayton Accords. However, it took another four years for the situation to be stabilised. In 1996, American peacekeepers arrived to enforce the Accords and to ensure the end of the 'ethnic cleansing'. It was the first time the US military had been deployed in Europe since the World War II.

1870 Brooklyn Bridge: Construction of New York's graceful landmark began. It was completed in 1883.

1929 The USA and Canada met to discuss how best to preserve the beautiful Niagara Falls, which makes a border between them.

1936 Don Bradman, the Australian cricketer, scored 357 in a South Australia vs Victoria match in 424 minutes. It included 40 fours.

1971 Glasgow's Ibrox Stadium. Sixty-six soccer fans were killed and 200 were injured while leaving a game, when a barrier on a stairway gave way.

2005 Cyril Fletcher, the British comedian, died aged 91. He was most famous for his *Odd Odes*, on television's *That's Life*.

Sally Rand: the ostrich-plumed exotic dancer.

3 JANUARY

1882: Oscar Wilde

The witty Irish writer and dramatist Oscar Wilde told US Customs on his arrival for a lecture tour, 'I have nothing to declare but my genius.' He also wrote, 'Prayer must never be answered: if it is, it ceases to be prayer and becomes correspondence.' He loved being the centre of attention and dressed as a dandy. Wilde was imprisoned for two years for homosexuality at the height of his fame and wrote *A Ballad of Reading Gaol*. He also wrote *The Importance of Being Earnest*. He died in exile in Paris at the age of 46 in 1900.

1920: Babe Ruth

The fabled 'Curse of the Bambino' began when Herman 'Babe' or 'Bambino' Ruth was traded by the Boston Red Sox baseball team to their arch rivals, the New York Yankees. The Sox had won five World Series before the trade, including three with Babe, who played in more than 100 games, broke major league records and thrilled Sox fans. To everyone's shock and dismay the Sox's owner, Harry Frazee, sold Babe to the Yankees, using the money to underwrite his Broadway plays. Two generations of Bostonians wondered if their team would ever defeat the 'Damned Yankees'. After 84 years, on 27 October 2004, the curse was exorcised when the Sox won the World Series.

1969: Michael Schumacher

The Formula One driver was born in 1969 in Germany. He rakes in $100 million a year, making him the world's highest paid athlete. He is a seven-time world champion racing car driver. Formula One is one of Europe's most popular spectator sports.

106BC Cicero was born in Rome. He was a philosopher, orator and statesman. He wrote, 'Peace is liberty in tranquility' and 'Virtue is its own reward'.

1521 Martin Luther. The Roman Catholic Church excommunicated Martin Luther for his criticisms.

1939 Robert 'Bobby' Hull, an ice Hockey Hall of Fame left wing, was born at Pointe Anne, Ontario, Canada.

1969 John Lennon. New Jersey authorities confiscated 30 000 copies of John Lennon and Yoko Ono's album *Two Virgins*, after deciding it was 'pornographic', because the couple posed naked for the cover.

1980 Joy Adamson. A disgruntled employee murdered Joy Adamson in Kenya. Joy wrote the bestseller *Born Free* about Elsa, an orphaned lion cub she raised and returned to the wild. Through the book and movie of the same name, she started the preservation movement in Africa.

Oscar Wilde: 'I have nothing to declare, but my genius.'

4 JANUARY

1643: Sir Isaac Newton

One of the world's greatest scientific geniuses, Isaac Newton, was born in England (Gregorian calendar). By the age of 25, he had formulated his Three Laws of Motion, his theory of gravitation, invented calculus and discovered the spectrum of light. During his long life (he died at 84), he changed the way people understood the universe and Earth, moving from religious explanations to physical laws.

1809: Braille

Louis Braille, who liberated blind people by inventing a way to read and write by touch, was born. Blinded at the age of three, he developed his Braille system when he was a teenager. Each letter of the alphabet is made up of six dots—two across and three down—and can be felt by a fingertip. It is used internationally.

1960: Albert Camus

The Algerian Nobel laureate for literature and author of *L'Etranger* and *La Peste* (*The Stranger* and *the Plague*) died in a car crash at 46. He wrote, 'There is no need to wait around for the Last Judgment; it happens every day', and 'Don't believe your friends when they ask you to be honest with them. All they really want is to have their good opinion of themselves confirmed.'

1967: Donald Campbell

Seven-time world record holder Donald Campbell was killed instantly when his boat, *Bluebird K7*, disintegrated on Coniston Water, Cumbria, England. He was well above his 1964 record speed of 444.61 km/h when the accident occurred. This record stood for 14 years until Australia's Ken Warby broke it. Campbell's body and the wreckage were recovered 34 years later. He is the only person to hold both land and water speed records simultaneously.

Julia Ormand playing opposite Harrison Ford in *Sabrina*.

1936 *Billboard* **magazine,** founded in 1894, published its first music hit parade. It originally started tracking carnival music.
1951 Seoul, South Korea fell to the Communist North in the Korean War, a crushing defeat for America.
1961 Erwin Schrödinger, the Austrian physicist, who received the Nobel Prize for wave theory, died. As a young man he was prepared to give up physics for the woman he loved, but she turned him down. He lived out the Nazi regime in Oxford and Dublin. It enraged the Nazis that a non-Jewish, well-known German scientist would choose voluntary exile.
1965 Actress Julia Ormond was born in Surrey, England. She starred in *Legends of the Fall* and *Sabrina*.

5 JANUARY

1893: Paramhansa Yogananda

The first Indian spiritual leader and yoga master to permanently live and teach in the West was born. His own guru sent him to the USA to counter American materialism. Yogananda's *Autobiography of a Yogi* launched a spiritual revolution in 1946, with its nonsectarian and universal message. He wrote, 'The true basis of religion is not belief, but intuitive experience. Intuition is the soul's power of knowing God.' Hundreds of thousands of people attended his lectures. He was in constant demand to deliver his teachings until his death in 1952.

1931: Alvin Ailey

The African–American dancer and founder of the American Dance Theatre was born. He said, 'I always wanted to create an integrated dance company … to celebrate differences in people. I don't want all the same bodies … or all the same colour, in my company. I want my dancers to feel that they are not just black dancers. They are part of society.' He choreographed 79 modern dance ballets.

1943: George Washington Carver

He was not sure of the date he was born, as a slave, but Carver was probably 80 when he died on this day. He took his owner's last name and was freed after the US Civil War, became college educated and went on to be a distinguished agricultural botanist. His work helped revolutionise the economy of the Southern states. Carver taught crop rotation and disease prevention in farming. He developed more than 300 by-products from soybeans, peanuts and sweet potatoes and is internationally acclaimed.

1932 Umberto Eco, novelist and philosopher was born in Alessandro, Italy. He wrote *In the Name of the Rose* and *Foucault's Pendulum*, which has been dubbed 'the thinking man's *The Da Vinci Code'*.

1933 San Francisco's Golden Gate Bridge. Construction began across the deep channel of San Francisco Bay from the Marin County side.

1964 Embrace of Peace. Eastern Orthodox Church leader, Patriarch Athenagoras 1 and Roman Catholic Church leader Pope Paul VI met to talk about the Schism between their churches. It was the first time their church leaders had met in 500 years.

1969 Marilyn Manson the singer was born. His birth name was Brian Hugh Warner. He took his name from Marilyn Monroe and Charles Manson.

2004 Merrill Chase died aged 98. He was an immunologist who discovered in the 1940s how human T-cells and B-cells aided antibodies in protecting the body against disease.

The Golden Gate Bridge captured America's and the world's imagination.

1883: Kahlil Gibran

The Lebanese–American poet and artist was born. *The Prophet* is the best known of his works, with its timeless wisdom and mysticism. Portions are often read at weddings and baptisms. He wrote about marriage: 'But let there be spaces in your togetherness and let the winds of the heavens dance between you.' His life was marred by sadness; he lost his beloved to an abusive man to whom she had been promised as a child.

1884: Gregor Mendel

The father of modern genetics died, aged 62, in Austria. He has been described as a 'roly-poly twinkle eyed' monk who failed to advance in his teaching career because he 'lacked insight'. Mendel crossbred generations of a common variety of garden pea, recording how different traits would appear, disappear and reappear for generations. He was able to make accurate predictions to prove his theories. His work met with little interest when it was published.

1930: Donald Bradman

Known wherever cricket is played, 'The Don' was the greatest cricketer ever. On this day the self-taught cricketer, aged 20, scored a record 452-not-out for NSW against Queensland at the Sydney Cricket Ground. In 1930 on his first English tour, he scored 309-not-out in a single day at Leeds. His cricket career is legendary; an average of 99.94, a century in every third innings, the most double centuries and two triple centuries. He retired in 1949 and died in 2001, aged 92. A little known fact is that the Australian Broadcasting Commission, the ABC, uses The Don's score 9994 (without the decimal) as its post office box number in all major Australian cities.

Rowan Atkinson: the man behind Mr Bean.

1854 The 'birthday' of Detective Sherlock Holmes, the fictional character created by Sir Arthur Conan Doyle.

1907 Maria Montessori, the first Italian female medical school graduate, opened her first Montessori School in Rome. Her system is based on self-motivation.

1954 Anthony Minghella, director and writer, was born on the Isle of Wight, England. He wrote *The English Patient* and *The Talented Mr. Ripley.*

1955 Rowan Atkinson, the English comedian known as 'Mr Bean' and 'the Black Adder', was born in Newcastle-upon-Tyne.

2001 Al Gore, Jr., as President of the US Senate, tallied the Electoral College votes and certified George W. Bush as the US President, his opponent in the 2000 Presidential Election. It is known as the 'Stolen Election'.

7 JANUARY

1785: Dover to Calais by Balloon

The first successful balloon flight across the English Channel took place on this day. Aboard were Frenchman Jean-Pierre Francois Blanchard and American John Jeffries. When they nearly ditched they threw out all their equipment. Legend has it they even threw out their trousers.

1931: Sydney to New Zealand

Southern Cross Junior, a single-engine bi-plane piloted by 22-year-old Guy Menzies took off. His relatives thought he was attempting the Sydney–Melbourne–Perth flying record. His goal, however, was New Zealand, which only a three-engine plane had flown to from Sydney. Twelve hours and 12 minutes after takeoff, after flying very low to the water, Menzies arrived at Okarito on the South Island. He saw two gold prospectors and circled them. He dropped a message to them inside an egg sandwich, flew further south and startled a local by yelling at him that he wanted to land. Menzies was told to try Fox Glacier, but missed it. He landed in a swamp, upside down, but unhurt. The locals took Menzies from pub to pub to celebrate. He said, 'It's all been damned nice.' After three days of drinking, he repaired the plane and flew to Christchurch. His record stood for five years.

1976: The Third Cod War

UK and Iceland battled over fishing rights in the North Atlantic Ocean. The first skirmish took place in 1958 and the second in 1972–3. At its worst, guns were fired across ships' bows and ships were rammed. The UK deployed 22 vessels to protect British trawlers against Iceland's 16 vessels. An agreement was mediated in June 1976, enforcing a 321.8-km fishing zone.

The Harlem Globetrotters: entertaining basketball troupe who travel the world to promote their game.

1558 The French took Calais, the last English possession on the Continent.

1927 Transatlantic commercial telephone service began between New York and London.

1927 The Harlem Globetrotters, a dazzling performing road troupe of basketball players who helped popularise basketball, played their first game in Hinckley, Illinois.

1989 Japanese Emperor Hirohito died. He had ruled for 62 years.

2004 Oswald Garrison Villard Jr, the inventor of over-the-horizon radar, died. The radar bounced off an electrically charged layer in the upper stratosphere.

8 JANUARY

1885: John Curtin

Australia's wartime prime minister was born in Victoria. He took office as the Labor leader two weeks before the Japanese attack on Pearl Harbor. He stood up to Winston Churchill and worked closely with US Gen. Douglas MacArthur to prevent a Japanese invasion. The job stress and working with the two Allied leaders to protect Australia caused a heart attack. Curtin died at age 60, six weeks before the end of the War. His legacy is monumental. Australia changed its perspective from being a British offshoot, to having a more independent and international outlook.

1942: Stephen Hawking

The English physicist, who is frequently compared to Einstein, was born. Hawking studied mathematics, astronomy, physics and cosmology and holds a prestigious Chair at Cambridge University. He was diagnosed with amyotrophic lateral sclerosis (ALS or Lou Gehrig's disease) in 1962 and told he had two months to live. He depends on machines and constant care to stay alive. He is the most famous physicist to not be awarded a Nobel Prize. Hawking wrote the bestseller *A Brief History of Time*, which people joke 'may be brief but is so complex it takes a lot of time to read.'

1959: Charles de Gaulle

De Gaulle was proclaimed the first president of the Fifth Republic of France. His installation ended an eight-month transitional period following near civil war in Algeria, a former French territory. He came to world prominence during the Second World War when he resisted surrender to the German invaders. He escaped to London and led the French Resistance. After the War he was elected president, but withdrew after six months when a new constitution could not be agreed upon. He remained outside politics for 12 years until December 1958 when he was returned to power with a 78 per cent vote. There were 31 assassination attempts against him.

1324 Marco Polo died. With his father and uncle, he had travelled to China via the Silk Route where he spent 17 years, lived in the Kublai Khan's court and explored.

1746 Bonnie Prince Charlie occupied Stirling, Scotland.

1824 (William) Wilkie Collins was born. His novel *The Moonstone* was one of the first detective stories.

1947 Musician David Bowie was born in London. He was inspired by Little Richard as a child and became one of the most electrifying rock and rollers.

1990 Terry-Thomas, the gap toothed, British comic and movie star, often cast in 'twittish' roles, died.

Stephen Hawking: wheelchair-bound physicist who is expanding Einstein's legacy.

9 JANUARY

1898: Gracie Fields

One of the most famous British music hall singers, was born on this day. Audiences loved her wobbly, nasal, cheerful voice and comic songs like 'The biggest aspidestra in the world'. Her monologues appealed especially to soldiers and the working class. Fields was one of Britain's highest paid performers. Her signature song was 'Sally', which became the title of her first movie in 1931, *Sally in Our Alley*. The songs 'Sing as we go' and 'Wish me luck as you wave me goodbye' were famous wherever English was spoken.

1956: Dear Abby

The first 'agony aunt advice column' ran in the *San Francisco Chronicle*. Abby was born Pauline 'Popo' Esther Friedman. Her identical twin sister was Esther 'Eppie' Pauline Friedman. Eppie had launched a successful advice column under the name Ann Landers; Popo decided that she was equally good at giving advice, and began writing under the pen name 'Abigail Van Buren'. Both were syndicated in hundreds of newspapers worldwide.

1997: Tony Bullimore

'How about a nice cup of tea?' asked Tony Bullimore after he was rescued from his upside-down yacht, *Exide Challenger*, in the Southern Ocean. After five days he had been feared drowned. He survived by crouching in the yacht, with a little chocolate, water and sheer determination. Crew on the Australian Navy's HMAS *Adelaide* spotted his yacht and, although there were no visible signs of life, they investigated. They were amazed when they banged on the hull to hear him bang back. He was fortunately wearing a survival suit. Bullimore was taking part in the single-handed Vendee Globe non-stop round-the-world race. He still competes in races.

1768 Ringmaster Philip Astley staged the first modern circus in London.

1908 Simone de Beauvoir, the French philosopher, writer and early feminist was born. She died in 1986.

1951 The United Nations headquarters was opened in New York City.

1957 Sir Anthony Eden resigned as British Prime Minister over the Suez Canal Crisis and was succeeded by Harold Macmillan.

1972 Miner's Strike UK coal miners strike for the first time in 50 years.

Philosophers and lifelong companions: Jean-Paul Sartre and Simone de Beauvoir share a quiet moment.

10 JANUARY

49BC: Julius Caesar

Caesar crossed the Rubicon, a small river in northern Italy after Rome stripped him of his title as Governor of Gaul. A Roman law forbade a general from crossing it with a standing army, as it marked the boundary between a province and Rome's heartland. Crossing the river was like throwing down a gauntlet, so Caesar's action made civil war inevitable. 'To cross the Rubicon' is an expression still used today, meaning that a person has committed to an irreversible, risky course of action.

1868: Last Convicts Arrive in Australia

The last convicts transported from Great Britain to Australia arrived in Fremantle, Western Australia, on board the *Hougoumont*. Of the 229 convicts aboard, 57 were Irish revolutionaries, including John Boyle O'Reilly. O'Reilly made a successful escape from Australia the following year on board a whaler to America. From 1788 to 1868, Great Britain shipped 160 500 convicts to the Antipodes, often for very minor crimes, or for political reasons. A total of 24 700 women convicts were transported.

1929: Tintin

The comic book character created by Herge, first appeared. It is still very popular today, selling 200 million copies worldwide. It has been translated into 50 languages.

2004: Pete Cabrinha

Top pro windsurfer, kitesurfer and surfer, Pete Cabrinha surfed the largest wave for the Billabong XXL Awards. The wave known as Jaws, Maui, Hawaii had a face of 21.3 m. A partner in a jet ski towed Cabrinha into position, as it is impossible to paddle out in waves this size.

1908 Actor Paul Henreid was born in Trieste, Austria. He appeared in or directed over 300 movies. A staunch anti-Nazi, he was often cast as a German in *Goodbye Mr Chips* and others. He died in 1992.

1920 The League of Nations was founded on this day through the Treaty of Versailles, which ended World War 1. Unfortunately, the treaty sowed seeds for the Second World War. The League was dissolved in 1946.

1946 The United Nations General Assembly met for the first time, in London, with representatives from 51 countries.

1971 *Masterpiece Theatre,* the television show, premiered. Most of its episodes such as 'Upstairs Downstairs' were produced by the BBC.

1994 Lorena Bobbitt went on trial for severing her husband John's penis and throwing it in a field, in Manassas, Virginia, USA in a highly publicised trial. The penis was found and successfully reattached. Lorena was found innocent by reason of insanity.

Jaws: the biggest, scariest wave to be conquered by surfers and windsurfers.

11 JANUARY

1903: Alan Paton

The influential South African author and anti-apartheid politician was born. He used his writing to advance his political agenda as one of the South African Liberal Party (SALP) founders. His 1948 bestseller, *Cry the Beloved Country*, dealt with racial reconciliation after tragedy. It was made into two movies and a Broadway production, *Lost in the Stars*. At the SALP's last meeting in 1968, after the government banned it, Paton declared, 'Man was not born to go down on his belly before the state.'

1928: Thomas Hardy

The British novelist and poet died aged 88. Much of his work addresses the role of fate in human life. His *Jude the Obscure*, the riveting story of what Hardy described as 'a deadly war waged between flesh and spirit', includes what is perhaps the most gut-wrenching six word note in English literature: 'Done because we are too menny'. Among Hardy's great books are: *Tess of the d'Urbervilles, Far From the Madding Crowd* and *The Mayor of Casterbridge*, all of which have been reproduced in film.

1966: Hannes Kolehmainen

The first of the so-called Flying Finns, Finland's long-distance runners, Kolehmainen died. He was one of the stars of the 1912 Olympics, winning three gold medals. At that time, Finland was part of Russia and when the Russian flag was hoisted, Kolehmainen said, 'I almost wished I hadn't won.' He won gold in the 1924 marathon. Kolehmainen and his Finn protegé, Paavo Nurmi, lit the 1952 Helsinki Olympic Flame.

1787 William Herschel, born in Prussia but raised in England, was a musician, astronomer and telescope-maker. He discovered Titania and Oberon, Uranus' two moons. He was also the first president of the Royal Society.

1922 The first successful treatment of diabetes with insulin was achieved. Frederick Banting was knighted and won Canada's first Nobel Prize in Medicine for his work.

1934 Jean Chretien, Canada's 20th prime minister, was born in Shawinigan, Quebec. He was the Liberal Party leader in 1990 when he was elected.

1972 East Pakistan became Bangladesh. The division of India in 1947 to give separate homelands to Muslims and Hindus, with Muslims' homeland as 'bookends to India' in East Bengal and Pakistan, in hindsight, had been doomed to failure.

1973 UK Open Universities (OU) began granting degrees. The OUs ushered in a completely new attitude to learning, based on self-motivation, learning for life and credit for adult work experience. Today thousands of Internet courses are offered.

"TESS OF THE D'URBERVILLES"

BY THOMAS HARDY,

AUTHOR OF "FAR FROM THE MADDING CROWD," "THE MAYOR OF CASTERBRIDGE," &c., &c.

ILLUSTRATED BY PROFESSOR HUBERT HERKOMER, R.A., AND HIS PUPILS, MESSRS. WEHRSCHMIDT, JOHNSON, AND SYDALL.

Hardy's twelfth novel was begun in 1889 and published in 1891.

12 JANUARY

1729: Edmund Burke

The 'Father of Conservatism' was born in Dublin to 'mixed' parents: a Protestant father and a Roman Catholic mother. He was a politician and philosopher. He protested British misgovernment, whether in the American colonies or in Ireland. He wrote, 'There is but one law for all, namely, that law which governs all law, the law of our Creator, the law of humanity, justice, equity, the law of nature and of nations.' His belief that the French Revolution would destabilise Europe and his demands for English intervention destroyed his political career.

1876: Jack London

The author was born in poverty in San Francisco. He wrote thrilling adventure stories, based on his experiences in the Klondike gold rush and sailing the South Seas. His most well known book is *The Call of the Wild*, about a dog that returns to lead a wolf pack after its master's death. During London's lifetime he was the world's best known writer of novels and magazine articles.

1966: Batman

The comic book character, created in by Bob Kane in 1939, premiered on US television. Adam West starred as Batman, alias millionaire Bruce Wayne, who vowed to fight crime after his parents' murder. The crime-fighting series gave us the perennial favourites: the Batmobile, Gotham City, Robin the Boy Wonder, The Joker, The Riddler and Catwoman.

1966: Rhodesia

Three fact-finding British Labour Members of Parliament were assaulted. They were heckled and attacked by an audience of 400 white Rhodesians. Britain had sent the fact-finders to investigate the treatment of Black Africans by the minority white rulers and Rhodesia's illegal secession from UK the previous year. The situation deteriorated and black nationalists battled government troops for a decade until 1977, when Rhodesia negotiated for a transition to Black majority rule. In 1980, Robert Mugabe was elected prime minister under a new constitution for an independent Zimbabwe.

1628 Charles Perrault, the French storyteller, was born. His *Mother Goose Tales* are still beloved today.
1910 Luise Rainer was born in Vienna, Austria. She won Oscars for *The Great Ziegfeld* and *The Good Earth*. (Some sources believe she was born in 1912.)
1916 P.W. Botha, South Africa's hard-line apartheid leader, was born in Paul Roux. He was President from 1978–84 and 1984–89.
1964 Zanzibar's sultan was overthrown in 1964. Nationalist Abeid Karume proclaimed a republic. It is now called Tanzania.
1969 Led Zeppelin, the hard rock group, released its first album, taking its name from the Zeppelin airship.
1970 The Nigerian civil war ended with the surrender of Biafra.

Biafran refugees: a scene that has become all too familiar. The Ibo people of Nigeria were overwhelmed and decimated by Nigeria when they attempted to gain independence for thier traditional trible homelands. It should come as no surprise that the Biafran area of Nigeria is rich in oil.

13 JANUARY

1898: J'accuse–Emile Zola

France was rocked to its core by the publication of a letter that Emile Zola sent to President Georges Clemenceau. Zola's first sentence of *J'accuse (I accuse)* was inflammatory. He wrote, 'It is my duty to speak', and proceeded to challenge the trial and conviction of Capt. Alfred Dreyfus, a Jew, for treason. Zola was tried for libel and convicted. Fearing for his life, he fled to England for two years, from 1898–9. Dreyfus was tried again and condemned again, but this time 'with extenuating circumstances'. Dreyfus resumed his military career. Zola was pardoned. Zola's twenty novels are sombre social commentaries on poverty and misery. Some historians believe his death from carbon monoxide poisoning in 1902 in Paris was the work of his enemies.

1927: Dr Sydney Brenner

Brenner, the son of an immigrant Lithuanian unschooled shoe repairer, was born in South Africa. Brenner's brilliance shone through as a child and he never lacked for mentors and scholarships. He published his first scientific paper at 18. After studying both medicine and biology in South Africa, he arrived at Oxford University to study for a PhD. Fortuitously this coincided with the decoding of DNA by James Watson and Francis Crick. Crick and Brenner became collaborators in the new field of molecular biology. Brenner was awarded a Nobel Prize in 2002. His current interest is the question of human diversity, going far beyond the sequencing of the human genome. He once said, 'The problem of biology is not to stand aghast at complexity but to conquer it.'

1948: The Frisbee

The Frisbee started life as the Flyin-Saucer. Walter F. Morrison, its creator, sold his rights to the Wham-O Company in 1948. The first Frisbee aerodynamic disc was produced on this day in 1957. The toy's name is patented and trademark registered, but its name is also used generically for all flying discs. The name Frisbee comes from the Frisbie Pie Company of Bridgeport, Conn, USA, because Yale University students used that companies' pie pans for games before Wham-O's plastic discs.

1929 Lawman Wyatt Earp, best known for the Tombstone, Arizona OK Corral shootout, died in Los Angeles.

1941 James Joyce, the Irish novelist of *Ulysees* and *Finnegan's Wake*, died of a ruptured appendix, aged 58.

1967 Liberation Day in Togo commemorates the 1967 uprising.

1969 Cannons from the *Endeavour*, Captain James Cook's ship, were recovered off Cooktown, Australia.

1972 Dr Kofi Busia, Ghana's Prime Minister, was ousted in a bloodless coup by the military.

Wyatt Earp: his name is synonymous with the American Wild West.

14 JANUARY

1875: Albert Schweitzer

Dr Schweitzer was born in Alsace, Germany. He was an acclaimed musician and biblical scholar. He was considered J. S. Bach's greatest biographer and performer and also an accomplished organ master and organ builder. Instead of a life in the Church and music, he made good on a youthful commitment and entered medical school at the age of 30. After graduation, he established a medical clinic in Lambarene, the Congo. Turning from Christianity to a more Buddhist reverence for the sanctity of all life (including mosquitoes and other potential disease-carrying insects), his clinic attracted worldwide attention and volunteers from all walks of life. He received the Nobel Peace Prize in 1952.

1913: Henry Ford

The world's first modern assembly line, to mass produce cars, started production. Ford had always loved to tinker with machines on the family farm. He began his automobile career by racing cars. In 1903 he set up the Ford Motor Company and in 1908 began producing his famous Model T. His assembly line production, using a conveyor belt, was an industrial revolution not just for car manufacturing. Previously a car took one and a half days to assemble. Using Ford's production line cars rolled off the factory floor in just one and a half hours. It enabled him to make a car for just $500, within the reach of the average American. Ford said, 'A business that makes nothing but money is a poor kind of business.' He left his fortune to the Ford Foundation. It is one of the world's most generous benefactors to science and education.

1954: Joe DiMaggio

The camera bulbs flashed when one of the era's standout baseball players married the blonde bombshell movie star Marilyn Monroe. The wedding was as close as the USA could get to a royal wedding.

1900 Giacomo Puccini's *Tosca* premiered in Rome.

1935 Lucille Wheeler, Canadian Olympic downhill skier was born. She started skiing at age 2 and her Olympic bronze in 1956 was the first ski medal by a Canadian.

1949 The first non-stop trans-Canadian flight arrived in Halifax, Nova Scotia from Vancouver, BC.

1969 Sir Matt Busby, Manchester United's standout player and manager, retired.

2004 Republic of Georgia restored their national flag to official use after 500 years. The five-cross flag is similar to England's St George Cross.

Marilyn Monroe and Joe DiMaggio: America's 'royal wedding' couple bask in the limelight.

15 JANUARY

1759: British Museum and Library

The world famous institution opened its doors to the public. Its core was the personal collection of Sir Hans Sloane, a wealthy physician and naturalist. It contained not only books, but coins, medals and manuscripts. It is now the National Museum for the UK and the National Library is separate.

1919: Molasses in the Streets

The United States Industrial Alcohol Company (USIA) caused a disaster in Boston when a poorly made 90-foot tank with a capacity of 2.3 million gallons of molasses gave way near the harbour docks. The resulting wave of the sticky stuff was estimated to be as high as 5 metres. Pedestrians could not swim in it or move as the molasses engulfed them. USIA was found liable and paid damages to the 150 injured, 21 dead and to the owners of the destroyed buildings. For decades, Bostonians claimed they could smell molasses in central Boston.

1971: Aswan Dam

Egypt's mighty new dam was dedicated. Aswan was built to provide a reliable source of water for crop irrigation, the production of hydro-electricity and to control the Nile River floodwaters. Although Egypt has doubled its agricultural production there has been unexpected erosion of the Nile delta on the Mediterranean Sea, along with drainage and disease problems. The dam is 111 m high and 3.7 km long.

1559 Queen Elizabeth 1 was crowned in London's Westminster Abbey.

1891 Osip Mandelstam, the Soviet poet, was born. Stalin first admired him, but when he wrote about the peasants' plight, he was imprisoned.

1943 The Pentagon, the world's largest office building, opened in Washington, DC. It is the US military headquarters and also houses espionage and intelligence activities.

1987 Ray Bolger, The *Wizard of Oz*'s Scarecrow died. He was the last surviving member of the cast.

1997 Princess Diana called for a ban on landmines, after seeing mutilated Angolan children. She stirred up a row by criticising prominent British politicians and industrialists for not supporting the ban.

The late Diana, Princess of Wales, supported the Red Cross's anti-landmines campaign, bringing much needed media attention to the issue. Landmines continue to kill and maim innocent civilians long after wars have ended. Diana led calls for a worldwide ban on the manufacture and sale of mines.

16 JANUARY

1853: André Michelin

The French industrialist was born in Paris. With his brother Edouard, he founded the Michelin Tyre Company to manufacture bicycle tyres in 1888. Its Michelin Man is one of the world's oldest trademarks, dating from 1898. André said that the Michelin Man was based on his chubby brother Edouard who, he said, resembled a stack of tyres! The company also became famous for its European travel guides and its rating of restaurants using its coveted three-star system. Michelin Tyre invented the radial tyre and is now experimenting with computerised 'talking tyres'.

1874: Robert Service

The popular balladeer was born. He emigrated from England to Canada. He travelled widely and experienced the harshness of the 1895 Yukon gold rush and interacted with the prospectors who succumbed to 'gold fever'. Two of his best known ballads are 'The shooting of Dan McGrew' and 'The cremation of Sam McGee'. His ballads are popular for their witty rhymes and unusual subjects. In 'The Law of the Yukon', he wrote: 'This is the Law of the Yukon, that only the strong shall thrive/That surely the weak shall perish and only the Fit survive'.

1909: South Pole

One of the legendary Antarctic explorers, Sir Ernest Shacklelton reached the South Magnetic Pole on this day. As a young man, born in Ireland and raised in England, he said, 'I feel strangely drawn to the mysterious South.' He followed his destiny. He is considered one of the most selfless, model leaders, never expecting his men to do tasks in the dire circumstances that he would not do himself. Sir Edmund Hillary of Everest fame said that Shackleton was his hero.

1793 The first free immigrants arrived in Australia to settle. The first convicts had arrived in 1788.

1902 Eric Liddell was born. The Englishman was an Olympic runner and missionary, portrayed in the movie *Chariots of Fire*.

1932 Dian Fossey was born. She studied Rwandan gorillas and was apparently murdered in 1987. Her life was portrayed in the movie *Gorillas in the Mist*.

1979 Ayatollah Khomeini ousted the Shah of Iran, Mohammed Reza Pahlavi.

1991 Gulf War. A United Nations coalition led by the USA, began bombing Iraq after Saddam Hussein refused to withdraw from Kuwait. This war is known as the Persian Gulf War. It ended four months later.

Dian Fossey, with a poster of one of 'her' gorillas. Sadly many of the gorillas have since perished in the protracted civil war in the eastern Congo which is forcing farmers off their land into the forests, where 'bush meat' is a prime source of food.

17 JANUARY

1706: Benjamin Franklin

The fifteenth of seventeen children, Franklin was born in Boston, Massachusetts. He was a writer, newspaper publisher, ambassador and one of the drafters of the Declaration of Independence. At age 17 he moved to Philadelphia and was apprenticed to a printer. His *Poor Richard's Almanac*, which he published, included aphorisms such as 'Early to bed, Early to rise/Makes a man healthy, wealthy and wise.' He also invented bifocal glasses, the lightning rod and the Franklin stove. At age 81, three years before his death, he was the oldest signer of the US Constitution.

1899: Nevil Shute Norway

Better known as Neville Shute, the author was born in London. He worked as an aeronautical engineer at Vickers before setting up his own airship company. Worried that his reputation as a fiction writer would damage his engineering career, he wrote under the pseudonym Neville Shute yet still incorporated technical aspects to his writing. He was one of the most popular novelists from 1930 to 1957. He moved to Australia after the Second World War with his family. Shute immortalised Alice Springs in *A Town Like Alice*. The possibility of Australia being the last place on earth in a nuclear attack was chillingly portrayed in his book *On the Beach*, which was also made into a movie. He wrote about twenty books and an autobiography, *Slide Rule*.

1928: Vidal Sassoon

The 'father of modern hairdressing' was born in the tough East End of London. His immigrant Jewish family struggled to survive, and after his father abandoned the family the five-year-old Sassoon and his younger bother were placed in an orphanage. The family was reunited when his mother remarried six years later. When Sassoon was a teenager, his mother dreamed she saw him in a barbershop and took him to a shop to be an apprentice. He decided if this was to be his fate he might as well excel, so attended the theatre to learn to speak better English. After the creation of Israel in 1948, he lived there for a few years, serving in the military, using the street fighting skills learnt in his East London youth. Upon his return to London, he set up his first shop. By 1963, he had pioneered cuts that did away with curling irons, hairdryers, permanent waves and hairspray, such as the 'Bob and Five-Point Cut', the 'Nancy Kwan' (for the ice skater) and other geometric shapes that brought out the hair's natural luster. Sassoon became an international celebrity with his hair products and his chain of uni-sex saloons throughout the UK and USA. In 1982 he established the International Centre for the Study of Anti-Semitism at Hebrew University of Jerusalem.

1877 May Gibbs, author of the Australian classic *Snugglepot and Cuddlepie*, was born.

1893 Queen Liliuokalani, the last monarch of Hawaii, was overthrown by white businessmen. They wanted Hawaii annexed by the USA.

1931 James Earl Jones was born. He overcame stuttering to become one of the most recognised voices and actors worldwide.

1949 Andy Kaufman the comedian was born. His complicated personality was revealed in *Man on the Moon*, played by Jim Carrey.

1966 Simon and Garfunkel's best-selling *Sounds of Silence* album was released.

1975 Bob Dylan's *Blood on the Tracks* was released.

Bob Dylan relaxes with friend and fellow folk singer Joan Baez.

18 JANUARY

1788: The First Fleet

The British ship *Supply* arrived at Botany Bay, Australia under the command of Captain Arthur Phillip, whose orders were to establish a convict settlement. Within two days the other ten boats of the First Fleet arrived. Aboard the *Supply* were: 736 convicts (548 men, 188 female and 13 children), 211 marines, 27 marine/officers' wives and 16 children, plus merchant seamen and the ship's crew. They were supposed to establish a sustainable food supply from just : two bulls, four cows, two stallions, four mares, 19 goats, 74 pigs, 29 sheep, five rabbits, 18 turkeys, 29 geese, 35 ducks and 209 fowl. Two weeks after their arrival, lightning killed six sheep and one pig. In April, dingoes took six sheep and the cattle strayed. Hunger was a serious problem. Although there was abundant seafood and edible bush plants, the English didn't consider researching what the Aborigines ate.

1893: Jim Thorpe

The Native American, who won Olympic gold medals in the pentathlon and the decathlon at the 1912 Olympics, was born into the Sac and Fox tribe. Thorpe is one of the standout athletes of all time. Sweden's King Gustav V told him: 'Sir, you are the greatest athlete in the world.' Thorpe replied, 'Thanks King.' Thorpe was also an outstanding baseball and football player. The International Olympic Committee (IOC) stripped him of his medals and purged his records in 1913 when it learned that Thorpe had accepted a few dollars in 1909 to play baseball. This was in violation of the IOC's 'amateur status rules'. On this day, the IOC returned his Olympic medals to Thorpe's family, 30 years after he died in poverty.

1904 Cary Grant, a screen romantic lead for three decades was born Archibald Alexander Leach, in Bristol, England. His movies include *Bringing Up Baby* and *The Awful Truth.* He died in 1986.

1912 Englishman Robert Falcon Scott reached the South Pole and found that his rival, Norway's Raol Amundsen, had beaten him there, about one month before. All of Scott's team perished.

1913 Comedian Danny Kaye was born in New York. His most notable movies are *The Secret Life of Walter Mitty* and *Hans Christian Andersen.* He raised millions of dollars as a UNICEF ambassador. He died in 1987.

1933 John Boorman The English moviemaker was born in Shepperton. His movies include *Deliverance* and *Excalibur.*

1980 Sir Cecil Beaton, the English photographer, best known for his portraits of Royalty died in Broadchalke, aged 76.

Cary Grant: silver screen heartthrob to millions of women.

19 JANUARY

1839: Paul Cézanne

The French artist, best known for still life and landscape was born in Aix-en-Provence. He was one of the founders of Post-impressionism and one of the 19th century's great artists. Pablo Picasso called him 'the father of us all', yet his work was publicly ridiculed and poorly reviewed. Cézanne was humiliated as a child for being illegitimate because his parents did not marry until he was 10 years old, and he carried the stigma for life. Cézanne enjoyed rambling alone around the countryside near his home observing nature and painting. Often he painted the same subject from different angles. He once said, 'The day is coming when a single carrot, freshly observed, will set off a revolution.'

1946: Julian Barnes

The prolific contemporary writer, literary and television critic and translator was born in Leicester, England. He writes on themes as varied as history, cooking, love and reality. Two of his ten novels are *Flaubert's Parrot* and *England, England*, which were both Booker Prize nominees. Under the pseudonym Dan Kavanagh, he has written a crime series about a freelance security systems specialist. He also writes short stories and essays. Barnes worked as a lexicographer on the *Oxford English Dictionary Supplement* for three years, followed by a stint as a reviewer and literary editor for *The New Statesman* and *The New Review*. He has won major literary awards from four European countries, including France's distinguished Commandeur de l'Ordre des Arts et des Lettres in 2004. He wrote: 'Books say: she did this because. Life says: she did this. Books are where things are explained to you, life where things aren't.'

1988: Christopher Nolan

The 21-year-old Dubliner won the Whitbread Book of the Year award. *Under the Clock* was typed on a computer by a wand attached to his forehead, because of his severe cerebral palsy. On hearing the news, Nolan typed, 'I want to shout with joy. My heart is full of gratitude. You all must realise that history is now in the making. Crippled man has taken his place on the world's literary stage.' His first publication, a book of poems called *A Dam-burst of Dreams*, was published when he was 14 years old.

1809 Edgar Allan Poe, master of mystery and macabre and poetry such as *The Raven*, was born. *The Edgar Award* for suspense fiction is named after him.

1736 James Watt, who improved on previous steam engines to build the first steam locomotive, was born in Greenock, Scotland.

1942 Singer Michael Crawford, who starred in *Phantom of the Opera* was born in Salisbury, England.

1943 Janis 'Pearl' Joplin, the blues singer, was born in Port Arthur, Texas. She rapidly achieved superstar status with 'Piece of my heart', 'Mercedes Benz' and 'Ball and Chain'. She died of a drug overdose in 1970.

1955 Simon Rattle, the symphonic conductor, was born in Liverpool, England

Janis Joplin: the white girl who gave the Blues a big shake, rattle and roll.

20 JANUARY

1957: Antarctica

In November, two groups of explorers set off from the opposite sides of the Antarctic Continent, to attempt the first surface crossing. They used motorised vehicles. New Zealand's team, led by Sir Edmund Hillary, set up food and fuel depots for the British team led by Dr Vivian 'Bunny' Fuchs. They met on this day in 1958 at the South Pole. The weather worsened and they considered abandoning the rest of their trip, but waited it out and reached their destination, Scott Camp, on 2 March.

1966: Sir Robert Menzies

The longest serving Australian prime minister retired, aged 72, after a record sixteen years as prime minister and head of the Liberal Party. He saw Australia through part of the Second World War, the Korean War, the Petrov espionage case, the Suez Crisis and the Vietnam War. He was unswerving in his loyalty to Queen Elizabeth II. Students enjoyed heckling Menzies at public appearances and delighted in his rapier sharp repartee. On one occasion a heckler shouted, 'I wouldn't vote for you if you were the Archangel Gabriel.' He replied, 'If I were the Archangel Gabriel, madam, I'm afraid you would not be in my constituency.' A collection of King Ming's repartee was collated in a book: *The Wit of Sir Robert Menzies* by R Robinson. Menzies died in 1978.

1993: Audrey Hepburn

The pixie-like movie star died. She was born in 1929 near Brussels, Belgium and suffered from severe malnutrition as a child. She won an Oscar for her first major movie, *Roman Holiday*. Her most famous role was as Holly Golightly in *Breakfast at Tiffany's*. She was a UNICEF goodwill ambassador for many years.

1920 Federico Fellini, Italian movie director and screenwriter, was born at Rimini. He won four Oscars. Two of his best known movies are *La Dolce Vita* and *Juliet of the Spirits*. He died in 1993.

1926 Patricia Neal, who starred in *Hud* and *The Subject was Roses,* was born in Packard, Kentucky. She is also admired for her recovery from a near fatal stroke at the peak of her career.

1948 Natan Scharansky, the expatriate Soviet dissident, was born in Donetsk.

1969 The first pulsar was discovered, in the Crab Nebula.

1982 The Camcorder went on sale, the result of collaboration between five rival companies.

1989 Comedian Beatrice Lillie died aged 94 in London. She was born in Toronto and appeared in *Auntie Mame* and *Thoroughly Modern Millie*.

Audrey Hepburn: the 'pixie' won an Oscar for her first major role in *Roman Holiday*.

21 JANUARY

1793: King Louis XVI

The King of France was executed by guillotine during the French Revolution. He was ill equipped to be King during such a time of political upheaval. He never understood the seriousness of the revolutionaries' demands. His refusal prompted the storming of the Bastille to release political prisoners on 14 July 1789. He enraged revolutionaries when he refused to approve the abolition of feudalism. The last straw to the revolutionaries was the King's attempt to involve other countries' militia in France's problems. He was charged with treason and executed. His wife, Marie-Antoinette, followed him, nine months later.

1863: Burke and Wills

A public funeral was held for two Australian explorers, Robert O'Hara Burke, about 40 years old and William Wills, about 27 years old, in Melbourne. They had died in 1861, after reaching the Gulf of Carpentaria, in the Northern Territory. When they returned to their depot, their relief party had left the day before. Food was left buried for them, but for unknown reasons they failed to find it. They apparently died of hunger.

1951: Mount Lamington PNG

A Qantas airplane was flying over the extinct Mount Lamington volcano in Papua 'New Guinea when the volcano suddenly blew out its side. The plane was pounded by pumice and rock, but the pilot kept a cool head, diverted and flew out of danger. The volcano spewed lava and smoke as high as 10 000 m and decimated the surrounding area. At least 3000 villagers were killed.

MASSACRE of the Unfortunate FRENCH KING, with a View of LA GUILLOTINE, or the Modern French BEHEADING MACHINE.

1 The Monarch 3 General Santerre
2 His Confessor 4 The Mayer of Paris.

Published by Alex.^r Hogg. March 1 17.93.

1855 John Browning. The gun-maker was born in Ogden, Utah. He designed guns for Winchester, Remington, Stevens and Colt and held more gun patents than anyone else. He died in 1926.

1922 Paul Scofield, English dramatic actor, was born in Hurstpierpoint. One of his major roles was as Sir Thomas More in *A Man for All Seasons*.

1950 George Orwell (pen name for Eric Blair) died, aged 46, after a long battle with tuberculosis. The word 'Orwellian' means an oppressive system. His most famous works are *Animal Farm* and *1984*, which attack oppressive autocratic regimes.

1976 The supersonic Concorde, built by British and French aeronautical companies, was put into service.

1981 Fifty-two US hostages held at the Embassy in Tehran, Iran were freed after 444 days of captivity.

King Louis XVI of France was executed by guillotine during the French Revolution.

22 JANUARY

1788: Lord Byron

One of English literature's 'bad boys', Lord George Gordon Byron (the sixth Baron Byron) was born in London. A charismatic, gifted poet, he shocked Londoners with his affairs and his alleged incestuous relationship with his half-sister. Byron is best known for *Childe Harold's Pilgrimage* and *Don Juan*. In *Childe Harold* he wrote: 'Fame is the thirst of life', which describes himself. He was also a Liberal Member of Parliament and supporter of social reform.

1901: Queen Victoria

The imposing 82-year-old English Queen died after the longest reign in British history. Victoria ruled the world's largest Empire, on which 'the sun never set', for sixty-four years. She was happily married to Albert and had nine children. She barely endured his premature death at the age of 41. When her children married, she was linked to nearly every European ruling family.

1931: Sir Isaac Isaacs

The first native-born Australian Governor-General was appointed. The distinguished jurist was Jewish, which made his appointment extremely controversial.

1980: Dr Andrei Sakharov

The famous dissident and his wife, Yelena Bonner, were arrested for speaking out against the USSR's invasion of Afghanistan. One of the USSR's leading scientists, he became one of its leading dissidents. The couple was given two hours to pack and sent into internal exile in Gorky, a city off-limits to the Western press. Sakharov, the winner of the 1975 Nobel Peace Prize, continued to write letters and to stage hunger strikes during their seven-year exile. President Gorbachev ordered his release in 1986. Sakharov helped draft a new constitution and was active in parliament, but died just before the dissolution of the Soviet Union.

1775 Andre Ampere, the French physicist was born. The ampere ('amps') unit of electrical current was named after him. His life was so tragic that his epitaph read. 'Happy at last'.

1849 August George Strindberg, Swedish playwright, was born. His dark, tense dramas influenced writers of the Theatre of the Absurd.

1904 George Balanchine was born in Russia and was enticed to the USA by a philanthropist. A leading influence on 20th century ballet, he choreographed more than 200 works.

1918 Ukraine declared its independence from Russia; by 1921 it had become part of the USSR. Its independence was finally restored on this day in 1991.

1973 The Roe v Wade case making abortion legal, was passed by the US Supreme Court.

Queen Victoria: Britain's longest serving monarch.

23 JANUARY

1849: Elizabeth Blackwell

Born in Bristol, England, Blackwell graduated from medical school in upstate New York as the first female doctor in the USA. Her sister Emily also became a physician. They specialised in services to women and children, in New York and later in London.

1884: Ralph de Palma

De Palma was born in Italy. He immigrated to the USA in 1893. In his quarter-century career car-racing career, he entered 2889 races and won 2557. He is remembered for two races. In the 1912 Indianapolis 500, he was leading when his car broke down. He and his 'mechanician' pushed the car the last mile. He was disqualified, but won a standing ovation. His rivalry with Barney Oldfield thrilled spectators and he supposedly said, 'I would rather beat Oldfield than eat five plates of spaghetti in a row.' In a 1914 race, Oldfield was leading. When de Palma realised he could not catch him, he signalled to make a pit stop. Oldfield, driving on a worn tyre, also pulled in. Just as he did so, de Palma roared off to victory.

1933: Bodyline Cricket

One of cricket's biggest furores took place during the English Marylebone Cricket Club (MCC) team's Australian Test tour of 1932–33. The MCC watched films of their main rival, Donald Bradman, and decided on a new tactic. They authorised 'bodyline' bowling aimed directly at the batsman. On 18 January, Australian officials sent a telegram to the MCC to complain. The reply on this day in 1933, said 'MCC has full confidence in team.' The Third Test came to a head in Adelaide. A riot nearly broke out when one Aussie was hit above the heart and another had his skull fractured. The MCC won, but the victory was controversial. In 1934, cricket rules were revised, allowing umpires intervention if there was a danger of batsman injury.

Vietnam: the American airforce halted its bombing raids on North Vietnam. Ground troops realised that they would soon be going home.

1832 Eduoard Manet, the Impressionist painter, was born in Paris. He outraged the public with his painting *Dejeuner sur l'Herbe*, featuring an outdoor scene of a naked woman surrounded by clothed men.

1943 The Allies prevailed against Japan in New Guinea in the Second World War.

1957 Princess Caroline of Monaco was born, the first child of Prince Rainier and Princess Grace.

1973 The Vietnam War. America stops bombing the North and moves towards withdrawal of troops from the South. Dr Henry Kissinger presented President Richard Nixon with a draft peace proposal that became known as the Paris Accord. It was signed on 27 January. Although attacks against the North stopped, air assaults continued against communist forces in South Vietnam, Laos and Cambodia.

1986 The first rock and roll musicians were inducted into the new American Rock and Roll Hall of Fame. They were Chuck Berry, James Brown, Ray Charles, Fats Domino, the Everly Brothers, Buddy Holly, Jerry Lee Lewis and Elvis Presley.

24 JANUARY

1848: Gold Rush

Gold was discovered near Sacramento, California. This led to the biggest mass migration of people in modern history. The amount of gold discovered in the first year was more than the total world's production. San Francisco was the arrival point for most people. That is why the city's famous bridge is known as the Golden Gate.

1965: Winston Churchill

Sir Winston Churchill, the former British prime minister, died on this day at age 90. In worldwide votes for Millennial Heroes, his name was often first. He was the first person to be made an honourary US citizen in recognition of courageous leadership against Nazi Germany. His life was one of great successes and great defeats. He did poorly in school, so entered the Army, where he quickly emerged as a leader. Once Churchill entered politics he made some unwise decisions, such as his lack of foresight as First Lord of the Admiralty in the Gallipoli campaign, which led to thousands of ANZAC deaths. Yet, it is hard to imagine a more effective and inspirational leader than Churchill in the Second World War, during the UK's 'darkest hours'. England and especially London was barraged round the clock by Nazi bombs. He rallied the troops and civilians, telling them this could be 'the British Commonwealth's finest hour'. Eventually, Hitler called off his invasion plans when a revitalised and determined Royal Air Force brought down increasing numbers of Nazi aircraft. Churchill acknowledged the sacrifices the Air Force had made: 'Never in the field of human conflict was so much owed by so many to so few.' He summed up his political philosophy in 1948: 'In War: Resolution. In Defeat: Defiance. In Victory: Magnanimity. In Peace: Goodwill.'

1862 Author Edith Wharton was born. Her forty books about 'society's tribal behaviour' include *The Age of Innocence* and *The House of Mirth*.

1935 Canned beer was introduced. When, the Gottfried Kreuger Brewing Company in Newark, New Jersey, USA produced 'Krueger's Special Beer', an industry analyst predicted, 'Men would stay home with their families more.'

1941 Neil Diamond, the all-round entertainer singer, was born in New York. Favourites include *Cracklin' Rosie*, *Sweet Caroline* and *Solitary Man*.

1960 Actress Nastassja Kinski was born in Berlin, Germany. She appeared in *Hotel New Hampshire* and *Tess*.

1972 Shoichi Yokoi was found in a cave on Guam. He did not know that the Second World War had ended with Japan's surrender, nearly three decades before.

Shoichi Yokoi: the Japanese soldier who spent more than a quarter of a century in the jungles of Guam comes face to face with the modern world.

25 JANUARY

1759: Robert Burns

'Robbie' Burns, whose statues grace parks worldwide, was born in Ayrshire, Scotland into a poor farming family. Very handsome and outgoing, he began writing while young and, despite dying at age 37, his legacy is remarkable. Writing in both English and Scot, some of his best known works include *Auld Lang Syne, O My Luve's Like a Red Red Rose* and *Ye Banks and Braes*. Since 1796, members of the Burns Society celebrate his birthday worldwide with readings and a glass or two of good Scotch.

1882: Virginia Woolf

The controversial author was born in Hyde Park Gate, England. She later lived in Bloomsbury. She is considered one of the most innovative English writers in her use of stream of consciousness. Her writing delights each new generation, especially feminists. She and her husband formed the nucleus of the famed Bloomsbury literary circle. Together they founded the esteemed Hogarth Press. Between bouts of mental illness, she wrote *Mrs Dalloway, A Room of One's Own, To the Lighthouse* and others, as well as writing for the *Times Literary Supplement*. She drowned herself in 1941. Her life story was brought to the screen by Nicole Kidman in the Academy Award winning movie *The Hours*, based on a book of the same title.

1996: Rent

The musical opened to rave reviews on Broadway. Set in the low-rent area of New York City, it was inspired by Giacomo Puccini's opera *La Boheme*. Sadly, the playwright Jonathan Larson died that same day from an aortic aneurysm. The play won four Tony awards and a posthumous Pulitzer Prize for Larson.

1858 Felix Mendelssohn's 'Wedding March' debuted at the wedding of Queen Victoria's daughter, for which it had been commissioned.

1874 W. Somerset Maugham, the English novelist, short story writer and playwright, was born in Paris. His books include *Of Human Bondage, The Razor's Edge* and *Cakes and Ale*.

1924 The first Winter Olympic Games were held at Chamonix, France.

1947 Al Capone, the Chicago mobster of the Prohibition era died, aged 48. Capone was a ruthless operator, organising many murders including the Valentine's Day Massacre, but only served ten years in prison for tax evasion.

1949 Israel, the newly created homeland for Jews, held its first election. David Ben-Gurion was elected president.

1993 Akebono (Chad Rowan) of Hawaii became the first foreign-born sumo grand champion. He was 2 metres tall and weighed 235 kilograms. Sixty-two per cent of Japanese households watched his victory on TV.

Alphonso 'Scarface' Capone: the Chicago mobster who turned Italian immigrant crime into a modern corporate mega business.

26 JANUARY

1788: Sydney Cove

After Captain Arthur Phillip of the First Fleet determined that Botany Bay was unsuitable for settlement, he investigated Port Jackson to the north. On this day the British flag was raised at the Tank Stream camp, Sydney Cove, near today's Circular Quay. The first three years were extremely difficult. The colony was wracked with hunger, violence and lawlessness. Australia Day, a public holiday, is celebrated every year to commemorate the event.

1893: Bessie Coleman

The first female African–American aviator was born in Texas. Denied admission to aviation school in the USA because of her race and sex, she went to flight school in Paris. She inspired other women to take up flying. She died at age 33 in a plane crash.

1905: Maria von Trapp

Maria von Trapp was born in Austria. After she became a nun a widower hired her as a governess, but the couple fell in love and married. With his seven and their three children, they toured the world as the Trapp Family Singers. *The Sound of Music* which starred Julie Andrews, was based on their life. It includes the songs *Do-Re-Me*, *Edelweiss* and *Climb Every Mountain*.

1925: Paul Newman

The humanitarian, actor, businessman and car racing enthusiast was born. He starred in *Hud*, *The Sting* and *Butch Cassidy and the Sundance Kid*. After six nominations, he finally won an Oscar for *The Color of Money*. Fans still cringe at his eating fifty eggs in one hour in *Cool Hand Luke*. In 1982, Newman established Newman's Own to make salad dressing, popcorn, lemonade, sauces, etc. He donates all the profits to charity. Newman took up auto racing in his 40s and at age 70, is the oldest driver of a major sanctioned event. He was 19th on President Nixon's 'enemies list' for his liberal politics.

1955 Guitarist Eddie van Halen was born in the Netherlands. Two of his works are *Jump* and *Right Now*.

1965 Hindi was made the official language of India, and a month-long riot convinced the government to also retain English as an official language.

1969 Prague, Czechoslovakia. Hundreds of protestors rioted after police tried to break up a peaceful march in honour of Jan Palach, a philosophy student who set himself on fire in protest of the Soviet occupation of his country.

1972 Vesna Vulovic, a Yugoslavian flight attendant, fell from an exploding airplane without a parachute from 10 160m. In a coma for three days, she made a full recovery.

1983 IBM introduced its Lotus 1-2-3 spreadsheet.

Paul Newman in one of his iconic roles, in *Butch Cassidy and the Sundance Kid*. Newman (right) played Butch opposite Robert Redford as Sundance. Katharine Ross rounded out the cast of the romantic, comic western that became a classic.

27 JANUARY

1606: Guy Fawkes

Eight conspirators were convicted of having attempted to blow up Parliament and King James 1, in the infamous 'Gunpowder Plot'. They were executed and their heads were placed on spears on London Bridge and other body parts were displayed on Parliament House. The day when the Plot's leader, Guy Fawkes was arrested, 5 November, is commemorated annually in parts of the British Commonwealth. His effigy is blown up, or burned on a bonfire and celebrated with fireworks.

1756: Mozart

Wolfgang Amadeus Mozart was born in Salzburg, Austria, into a musical family. He was one of the most astonishingly gifted musical prodigies ever, but he is much more appreciated now than during his lifetime. He began studying music at age three, composing at age five and performing in Paris and London and other European cities from age seven. Although he worked hard and wrote over 600 compositions and 22 operas, he had trouble paying his bills and supporting his family. His last work was a requiem, presaging perhaps his own death, at just 35 years old. He was buried in a pauper's grave.

1832: Lewis Carroll

The mathematician Charles Dodgson, known to readers as Lewis Carroll, was born in Cheshire England. His *Alice's Adventures in Wonderland* was written for his friend Alice Liddell, in 1886. *Through the Looking Glass* followed it. The stories are fun and have no preaching and sermonising, unlike other children's books of the time. Carroll created the characters the March Hare, the Mad Hatter, Tweedledum and Tweedledee. The Duchess told Alice, 'If everybody minded their own business … the world would go round a good deal faster than it does.'

Alice meets Tweedledum and Tweedledee in Wonderland.

1721 Quebec City and Montreal, Canada, were linked by a regularly scheduled mail coach service.
1888 The National Geographic Society was incorporated.
1903 Australia's Sir John Eccles was born. In 1963 he was awarded a Nobel Prize for his work on nerve impulses and was also named 1963 Australian of the Year.
1931 Mordecai Richler, the prolific Canadian writer and commentator, was born in Montreal. His books include *Cocksure* and *St. Urbain's Horseman*, named after the street he lived on.
1944 The Siege of Leningrad ended. Half its population had starved to death because of a Nazi blockade since July 8th 1941. Despite overwhelming odds, freezing weather and lack of ammunition, the Russians stopped the German invasion here.
1974 When Brisbane, Queensland flooded, 7000 people were evacuated from their homes.

28 January

1884: Auguste and Jean Felix Piccard

The famous twins Auguste and Jean Felix were born in Basel, Switzerland. Both were scientists and explorers and usually worked separately. Auguste undertook space research and also deep-sea research. Jean Felix, researching cosmic rays, reached over 17 373 m in a sealed gondola piloted by his wife Jeannette in 1934. Auguste died in 1962 and Jean Felix died on their birthday the following year.

1986: Challenger

Seventy-three seconds after a flawless launch from Cape Canaveral, Florida, the space shuttle *Challenger* exploded. It had reached an altitude of 14 kilometres when the liquid oxygen tank ruptured. Millions of people watching on television worldwide were horror-stricken to see the wreckage plummet to earth. Killed were the first civilian in space, schoolteacher Christa McAuliffe, and astronauts Dick Scobee, Michael Smith, Judith Resnick, Ronald McNair, Ellison Onizuka and Gregory Jarvis. At a memorial service three days later, President Ronald Reagan, quoting a poem, said, 'we will never forget them . . . they waved goodbye and slipped the surly bonds of earth to touch the face of God.' All manned missions were put on hold for two years. An investigation showed that there had been a fuel leak through a simple faulty O-ring on the solid rocket booster.

1990: Romania

Ion Iliescu's interim pro-democracy government hit a stumbling block. Thousands of demonstrators poured into Bucharest's Victory Square demanding more changes that had been promised to them after Communist dictator Nicolae Ceausescu and his wife were executed on Christmas Day. Iliescu remained in power until 1996. In 2000 he was re-elected on his promise to accelerate Romania's entry into the European Community.

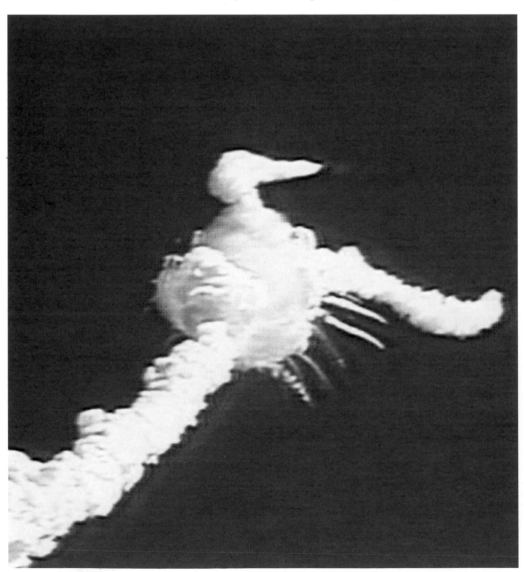

1547 England's Edward VI, aged seven, succeeded King Henry VIII, who died the same day.

1918 'In Flanders Field' is one of the best known poems about WWI. Its author, John McCrae, died in Guelph, Ontario.

1929 Sculptor Claes Oldenburg was born in Stockholm, Sweden. His works include *Standing Trowel.*

1943 Paul Henderson, the Canadian ice hockey great, was born. He scored the winning goal in the Canada/USSR Summit series in 1972, with just 34 seconds remaining.

1945 The Ledo Road was completed. It linked Burma and China, replacing the need for the US Flying Tigers to fly over 'The Hump' of the Himalaya, to re-supply the Chinese Allies against the Japanese.

The space shuttle, *Challenger* disintegrates shortly after launch, taking the lives of seven astronauts and halting America's shuttle program for two years.

3 JULY

2003: Kew Gardens

The Royal Botanic Gardens at Kew in West London, England became a World Heritage Site. Princess Augusta established the Gardens in 1750 with the ambitious plan that they would 'contain all the plants known on earth.' Kew's purpose has changed over the centuries. Its first gardener focused on medicinal plants. The botanist, Sir Joseph Banks, who accompanied Captain James Cook on his 1769-70 South Pacific voyage to Australia, New Zealand and Hawaii, brought back thousands of new specimens, which added a new scientific and botanical dimension to Kew. The Gardens rank among the world's most famous for their beautiful landscaping and variety of plants.

1951: Paddles Hadlee

Sir Richard Hadlee the left-handed cricketer was born in Christchurch, New Zealand. He is known as 'The Master of Rhythm and Swing' for his playing style and also as 'Paddles' for his large feet. His father, Walter and his brother Dayle also played NZ Test cricket. Hadlee is an outstanding medium-fast bowler and excellent batsman. He took five wickets in an innings over 100 times in first-class cricket and more than 35-times in Test cricket. He was the first bowler to take 400 wickets in Test cricket, which he achieved at his home ground of Lancaster Park. His career total of 431 wickets was a record that stood until 1994, when India's Kapil Dev, broke it. He retired in 1990.

1971: Light my Fire no more

The Doors lead singer, Jim Morrison, died on this day, aged 27, in Paris. Morrison, 'The Lizard King' thought of himself as a poet as well as a contemporary rock musician. He went to Paris to escape the hectic Californian pace of life. He was a songwriter and singer and is best known for the classic 'Light My Fire'. He died of heart failure possibly caused by a mixture of alcohol and drugs. He was both plagued and inspired by LSD, heroin, alcohol and fan adulation. The talented Jimi Hendrix and Janis Joplin had died the year before from overdoses and Morrison often said, 'You're drinking with number three.' His death was kept secret until after his burial. His grave in Père Lachaise cemetery is a mecca for alienated youth, who leave letters, cigarettes and whisky.

1844 Great Auk became extinct. Once prolific in Greenland, Iceland, Norway and the UK, the flightless bird was hunted for its feathers to make mattresses. It was like a large penguin.

1848 The Danish West Indies, now called the US Virgin Islands, freed all its slaves.

1908 M. F. K. Fisher was born in Albion, Michigan. Her focus was food, in books such as *How to Cook a Wolf* and *Consider the Oyster*. She died in 1992.

1919 The super dirigible R34 was the first aircraft to cross the Atlantic Ocean from the east to the west and then to make the return voyage by air. It carried eight officers, twenty-two crew and two stowaways, plus a bottle of brandy, which remains unopened.

1938 The Mallard, an English steam railroad locomotive, set a world record of 203 kmh. It retired in 1963 after 2 400 000 km.

Jim Morrison, the lead singer of the rock band the Doors, in a 1968 studio shot.

4 JULY

1776: Americans Revolt

The thirteen American colonies declared their independence from England during the American Revolutionary War. Some members of the newly formed Continental Congress signed what has become one of the world's most famous documents—*The Declaration of Independence*. The background is this: England's King George III considered colonists to be English citizens who chose to live abroad in America. Several generations of colonists had been raised in America, felt no allegiance to England and knew very little about England. Yet the King thought that they should pay taxes to England, even though the Colonists were not living in England, could not vote in English elections and had no representation in the British Parliament. At first, when the King instituted a new tax, the Colonists' rallying cry was 'No taxation without representation.' England dispatched troops to bring the rebellious colonists back into line and the American Revolutionary War broke out on 19 April 1775 in Concord and Lexington, Massachusetts. It would last for nearly six years, with an American victory. The American leader, General George Washington, became the first American President.

1826: Jefferson and Adams

In one of the most fascinating coincidences in American history, two of the main architects of the American independence died hours apart on the fiftieth anniversary of the Declaration of Independence: John Adams the second American President and Thomas Jefferson, the third American President. Jefferson was the author of *The Declaration of Independence*.

1999: Becks and Posh

The celebrity English couple married at Luttrellstown Castle near Dublin, chosen for its seclusion so that they could avoid the paparazzi. 'Becks' is David Beckham, a well-known soccer player and 'Posh,' Victoria Adams is a singer, formerly with the Spice Girls. They are a popular tabloid couple with good looks and what appears to be a relaxed yet extravagant lifestyle. 'Becks' is known for his frequent changes in hairstyle to the delight of his fans. They both became multi-millionaires from endorsements for a vast array of commercial products that are especially popular in Asia and Europe.

1790 Sir George Everest was born in Powys, Wales. He accurately surveyed the Indian subcontinent in the Great Survey and created new survey techniques. Peak XV was named Mount Everest in his honour.

1848 Francois-Rene, the Vicomte de Chateaubriand, the founder of French Romanticism, was born in Brittany. He was also a diplomat who travelled widely, including North America, which he wrote about in his novels.

1917 Manuel Rodriguez Sanchez, considered by many the greatest bullfighter of all time, was born in Cordoba, Spain. He died aged 30, leaving Spain in shock.

1928 Gina Lollobrigida was born at Auviaco, Italy. She began in Italian language movies. She has appeared in about 30 movies, including *Bread, Love* and *Dreams*.

1954 Wartime rationing ends in Great Britain.

1991 Victor Chang, Australian of the Year and world-renowned transplant surgeon, was murdered in Sydney in an apparent extortion attempt.

Portrait of Victor Chang at the Garvan Institute of Medical Research in Sydney, Australia.

5 JULY

1975: Ashe nails Wimbledon and Connors

Arthur Ashe became the first black man to win the singles title at Wimbledon. His victory was especially sweet because he defeated Jimmy Connors, who two weeks previously had announced a US $5 million libel suit against Ashe, President of the Association of Tennis Professionals. Ashe had criticised Jimmy Connors for his refusal to join the American Davis Cup team. Ashe was also the first African-American to win the US Open in 1968 and the Australian Open in 1970. When he retired from tennis he became a respected scholar and civil rights activist. He suffered from poor health later in life and died at 49-years-of-age from AIDS contracted from a blood transfusion during heart surgery.

1996: Dolly

Dolly, the cloned sheep, was born in the late afternoon at the Roslin Institute, near Edinburgh, Scotland. She was created from an adult mammary gland cell of a six-year-old sheep and an unfertilised sheep egg that had been stripped of its chromosomes. The two were fused with an electrical jolt and surgically implanted into a surrogate ewe. It took researchers Ian Wilmut and Keith Campbell ten years to succeed. Scientists doubted for a quarter of a century that cloning was possible from anything other than embryonic material. Dolly's birth led to religious leaders, ethicists, politicians and others debating the case for and against human cloning. Since then, cloning has been successful with mice, horses, cats and other species. The possibility of saving species of animals from extinction is being pondered, but human cloning remains a volatile issue. Dolly was put down in 2003 after doctors found she had progressive lung disease.

A.D. 863 Saint Cyril and Methodius Day celebrated in Slovakia. They were Greek priests who were invited by Prince Ratislav of Great Morovia to introduce Christianity and the first Slavic alphabet.

1811 Venezuela achieved its independence from Spain, by proclamation, but not in actuality until 1821.

1853 Cecil Rhodes was born in Hertfordshire, England. He controlled the world's diamond production, based in Africa. Rhodesia (Zimbabwe) was named for him. His will endowed scholarships for Oxford University.

1962 Algeria gained its independence from France, after years of bitter fighting. It is celebrated as a national holiday.

1979 The Tynwald, the Isle of Man Parliament, celebrated its 1000th anniversary, although the exact date of its founding is unknown. Tynwald Day is the National Holiday for the Isle. Vikings settled the Isle, off the English coast.

Arthur Ashe of the United States competes at Wimbledon in London, England.

1907: Frida Kahlo

The artist Magdalena Carmen Frida Kahlo Calderon was born in Coyoacan, Mexico. She had polio as a child and was severely injured in a traffic accident when she was 15-years-old. She started painting during her convalescence and sent some of her work to Mexico's famous muralist Diego Rivera. He encouraged her and they married in 1929. They divorced, but later remarried. Andre Breton, the surrealistic artist, said that her vibrant, brightly coloured work was 'like a ribbon around a bomb.' Kahlo often scandalised the public with her turbulent private life and her communist leanings. She became an alcohol and drug user to cope with the pain of her many operations, a leg amputation and emotional upheavals. She died aged 47, in her sleep, perhaps a suicide. A major movie, *Frida*, was made about her in 2002.

1951: Geoffrey Rush

Australia's late blooming actor was born in Toowoomba, Queensland. Rush was a graduate of Sydney's National Institute of Dramatic Arts, where he was a roommate with Mel Gibson. His first real hit was as Snoopy the dog in the musical *You're a Good Man Charlie Brown*. He appeared in many Australian stage productions and four movies, before his 1996 international breakthrough movie, *Shine*. *Shine* received seven Oscar nominations and was a box office sensation. Rush won an Oscar for best actor. Since then Rush has appeared in dozens of movies, including *Les Miserables*, *Elizabeth* and *Lantana*. He received Oscar nominations for *Quills* and for *Shakespeare in Love*.

1957: Gibson smashes tennis colour bar

29-year-old Althea Gibson became the first black person to win a tennis final at Wimbledon. Queen Elizabeth II presented Gibson with the singles trophy. Gibson had learned to play tennis on the asphalt streets of Harlem, New York and was mentored by a black physician, Dr Walter Johnson, who also mentored Arthur Ashe. After her victory in England, she was given a ticker tape parade on Broadway and a Mayoral reception. Gibson went on to win the US Open two months later. She was voted Female Athlete of the Year by the *Associated Press* in 1957, the first black person to be honoured. She died in 2003, aged 76.

1953 Nanci Grifiith, singer, guitarist and songwriter, was born in Seguin, Texas. Her best-known song is *From a Distance*, written by Julie Gold. She won a Grammy in 1994.

1957 Australia and Japan signed a trade agreement, eliminating trade discrimination. Previously, there had been strong anti-Japanese feelings based on atrocities committed in the Second World War against Australian prisoners of war.

1966 Malawi received its independence from Great Britain after becoming a republic in 1965. It was previously known as Nyasaland.

1973 Otto Klemperer, German conductor and composer, died in Zurich, aged 88. He was one of the greatest 20th century conductors. He fled the Nazis and was appointed Los Angeles Symphony Orchestra conductor.

1999 Joaquin Rodrigo, Spanish classical composer died in Madrid, aged 97. He was blind from age three. His most famous work was *Concierto de Aranjuez*, a haunting concerto for classical guitar and orchestra.

Australian actor Geoffrey Rush during a photo call for the film *The Life and Death of Peter Sellers* at the 57th Cannes Film Festival in 2004. The film is based on a controversial biography of the *Pink Panther* star by author Roger Lewis

7 JULY

1978: Chariots' Anniversary

Every year, New Zealand's Lord Arthur E. Porritt and Englishman Harold Abrahams had dinner on this day, with their wives at 7.00 p.m for over 50 years until Abrahams' death in 1978. That was the exact time of the final of the 1924 Paris Olympics 100-metre race, which Englishman Abrahams won. The race was immortalised in the movie *Chariots of Fire*. The movie did not mention Porritt by name, but he had won the bronze medal. Porritt was an outstanding athlete and captained the New Zealand team at the 1924 and 1928 Olympics. He was a leading coach and advised fellow Kiwi and Oxford Rhodes scholar, Jack Lovelock, to enter the 1500 metre race instead of the 5000 at the 1936 Berlin Olympics. Lovelock won New Zealand's first gold track medal. Porritt was later a member of the International Olympic Committee. He trained as a physician in Otago and Oxford and became Surgeon to the Royal Family. Porritt was the first New Zealand-born Governor General, serving from 1967–72. He died in 1994, aged 93.

1985: Boom Boom Becker

Seventeen-year-old tennis player Boris Becker became the youngest Wimbledon champion. Becker, known as 'Boom Boom,' was also the first unseeded champion and the first German winner. His gymnastic style brought renewed popularity to the game. He defeated Kevin Curren, a South African-born American, in four sets in three hours and 18 minutes.

1990: The Three Tenors

The trio of Jose Carreras, Placido Domingo and Luciano Pavarotti sang together for the first time. They always list their names in alphabetical order. *The Three Tenors* sang in Rome at the 1800 year-old Baths of Caracalla on the eve of the World Cup Final. Planes from Rome's Leonardo da Vinci airport were re-routed to avoid drowning them out. The concert proceeds were donated to charity. The Roman concert launched the trio's highly successful career on stage, radio and television. Carreras was born in Barcelona, Spain in 1946. The concert marked his return from a successful battle against leukemia. Domingo was born in Madrid, Spain in 1941 but was raised in Mexico. Pavarotti was born in 1935 in Italy. He is probably the best known of the trio for his exuberant, larger-than-life personality.

1887 Marc Chagall, the Russian artist was born. He was known for his dreamlike, whimsical canvases and huge murals. He designed the sets for Igor Stravinsky's *The Firebird*. He died in 1985.

1922 Pierre Cardin was born in Venice, Italy to French parents. He pioneered geometric shapes and unisex designs. The fashion designer also owns the *Maxims* Restaurants.

1942 Carmen Duncan was born in rural Cooma, NSW. She appeared in Australian soap operas *Number 96* and *Skyways*. For six years she appeared in the American soap opera *Another World*.

1984 Dame Flora Robson died aged 82. She was born in Durham, England and appeared in about sixty movies, including *Wuthering Heights* and *Fire Over England*.

Placido Domingo (L) of Spain, Jose Carreras (C) of Spain and Luciano Pavarotti (R) of Italy share a laugh during the Three Tenors New Year 1999 Concert in Tokyo, in front of more than 34,000 people.

8 JULY

1926: Death Dissected

Identical triplets Elisabeth, Eva and Erika Kübler were born in Zurich, Switzerland. Elisabeth pursued a medical career and married a fellow doctor, American Emmanuel 'Manny' Ross. She spent most of her life in America. In 1969 she wrote the block-buster book *On Death and Dying*, written at a time when death was never discussed in medical school. From her work with terminally ill patients, she identified five stages of emotional preparation for death: denial, anger, bargaining, depression and acceptance. She died in August 2004, in Scottsdale, Arizona.

1943: Jean Moulin–Freedom Fighter

The celebrated hero and unifier of the French Resistance, Jean Moulin was tortured to death by the notorious Nazi, Klaus Barbie. Moulin escaped Nazi-occupied France in September 1941 to meet General Charles de Gaulle in London. In 1942 he secretly parachuted back into France to implement de Gaulle's plan to unify the eight major resistance groups. He helped restore French pride and unity, yet a fellow countryman betrayed him to Barbie. A German soldier wrote about Moulin, 'I compliment you on the energy with which you defend … your country's honour.' After the war Barbie was recruited by American counter-intelligence who provided him with a false identity and a new life in La Paz, Bolivia. In 1983 he was extradited to France for crimes against humanity and sentenced in 1987 to life imprisonment. He died of leukemia in Lyon's prison hospital in 1991.

1977: Young Gun Golfer

Twenty eight-year-old Tom Watson took on golfing giant, 37-year-old Jack 'Golden Bear' Nicklaus in the British Open. They both shot a 65. The next day, 9 July, they shared the lead at 17 under. When both Watson and Nicklaus birdied 18, Watson won by a stroke after the second consecutive 65. Watson's score of 268 broke the British Open record of 276 and the major championship record of 271. Nicklaus was a golf prodigy, starting from age ten. At 13, he shot a round of 69 over a 6.5 km course. Sportswriters later voted the Golden Bear Golfer of the Century.

1497 Vasco da Gama set sail for India. He landed in Goa, which still bears strong Portuguese influence.

1889 The Wall Street Journal, New York's financial newspaper, was first published. To this day, it still does not run photographs.

1889 The last bare-knuckle boxing match was held. John L. Sullivan beat Jake Kilrain in 75 rounds.

1990 West Germany beat world champion Argentina in football's (soccer) World Cup Final with a controversial penalty kick. The score was 1:0.

1994 Kim Il Sung, North Korea's 'Great Leader', died. Revered as a god-like figure his death stalled planned talks of conciliation between the America and South Korea. His reclusive son, Kim Jong Il, succeeded him.

French Forces of the Interior capture a German prisoner in southern France, in1944.

Inset: Jean Moulin, the brains and charisma behind the National Council of the French Resistance in World War II. Codenamed 'Max', he was arrested by Klaus Barbie of the Gestapo in 1943 and died in custody after weeks of torture.

9 JULY

1927: Alaska flies state flag

Alaska's state flag was flown for the first time. The flag design was chosen as the result of a contest for intermediate and high school students, when Alaska was still an American territory. The winner from the 700 entries was 13-year-old orphan, John Bell 'Benny' Benson. His design was a dark blue background to depict the huge overarching night sky and the Forget-Me-Not flower with the North Star symbolising Alaska as the most northerly American possession. Benson included the predominant feature of the night sky, Ursa Major, the Big Bear constellation. The prize was a $1000 scholarship and an engraved watch. Benson himself represented Alaska—part Russian, Aleut and Swedish. He later worked for Kodiak Airways and died in 1972.

1984: York Minster Burns

The historic church York Minster in northern England was engulfed with flames causing more than £2 million in damages. The fire was probably caused by lightning. It is a Norman/Gothic Church and one of the largest and finest examples of Medieval architecture in Europe. Work started in 1220 and was not completed until 1480. The present building is awe-inspiring in its size—160–metres long, with 60–metre high towers. The Church was the seat for the powerful Archbishop of York, ideally suited on the main North-South thoroughfare from London to Scotland. The Minster was restored by 1987.

2000: Nkosi Johnson

Eleven-year-old Johnson addressed 10 000 delegates at the 13th International AIDS Conference in Durban, South Africa. He had been born HIV positive in poverty in KwaZulu-Natal, one of the provinces hardest hit by HIV-AIDS. He was raised by Gail Johnson, his foster mother, as his HIV infected mother could not care for him. In his speech, Johnson talked of the need to overcome AIDS stigma and of his own fight for admission to primary school. He said that 200 AIDS babies were born every day in South Africa and that 11 per cent of the country's population was infected. Johnson spoke of the need for more government action. He inspired millions with his courage. Johnson said, 'Do all you can, with what you have, in the time you have, in the place you are.' He died on 1 June, 2001, the longest surviving AIDS child in South Africa.

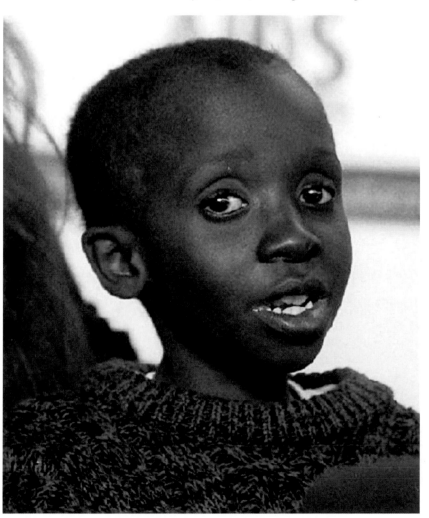

1816 Argentina declared its independence from Spain. Its name comes from argentum, Latin for silver. It had been a source of wealth to Spain since the 16th century.

1893 Daniel Hale Williams, African-American surgeon, performed the world's first successful open-heart surgery in Chicago.

1956 Tom Hanks was born in Concord, California. He won Oscars for *Forrest Gump* and *Philadelphia*.

1991 The International Olympic Committee reinstated South Africa, now that apartheid was banned. The next day, the America lifted its economic sanctions.

2001 The highest transfer fee paid for a soccer player was $66 million for Zinedine Zidane who transferred from Turin, Italy's Juventus to Real Madrid.

Eleven-year-old HIV-Positive Nkosi Johnson addresses a media conference in 2000, at the launch of a global campaign 'Action for Orphans' at the 13th International Aids Conference in Durban. Nkosi appealed for greater care by the world community for children like himself living with Aids. He died the following year.

10 JULY

1915: Saul Bellow

Usually thought of as a Yiddish-American writer, Bellow was, in fact, born in Lachine, Quebec, to Russian parents on this day. When he was nine, the family moved to Chicago, Illinois, where he lived until he died on 5 April 2005. Bellow has written novels, plays and essays and has received the Pulitzer Prize, the National Book Award (three times) and the 1976 Nobel Prize for Literature. Some of his best-known books are *Herzog, Henderson the Rain King* and *The Adventures of Augie March*. He has received numerous international literary awards. In 2000, when he was 84-years-old, he surprised everyone when he announced the birth of his daughter.

1985: Rainbow Warrior Goes Down

The French Secret police were accused of committing an act of terrorism when they sank the *Rainbow Warrior* in Auckland Harbour, New Zealand. The boat, owned by Greenpeace, the environmental and peace activist group, was en route to Tahiti to protest and to try to prevent French atomic weapon testing. One crew member died when the *Rainbow Warrior* sank. Relations between the two countries were strained. After an inquiry by *Le Monde* newspaper identified who was responsible, the French Defence Minister resigned along with the head of the Secret police.

1996: White Cloud

An extremely rare albino buffalo was born at the Shirek Buffalo Farm near Michigan, North Dakota. The female buffalo was named White Cloud. She is considered sacred and a good omen to the Lakota Indians. Once there were millions of buffalo (also called bison) on the Western Plains, but White settlers hunted them almost to extinction.

1899: Age Race

Sprinter Philip Rabinowitz broke the world record for the 100-metre race at a Cape Town, South Africa stadium. His time was 30.86 seconds. Never mind that Olympians can run the distance in under 10 seconds; Rabinowitz is 100 years old! He stays in shape by walking nearly four miles a day and eating healthily, he said.

1099 English Christian Crusaders captured Jerusalem. The city's entire Jewish and Muslim population had been massacred by the following week.

1871 Marcel Proust, one of the greatest 20th century writers, was born near Paris. He is best-known for his multi-volume *In Search of Lost Time (Remembrance of Things Past)*. He suffered from severe asthma his whole life and died aged 61.

1985 Coca Cola re-introduced its popular Coke, which company executives had tried to replace with a 'New Coke' in a textbook case of 'don't mess with success'.

1991 Boris Yeltsin took office as President of Russia. This was the first popular election in the 1000-year-old country's history. He was President for eight turbulent years, during the dismantling of the USSR.

1997 DNA evidence from a Neanderthal skeleton supported the theory that humans evolved from an 'African Eve,' perhaps 100 000 to 200 000 years ago, was confirmed by British scientists..

The Rainbow Warrior, sunk by a bomb while docked in Auckland, New Zealand. One crew member died in the attack by the French Secret Service.

11 JULY

1893: Mikimoto Pearls

Kokichi Mikimoto became fascinated with pearls as a child and would eventually go on to develop the cultivated pearls that bear his name, Mikimoto. When he was 30-years-old, he and his wife Ume borrowed money to start a pearl farm in the Mie Prefecture, Japan. It took five years before they succeeded with their first, imperfect, cultivated pearl on this day. Another decade passed before Mikimoto harvested completely spherical pearls that are indistinguishable from natural ones. His first Mikimoto store opened in 1899 in Tokyo and it soon became an international empire. He died in 1954, aged 96.

1899: E B White

The children's author was born in Mount Vernon, New York. Elwyn Brooks White wrote essays, articles and literary criticism. He is the beloved author of the children's classics *Charlotte's Web*, *Stuart Little* and *The Trumpet of the Swan*. He was a *New Yorker* magazine staff writer, where he was considered a writer of grace, good humour and control. In 1963 American President John F. Kennedy awarded him the Presidential Medal of Freedom, the highest peacetime civilian honour. In middle age, he moved to Maine to farm and wrote a collection of delightful articles, *One Man's Meat*.

1951: Bonnie Pointer

One of the four Pointer Sisters was born in Oakland, California. The four sisters are preacher's daughters and bring a soulful tone to their Rhythm and Blues music. They were the first African-American women to appear at the Grand Ole Opry, a live radio recording studio in Nashville, Tennessee, which has an audience capacity of 4400. Bonnie went solo in 1978.

1754 Thomas Bowdler, the priggish physician, was born near Bath England. He 'cleaned up' Shakespeare, the Old Testament and other major literary works, to remove 'naughty' words. The word 'bowdlerise' is named for him. He died in 1825.

1936 Giorgio Armani, fashion designer, was born in Romagna, Italy.

1960 Three former French colonies gained their independence. Dahomey changed its name to Benin, Upper Volta to Burkina Faso and Niger retained its name.

1975 6000 clay warriors and their armaments were unearthed in a major archaeological find in China. The terracotta soldiers date from 221 to 206 BC.

1987 The world population reached five billion, reported the United Nations. It was at 6.5 billion as this book was published and is doubling every 35 years.

China's army of terracotta soldiers at the museum located about 40 km from the ancient capital of Xian in northern China. The statues, modelled after the soldiers serving Emperor Qin Shihuang (259 to 210 B.C.), the first ruler of a unified Chinese empire, have become one of the country's largest tourist attractions.

12 JULY

1730: Wedgwood

Josiah Wedgwood, 'the father of English potters', was born in Burslem, England. He came from a long line of potters. At the age of nine he began working in the family business. An attack of smallpox led to a partial leg amputation and although this slowed his mobility, it gave him the opportunity to analyse processes more carefully. Wedgwood set up his own factory in 1759 in Burslem. His experiments led to manufacturing, glazing and design changes. Queen Charlotte liked his new durable cream-coloured earthenware so much she appointed him the Official Royal Supplier of Dinnerware. His invention of a kiln temperature gauge earned him membership of the Royal Society. In 1774 Wedgwood produced a 952-piece dinner service for Russia's Catherine the Great. His Jasperware is world-renowned—white relief portraits of Greek or classical scenes on blue pottery. Potters have tried to imitate his work, but none have succeeded. The Wedgwood company continues to produce fine pottery.

1895: Buckminster Fuller

The visionary philosopher, inventor and architect, was born in Milton, Massachusetts. His best-known invention remains the Geodesic Dome. It first went on display at the Museum of Modern Art in 1952. Hundreds of thousands of domes have since been constructed around the world, used for many different purposes, such as military shelter, inexpensive housing in Africa, aeroplane hangars and even as the headquarters for the Ford Motor Company. In 1963, Fuller received a patent for an underwater submarine base. His name was also given to a chemical compound buckminsterfullerine or 'bucky balls'. He died in 1983 in Los Angeles.

1972: Shirley Chisholm

The American Congresswoman came fourth in the Democratic National Convention as a candidate for the American presidency, winning 151 delegate votes. She was the first major party African-American woman to run. Chisholm first became involved in politics in college after encountering racism. She won the election for the New York State Assembly in 1964. When she was elected to Congress, in 1968, she was the first African-American congresswoman. Chisholm hired an all-female staff and worked on civil rights issues, women's issues and anti-war activities. She was a much sought after public speaker and co-founded the National Organisation for Women. Chisholm served in Congress until 1982 and died in 2005.

1690 Orangeman's Day in Northern Ireland commemorates the Battle of Boyne, when English King William III, the Prince of Orange, defeated James II. A public holiday is held on the date, or close to it.

1817 Henry David Thoreau author, philosopher and non-violence advocate, was born near Concord, Massachusetts. He wrote the classic *Walden*.

1849 Sir William Osler, author of *The Principles and Practice of Medicine* was born at Tecumseh, Ontario Canada. He was the world's best-known physician at the beginning of the 20th century. He died in England in 1919.

1971 Kristi Yamaguchi, Olympic gold medallist ice skater, was born in Hayward, California.

A Black man gestures with his thumb down to an armed National Guardsman, during a protest in the Newark race riots, Newark, New Jersey, 1967.

13 JULY

1771 and 1772: Cook comes and goes

This day is significant in the life of one of the world's greatest explorers, Captain James Cook, for two events. In 1771 he arrived in Dover, concluding his first voyage of discovery, which had taken three years. Cook had sailed Endeavour around Cape Horn to Tahiti to observe the transit of Venus. He unsealed secret orders and sailed south in search of a rumoured 'Great South Land'. He made contact with Maoris in New Zealand while mapping most of its two islands. He mapped part of Australia's east coast and claimed it for the Crown, before returning home. One year later on this day, he set sail for the Antarctic Circle and was the first to explore it extensively. Cook returned to England in 1775. His third expedition in July 1776 in search of a Northwest Passage above Alaska was unsuccessful. Cook then sailed to Hawaii, naming them the Sandwich Islands. In a skirmish with Hawaiians, he was killed in 1779.

1934: Wole Soyinka

The writer was born near Ibadan in western Nigeria. With his parents' encouragement, he received a solid education and pursued a doctorate in drama at Leeds University. On his return to Africa, Soyinka founded the Orisun Theatre Company. He was arrested and imprisoned during the Nigerian civil war, from 1967. During his 22-months imprisonment he wrote the auto-biographical, *The Man Died: Prison Notes*. He has published about 20 volumes of novels, poetry and plays, exploring African mythology, music and dance. Soyinka won the Nobel Prize for Literature in 1986.

1985: Live Aid

A huge concert was held at Wembley Stadium, England as a fundraiser for starving Ethiopians. The concert attracted 72 000 people and was watched worldwide by 1.5 billion people. Bands included Dire Straits, Wham and David Bowie. The organiser, Bob Geldorf pleaded between acts, 'Don't go to the pub tonight, please stay in and give us your money.' Dubai's ruling family pledged £1 million. The concert raised over £30 million.

CAPTAIN COOK

London Published as the Act directs Sept 20 1800 by J Wilkes

1837 Queen Victoria moved into London's Buckingham Palace. She was the first British monarch to live there.

1878 The Treaty of Berlin re-drew the map of Europe. The Balkans, Montenegro and Serbia were now wholly independent of the Ottoman Empire.

1933 David Storey, English author and playwright, was born in Wakefield. He wrote *The Performance of Small Firms*.

1935 Earl Lovelace, the writer, was born in Toco, Trinidad. His first novel, *While Gods are Falling*, was acclaimed for its description of West Indian culture.

1944 Erno Rubik, inventor of the puzzle named for him, the Rubik's Cube, was born in an air-raid shelter in Budapest, Hungary.

1940: Patrick Stewart, the British actor was born in Mirfield England. He enrolled in the Bristol Old Vic Theatre School in 1957 and began a distinguished career on the stage, in Shakespeare, classical and contemporary work. He is known for his character Captain Jean-Luc Picard on the television classic *Star Trek: The Next Generation*.

English explorer Captain James Cook (1728-1779), whose expeditions to the Pacific, North America and Antarctica vastly increased contemporary cartographical knowledge of these areas.

The inset below depicts his death at the hands of irate islanders on Hawaii. A print by J Chapman, published in 1800.

14 JULY

1858: Great Eastern

One of the most extraordinary ships ever built was one that few people have ever heard of, *The Great Eastern* (GE), was launched. It was the first large iron steamship and the first to use a screw propeller. It took four years to build, used three million rivets and was six times the size of a regular ship. Isambard Kingdom Brunel, known for building railroads, designed it to use both steam and sail. It carried enough coal to avoid refuelling stops, but was unprofitable once the Suez Canal opened. In 1864 it was offered for sale, but no one was interested until the Telegraph Construction Company chartered the ship to lay a second wire cable between England and America. It took five months just to load the cable. After the telegraph cable was laid 200 men took two years to break up the GE for scrap. An admirer wrote, 'Poor old ship: you deserved a better fate'.

1912: Woody Guthrie

The American folk singer was born in Okemah, Oklahoma. He developed a love for 'riding the rails,' when he was forced to travel to find work to support his family during the 1930s Great Depression and the Great Dust Bowl. He became a supporter of the downtrodden. He was patriotic and wrote the anthem-like *This Land is Your Land*. Guthrie spent his final years in and out of institutions. Misdiagnosed as schizophrenic, he had inherited Huntington's chorea, a degenerative disease. His work influenced singers as diverse as Bruce Springsteen, Bob Dylan, Pete Singer and his son, Arlo. He died in 1967.

1918: Ingmar Bergman

The prolific writer for stage and screen and movie director was born in Uppsala, Sweden. He once said, 'the cinema was an exciting mistress but the theatre was his faithful wife.' Known for his probing exploration of characters' psychological makeup, he explores metaphysical themes, the existence of God and difficulties in male-female communication. Some of Bergman's best known works are *Cries and Whispers*, *Wild Strawberries* and *The Seventh Seal*.

1950: Young Maori

Sir Apirana Turupa Ngata, one of the earliest Maori university scholars, lawyers and Maori activist, died at Waiomatatiri age 76. Initially he advocated change and progress through the Europeanisation of his race, but when he was elected to Parliament, his crusade changed to one of preserving Maori language, traditions and culture. Ngata was one of the founders of the Young Maori Party, along with Sir Peter Buck, Maui Pomare, (the first Maori physician) and clergyman Frederick Bennett.

1486 Andrea del Sarto was born near Florence, Italy. He was one of the most renowned painters of his time.

1769 Gaspar de Portola, the Spanish explorer, set out with a party of 64 from San Diego to explore Northern California. His missions included the famed San Juan Capistrano and Santa Barbara.

1789 The French Revolution began with the fall of the infamous Bastille prison. It is a national holiday in France and many other countries.

1867 Alfred Nobel, an explosives manufacturer, demonstrated his invention, dynamite, in a Surrey, England quarry. His will endowed the prestigious Nobel prizes.

1990 Ulrich Inderbinen, a 90-year-old Swiss mountain guide reached the peak of the 4,481-metre Matterhorn on the 125th anniversary of its first ascent.

Isambard Kingdom Brunel's massive, double-hulled steamship the *Great Eastern* was launched on 31st January 1858 and broken up in 1888.

15 JULY

1606: Rembrandt Van Rijn

The painter and etcher was born in Leiden, the Netherlands. Rembrandt's masterpieces are renowned for their rich colours, brushwork and interplay of light and dark. His paintings offer an insight into the Amsterdam of his day. Some of his most famous works are *The Night Watch* and his series of self-portraits. He painted his own portrait more than 90 times, leaving a record of how he looked throughout his life. He outlived his wife and all four children making his later years very lonely. His paintings reflect his melancholy and attempts to reveal the personality behind the face. He died in 1669.

1933: Julian Bream

The English virtuoso and classical guitarist, was born in London. He grew up in a musical family and first learned piano. For his eleventh birthday, his father gave him a classical guitar. From 12-years-old, he studied cello and piano at the Royal College of Music. He also studied lute playing and has helped audiences discover the pleasures of the little known instrument. Contemporary composers often write pieces with Bream in mind, for example, Benjamin Britten wrote *Nocturnal* for him.

2003: Cathy Freeman

After saying, 'My heart's not in it,' Cathy Freeman retired. *The Melbourne Age* described her as 'Australia's greatest athlete in recent history and arguably its greatest ever' in terms of the impact she had on sport. Freeman had lit the Olympic flame at the Sydney 2000 Olympics and had thrilled her countrymen when she won gold in the 400 metres. She ran a victory lap holding the Aboriginal flag. There was so much stamping and so much applause and cheers that the Stadium actually shook. Freeman was also part of the Aussie team that came in fifth in the 4 x 400 m relay that broke an Australian record that had stood since 1976. Freeman was born in Mackay Queensland in 1973. She is very proud to be the first Aboriginal sprinter to win a gold medal at the Commonwealth Games in 1990 and then at the Olympics in 2000. She was voted Young Australian of the Year in 1995 and Australian of the Year in 1998, the first person to be honoured with both awards

1870 Manitoba and the vast Northwest Territories joined Canada.

1918 The last great offensive by the Germans in World War I, known as the Battle of the Marne. The Germans were defeated by American, Italian and British forces and soon after Germany sued for peace.

1946 Linda Ronstadt was born in Tucson, Arizona, America. She started the group, *The Stone Poneys*, before going solo. Her first big hit was *Different Drum*.

1997 Gianni Versace, head of an Italian fashion house, was murdered by a fan. He was 50-years-old.

2004 The Secret Agent, a BBC documentary about the British National party, revealed that the far-right political group, founded in 1982 by John Tyndall, was racist.

Australian sprinter Cathy Freeman crosses the finish line ahead of her rivals after winning the Women's 100 Metre A final with a time of 12:05 seconds at the Emil Zatopek Classic at Olympic Park, Melbourne, Victoria, Australia.1999:

16 JULY

1801: Hartog's Time Capsule Found

After the British established their Sydney penal settlement, there was lively interest in Australia throughout Europe. The French sent an expedition, under Captain Nicolas Baudin on board *Le Geographe* and Emmanuel Hamelin on board *Le Naturaliste* to explore the west coast. When Hamelin went ashore at Dirk Hartog Island, he was surprised to find a pewter plate nailed to a post that had been left in 1697 by the Dutch explorer Willem de Vlamingh. For hundreds of years, Dutch ships had either explored or had encounters with the west coast, the latter from when they were blown off course on their way to the Javanese Spice Islands. Captain Dirk Hartog was the first known European to land on Australian soil in 1616. He commemorated his landing by leaving an engraved pewter plate. This is the plate that de Vlamingh found 81 years later and took back to the Netherlands. De Vlamingh left his own plate behind, which Hamelin found.

1994: Shoemaker-Levy Lightshow

The first fragments of the Shoemaker-Levy comet began crashing into and exploding on the planet Jupiter. It had been anticipated and astronomers were ready to catch it on video. The Hubble Space Telescope provided vivid images of each successive impact, which were more than the planet Earth's arsenal of weapons, combined. The bombardment lasted for five days.

1995: Amazon.com

The online store *Amazon.com* was launched. It sells books, music, DVDs, videos and other products, including clothing, toys, cameras and barbeques. Jeffrey P. Bezos, its founder, was always an inventor. He graduated from college with a degree in engineering and computers. In 1994, Bezos wondered if the Internet had commercial capability. He reviewed mail order catalogues to see what might be viable and decided to try selling books. He set up three computers in his garage and told 300 friends to test his site. It worked perfectly, so he launched it on July 16. By July's end, Bezos had sold books in 45 countries and all American states. He originally called Amazon 'Cadabra,' like 'Abracadabra', but people misheard it as 'cadaver,' so he changed it. The store has 700 000 active sellers in its virtual marketplace and 41 million active customers.

1782 Wolfgang Amadeus Mozart's comic opera *The Abduction from the Seraglio* opened in Vienna. It was commissioned by Joseph II, the Austrian Emperor.

1821 Mary Baker Eddy, the founder of Christian Science, was born near Concord, New Hampshire, America. She believed in the healing power of prayer. She also founded one of the world's most respected newspapers, *Christian Science Monitor*.

1880 Emily Stowe became the first female physician to practice in Canada. No school would admit her, so she trained in New York. Later, her daughter, Augusta, became the first female to earn a medical degree in Canada.

1951 Belgium's King Leopold III abdicated at age 50, in favour of his son, Crown Prince Badouin.

1951 J.D. Salinger's classic novel of teenage angst *Catcher in the Rye* was published in the America.

Full view of planet Jupiter with fragments of the comet Shoemaker-Levy 9 impacting, out of view, on Jupiter's dark side.

17 JULY

1938: Wrong way, Corrigan?

Douglas Corrigan helped build the plane for Charles Lindbergh's solo Atlantic crossing, which inspired him to visit his own ancestral land. However, government inspectors turned his application down for two years, as they did not think Corrigan's plane was safe enough. On this day in 1938, he was cleared to fly to California and left Long island airport, headed west. It was very cloudy and he must have read the compass backward, only realising it was Ireland below him, after a 28-hour flight. He told the press with a straight face that he was as surprised as they were to see him. People got a good chuckle out of the story and nicknamed him 'Wrong Way Corrigan.' The term is now used when people go the wrong way, especially in sporting events. On his return to New York, by steamship, he had a bigger ticker tape parade than Charles Lindbergh. He was also presented with an error-free compass. He died in 1995, never admitting that he intentionally flew to Ireland.

1955: Disney's Land

When people think of a theme park, they usually think of the world's first—Disneyland. It opened on this day in Anaheim, California. It covered 160 acres and cost $17 million. Projections were for five million tourists to visit each year, but upward of 12 million visit annually.

1999: Observation Post South

New Zealand's Phoenix Astronomy Society at Wairarapa near Wellington opened their first observatory. Its latest venture, Stonehenge Aotearoa, which is a calendar and map of the Southern Hemisphere skies opened in February 2005. Stonehenge Aotearoa is similar in size to its English namesake, but it is not a replica. The Society conducts talks and observations of the North Island's starlit skies.

180 Twelve Christians were executed in Scillium, Northern Africa. It was the first written record of Christians in Africa.

1762 Catherine the Great became Tzar of Russia, after the death of her husband, the pro-Prussian Peter III. Peter was murdered after just six months as tsar. His wife was probably involved.

1859 Luis Munoz-Rivera, the Puerto Rican patriot and writer, was born. He died in 1916. An annual public holiday commemorates his birth.

1995 Juan Manuel Fangio, a five-time Formula One world champion, died, aged 84.

2000 Tesco, a supermarket chain, restored Imperial measurements because too many customers were confused by metric. Metric is also used.

World champion Argentinian racing car driver Juan Manuel Fangio in action driving a Maserati at the 1957 Italian Grand Prix at Monza. He finished second behind Stirling Moss in a Vanwall.

18 JULY

1720: Nature Lover

Gilbert White, 'the Father of British Naturalists,' and the best known English naturalist until Charles Darwin a century later, was born in Selborne, Hampshire, England. He was a clergyman, but his hobby was studying nature. He is considered the first ecologist. His book, *The Natural History and Antiquities of Selborne* was an immediate success and has never been out of print. It describes the activities of earthworms and harvest mice, like a charming adult non-fiction prose version of Beatrix Potter's books. White inherited an estate, The Wakes of Selborne, which is now a museum for him and his work. He died in 1793.

1933: Yevgeny Yevtushenko

The Russian writer, poet and activist was born. He is a fourth-generation descendant of a Ukrainian family exiled to Siberia. He is the best-known poet of the post-Stalinist era. He was one of the first Soviet poets to tour widely, under Premiers Nikita Khrushchev and Leonid Brezhnev in the 1960s. He became a staunch critic of communism and attracted a huge following at home and abroad. After the publication of his autobiography he was silenced for a time, but his privileges were restored about two years later and he continued speaking out. In 1972 his play *Under the Statue of Liberty* was well received. In 1974 he protested the exile of Alexander Solzhenitsyn. In 1989 Yevtushenko became a member of the Congress of People's Deputies. After Mikhail Gorbachev became premier cultural restrictions eased and Yevtushenko introduced the works of Soviet writers whose work had been repressed. He also oversaw the erection of a statue for all victims of Stalin opposite the KGB's infamous Lublianka headquarters in Moscow. One of his best-known poems is about the June 1941 massacre at Babi Yar, one of the biggest massacres in history, when 34 000 Ukrainians were slaughtered near Kiev by the Nazis.

No Jewish blood runs among my blood,
but I am as bitterly and hardly hated
by every anti-Semite as if I were a Jew.
By this I am a Russian

1811 William Makepeace Thackeray, English novelist, was born in Calcutta, India. He wrote *Vanity Fair*. He died in London in 1863.

1873 Sir David Salomons, the first Jewish Lord Mayor of London, died. He was also the first English Jew in a political post and is remembered for removing a tablet from the British museum that blamed the 1666 fire on Catholics.

1939 Hunter S. Thompson, the counter-culture journalist was born in Louisville, Kentucky, America. He wrote *Fear and Loathing in Las Vegas*. He committed suicide in February 2005.

1980 Rohini I, India's first satellite, was successfully launched.

1993 Japan's Liberal Democratic Party, the ruling conservative party, lost its majority in a crushing defeat in the general election. It had been in power since 1955.

Russian poet Yevgeny Yevtushenko at the opening ceremony of Moscow Film Festival.in July 2003. Yevtushenko declaims poetry at the drop of a hat. Bright-eyed and stabbing the air he runs through half a dozen short poems, triggering a round of applause from reporters accustomed to more prosaic forms of speech. The author of 'Babi Yar', the angry denunciation of a wartime Nazi atrocity that had harsh words too for Soviet anti-Semitism, is clearly not about to lay down his pen. The poem, along with Alexander Solzhenitsyn's 'One Day in the Life of Ivan Denisovich' published the same year alerted Western audiences to a new tone in Soviet literature that heralded the stirrings of the dissident movement.

19 JULY

1695: Personal Classified

The first recorded matrimonial advertisement appeared in an English farming journal. The magazine was John Houghton's *Collections for the Improvement of Husbandry and Trade*, which seems like a most unusual place for an advertisement for a wife. Most likely, the gentleman who placed the advertisement was hoping a wealthy property-owning father would read it and see it as a way to marry off a spinster daughter. The advertisement read:

'A Gentleman about 30 Years of Age, that says he has a Very Good Estate, would willingly Match Himself to some Young Gentlewoman that has a fortune of 3000 pounds or thereabouts and he will make Settlement to Content.'

Other would-be-husbands followed suit and placed advertisements. When a woman placed an advertisement for a husband in 1727 in the *Manchester Weekly Journal*, she was committed to an insane asylum for four weeks.

1848: Sentimental Declaration

The first American women's rights convention began in Seneca Falls, New York. Lucretia Mott and Elizabeth Cady Stanton, two pioneering suffragettes, organised it. The convention program covered issues such as voting, property rights and divorce. The most controversial issue by far was women's right to vote. By the end of the next day the delegates had written a document called the *Declaration of Sentiments* modelled on the American *Declaration of Independence*, but addressing women's issues. The convention was the birth of the women's movement in America.

1921: Radioimmunoassay

Rosalyn Yalow was born in New York City. She was a 'medical physicist' who researched the medical applications of radioactive isotopes. Yalow developed radioimmunoassay (RIA) that measures minute concentrations of biological substances in the body. RIA has hundreds of applications, including the study of insulin concentration in diabetic patients' blood. She shared the 1977 Nobel Prize for Medicine.

1946: Ilie Nastase

The volatile tennis player was born in Bucharest, Romania. He won 57 singles titles and 51 doubles titles. He was ranked number one in the world in 1972 and 1973. Usually good-humoured on court, he acquired the nickname 'Nasty' after venting his anger in some tight matches. After his retirement he wrote novels and unsuccessfully ran for Mayor of Bucharest in 1996.

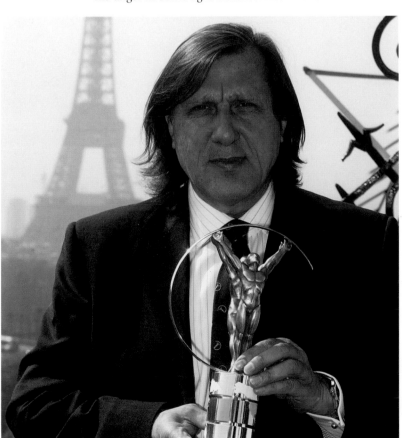

1873 W.C. Gosse was the first European to discover Ayer's Rock and the Musgrave Ranges in Central Australia. The area has been sacred to Aborigines for eons and is now known by its traditional name, Uluru.

1980 The Moscow Olympics opened, but were boycotted by athletes from more than 50 nations in an American led protest of the USSR invasion of Afghanistan.

1946 Marilyn Monroe was given her first screen test at Twentieth Century-Fox Studios. Her first movie was *The Shocking Miss Pilgrim.*. Her last was *The Misfits*. In all Monroe appeared in 31 films in 15 years.

1997 Daniel Komen, a Kenyan runner, became the first man to run two miles in less than eight minutes, with a time of 7:58:61.

Romanian tennis legend, Illie Nastase, at the announcement of the nominees for the 2003 Laureus World Sports Awards held at the Plaza Athenee Hotel in 2003 in Paris.

20 JULY

1969: A Big Step

Two American astronauts landed their lunar module *Eagle* on the moon at exactly 4.17 p.m. Millions worldwide watched on television. It had taken just over a decade create and to launch the complex spacecraft designed to fulfil the late President Kennedy's dream to land an American on the Moon and to beat the USSR in the so-called 'Space Race'. The USSR had pioneered space flight with its Sputnik program, to the American's chagrin. On Christmas Eve 1968 *Apollo 8* became the first manned spacecraft to fly to the Moon. Frank Borman, James Covell and William Anders successfully orbited the Moon, 403 000 km from Earth. No Moon landing was planned; scientists had to see how humans fared orbiting the Moon. *Apollo 8* paved the way for *Apollo 11* and the *Eagle's* Moon landing of 20 July, 1969. The first astronaut out was Neil Armstrong, who said, 'The Eagle has landed.' When he opened the module door and took his first step he said the unscripted historic words, *'One giant step for Man, one giant leap for Mankind.'* Edwin Aldrin Jr followed him onto the lunar surface. This left pilot Michael Collins alone to manoeuvre the mother spacecraft in its orbit around the Moon. Armstrong and Aldrin explored the Moon for two and a quarter hours, taking photographs and collecting rock samples. The trio made a successful return to Earth on 24 July.

1960: Widow Wins for Women

Mrs. Sirimavo Bandaranaike became the world's first-ever female elected government head when she was sworn in as Prime Minister, Foreign Minister and Minister of Defence in Ceylon. She was the widow of S.W.R.D. Bandaranaike, the Premier who had been assassinated the previous September. Bandaranaike had never been politically active yet her Freedom Party won a huge majority in the elections, running on a platform of nationalisation. In 1972 Ceylon achieved its independence from Great Britain and took the name Sri Lanka. She died in 2000.

1715 The English Riot Act was instituted. If more than twelve people assembled and were deemed a nuisance, a municipal authority was required to read them the Riot Act, which ordered them to disperse by Royal decree. It it still used to intimidate and move on protesters in many Commonwealth countries.

1810 Colombian nationalists began their independence movement against Spain. Nine years later, under Simon Bolivar, the Spanish were defeated. It is celebrated as a national holiday.

1924 Robert D. Maurer, American research physicist, was born in Louis, Missouri. He and colleagues invented optical fibre, which led to a revolution in telecommunications, because 65 000 times the amount of data could be transmitted than through a copper wire.

1930 Sally Ann Howes was born in London. She starred in *The History of Mr Polly* and *Dead of Night*.

1938 Diana Rigg was born in Doncaster, Yorkshire. She won a Tony Award for *Medea* and performed in *Witness for the Prosecution* and *King Lear*

American astronaut Edwin 'Buzz' Aldrin Jr. walks on the surface of the moon during the Apollo II mission on 20July 1969.. His footprints are scattered around the leg of the lunar landing module Eagle.

21 JULY

1899: Hemingway

Nobel Laureate Ernest Hemingway was born. He was a significant 20th century American writer with his terse, spare prose. He wrote, 'Poor (William) Faulkner. Does he really think big emotions come from big words? He thinks I don't know the ten-dollar words. I know them all right. But there are older and simpler and better words and those are the ones that I use.' Hemingway served as a correspondent in the Spanish Civil War, which led to two of his best books, *A Farewell to Arms* and *For Whom the Bell Tolls*. Hemingway drew on his life experiences in Africa and Mexico in his short stories. A complex man, he thrived on risk-taking, but could never vanquish his inner demons and killed himself in 1961.

1934: Comic Brain Surgeon

Would you want a comic genius as your brain doctor? Well, if it were the Britain's Sir Jonathan Miller, few would hesitate. Born on this day in London, he trained as a biologist and then became a neuro-psychologist. He launched a second career as a director and producer—stage, movies, opera and television and co-authored the zany revue *Beyond the Fringe* in 1960 with comedians Peter Cook, Dudley Moore and Alan Bennett.

1948: The Cat

Yusuf Islam was born Stephen Georgiou in London. Under the name Cat Stevens, he had a successful career as a songwriter, with songs such as 'Morning Has Broken', although he never wanted to be a star. When he became a devout Muslim he changed his name to Yusuf Islam. In a highly publicised case, he was denied entry by American customs in September 2004 because of questions about Islamic charities that he supported. In 2005 he released a new CD *Indian Ocean* to raise funds for victims of the Boxing Day Tsunami. His charity, Small Kindness, opened an Indonesian office to help orphans in Aceh.

2004: Pests Banned from Table Mountain

The Table Mountain National Park took a big step towards eradicating non-indigenous species when the South African High Court ruled that it would not hear the case presented by the Friends of the Himalayan tahr. The ruling meant the tahr, a goat-like animal, could legally be eradicated from Table Mountain. The issue was hotly debated because the tahr is endangered elsewhere in the world. Progress towards re-introducing native species was reported two months later. A group of reclusive native klipspringer, that had been re-introduced three years previously, were spotted with a newborn lamb.

1831 Leopold I became the first King of Belgium, after independence was granted from the Netherlands. It is a national holiday.

1952 Robin Williams, comic actor, was born in Chicago. He has appeared in dozens of movies, including *The Dead Poets Society* and *Patch Adams*.

1968 Arnold Palmer became the first professional golfer to win US $1 million in earnings in one year, when he placed second in the PGA championship.

1996 Miguel Indurian hoped to be the first person to win the Tour de France for the sixth time, but he was beaten in the annual cycling Tour by Bjarne Riis. Cancer survivor, Lance Armstrong. became the first person to win six times in 2004.

Author Ernest Hemingway standing in front of the harbour of a small fishing village in 1952.

22 JULY

1793: Canada Crossing

Sir Alexander Mackenzie arrived at the Pacific Coast with his dog, after travelling across Canada from the Atlantic Ocean on foot and by canoe. He was the first European to make the crossing. Mackenzie grew up destitute in Scotland and was sent by his family to New York to make money. He moved to Canada and became a fur trader and a Canadian hero. His first long expedition was in search of the 'Northwest Passage,' which he failed to find, but he discovered the river that bears his name. His second journey was further to the south. After encountering the Fraser River, his group borrowed an Indian canoe to travel further west, to where the river met the Pacific Ocean. Mackenzie later returned to Scotland a wealthy man and died there.

1844: Spooner says . . .

This is the anniversary for 'Spoonerisms' or verbal inversions, where initial sounds are transposed resulting in an unintended and different meaning, for example, 'votey heart' for 'hearty vote.' Spoonerism are named after Reverand William Spooner who was born on this day in London. He was a Dean and Warden of New College, Oxford University and became famous for his mangled and often hilarious English. The 'best' Spoonerisms are those that make sense, for example, a 'well-boiled icicle' for a 'well-oiled bicycle,' and 'go and shake a tower' for 'go and take a shower.'

1942 Gray Bartlett

Gray Bartlett was born in Auckland, New Zealand. A guitarist since the age of 15 with *The Phantoms*, he is very popular in Asia. His first big hit was in 1965 when his *La Player* soared to number 2 on the Japanese charts. His total output is more than 30 albums and 20 singles, selling in the millions.

1983: Chopper Circumnavigation

Thirty-nine-year-old Australian inventor, entrepreneur and adventurer, Dick Smith, completed the first solo around-the-world helicopter flight. He took off 2 August the previous year. An explorer, naturalist and risk-taker since childhood, Smith made a fortune with his electronic shops, *Australian Geographic* Magazine and Australian made food products. On 28 April 1987 he was the first person to reach the South Pole by helicopter, flying solo. He was Australian of the Year in 1986.

1962 Gary Player of South Africa was the first non-US resident to win the PGA golf championship.

1962 Valeri Brumel of the USSR broke his own and the world's high jump record by an astonishing 2.54 cm.

1939 Terence Stamp was born in London. The iconic actor has appeared on TV and movies mainly in 'working-class' roles. He appeared in *Alien Nation*, *Wall Street* and *The Adventures of Priscilla, Queen of the Desert*.

1968 Rhys Ifans, actor in *Notting Hill* and *Dancing at Lughnasa* was born in Wales.

1986 Archbishop Desmond Tutu spoke out about proposed American economic sanctions against South Africa, 'Your president (Reagan) is the pits as far as blacks are concerned. I think the West, for my part, can go to hell.'

South African Bishop Desmond Tutu addresses a press conference at the United Nations conference on racism in Durban 05 september 2001. He commented on the American and Israeli walk-out but stressed that tmany Americans from non government organisations (NGOs) remained and they are the ones who counted.

23 JULY

1942: Kokoda Track

Australian troops fought for the tiny village of Kokoda in Papua New Guinea (PNG). The Japanese had invaded New Ireland and Rabaul and by March were firmly embedded in PNG, preparing to invade Australia. They pummelled Port Moresby on the southern PNG coast from the air. The Japanese planned to trek across the mountainous Owen Stanley Range to invade Port Moresby, but Australians landed at Port Moresby, headed north and met the invaders at Kokoda. Outnumbered five to one, the Aussies fought to maintain Kokoda and its airfield, but were forced to retreat fighting as they went. The Japanese over-extended their supply lines and ultimately capitulated. PNG's indigenous people, dubbed 'Fuzzy Wuzzy Angels' by the troops, helped the wounded through the rugged terrain. In contrast to the soldiers' uniforms, the Angels wore a simple loincloth, elaborate feathers in their hair and shell necklaces, earrings and noserings. Soldier Bert Beros wrote in *Fuzzy Wuzzy Angels*:

Many a lad will see his mother and husbands see their wives
Just because the fuzzy wuzzy carried them to save their lives
From mortar bombs and machine gun fire or chance surprise attacks
To the safety and the care of the doctors at the bottom of the track…

With reinforcements, Australians launched an offensive and recaptured Kokoda on 2 November 1942.

1999: Chandra X-Ray in Space

The US$1.5 billion Chandra X-Ray Observatory was deployed by the Shuttle Colombia. It is sister to the Hubble Space Telescope and the Compton Gamma-Ray Observatory. It was named for India's astrophysicist Subrahmanyan Chandrasekhar, who immigrated to America in 1937. His last name was curiously prophetic, since Chandra means 'moon' or 'luminous' in Sanskrit. Chandra was awarded the 1983 Nobel Prize for Physics for his work on star evolution.

2003: Sacri Monti

The UNESCO World Heritage Committee inscribed the nine Sacri Monti (Sacred Mountains) in Piedmont and Lombardy in northern Italy. They are a group of 16th and 17th century Christian chapels, integrated into the landscape and house exquisite artworks.

1847 Wanganui was the last conflict in the protracted New Zealand War against the Maoris. In 1860, land disputes triggered the second New Zealand Wars, which lasted until 1872.

1932 Alberto Santos-Dumont died. He was a Brazilian aviation pioneer who studied aviation in Paris and won the Deutsch Prize for circumnavigating the Eiffel Tower in a balloon.

1952 Egypt's monarchy ended. King Farouk II was overthrown in a coup by Army officers. It is a national holiday.

1983 Seven Greenpeace activists who were imprisoned for protesting Soviet seal clubbing were freed.

1986 Prince Andrew and Sarah 'Fergie' Ferguson married. They separated in 1992 and divorced in 1996.

Papuan native helping a wounded Australian infantryman along road away from Buna during the World War II battle for Kokoda in Papua New Guinea.
The photographer, George Silk, is famous for highlighting the role of the Papuans in repelling the Japanese invasion.

24 JULY

1900: Aussie VC

The highest award for gallantry, courage and leadership for a military person in the British Empire was the Victoria Cross (VC). Australia's first VC winner was Sir Neville Reginald Howse. A Major-General and surgeon in the Boer War, Howse fought at the siege of Elands River at Vredefort, where the Australian Bushmen held out for 13 days in August 1900. Australia sent 16 175 troops to help the British in South Africa. Of these 251 were killed, 267 died of disease and 882 were wounded.

1911: Inca Glory Unveiled

Archaeologist Hiram Bingham re-discovered Machu Picchu after a local innkeeper led him to it. It was one of the most significant archaeological finds ever. High in the Peruvian Andes, it might have been spiritual centre with temples and an astronomical observatory or it may have been a royal estate, housing some 1200 women, children and officials. The well preserved buildings are more than 500-years-old and carved from huge blocks of solid granite. There is no mortar holding the huge stones and walls together, yet the construction has withstood the march of time and earthquakes. It was one of the last refuges of the Inca Indians and was not found by the Spanish invaders. It had long been abandoned and reclaimed by the jungle when found by Bingham. Today it is Peru's largest tourist attraction and provides an income for many of the area's indigenous people.

1982: Anna Paquin

The actor was born in Canada. She grew up in Wellington, New Zealand. When she was 9-years-old, she auditioned with about 5000 other children for the role of Flora in Jane Campion's movie *The Piano*. Until then, her only experience was playing a skunk in a school play. She won the part, won everyone's hearts and won the Oscar for Best Supporting Actress in 1993. Anna is the second-youngest Oscar winner. She also starred in the movie, *Fly Away Home* and is now a cellist.

1701 Fort Pontchartrain du Detroit, the French fortress at what is now Detroit, was established.

1783 Simon 'The Liberator' Bolivar was born at Caracas, Venezuela. He is a hero in many Latin American countries and his birthday is a holiday. Bolivia is named for him.

1802 Alexandre Dumas was born at Villers-Cotterets. He wrote about 300 books, including *The Three Musketeers* and *The Count of Monte Cristo*. He died in 1870.

1943 Operation Gomorrah was launched by The Royal Air Force. The pilots cleverly jammed German radar in attacks on Hamburg, Germany. The 791 bombers pushed bales of aluminium foil out their windows confusing the German radar that mistook them for dozens of aircraft. The Germans only succeeded in shooting down 12 planes.

1963 Julie A. Krone was born in Michigan. She was the first female jockey inducted into the National Racing Hall of Fame.

Machu Picchu, the 'lost city of the Incas' at the end of the 'Sacred Valley of the Incas' in Peru.

25 JULY

1978: Test-Tube Brown

Louise Brown, one of the most famous babies ever born was born in London, England. Her fame rested on the manner of her conception; she was the first of the so-called test-tube babies, although that name is inaccurate. After twelve years of research and failure, Dr. Robert G. Edwards and Patrick C. Steptoe pioneered a technique where a human egg is fertilised outside the body, (not in a test-tube) and then implanted in the womb. The technique permitted hundreds of thousands of infertile couples to have their own 'bundle of joy,' to an increase in multiple births, to ethical dilemmas and to surrogate parenting.

1981: Springboks Not Welcome

New Zealand showed its intense opposition to racial discrimination in sports when the South African all-white Springboks rugby team was scheduled to play at Waikato. Police cancelled the game when demonstrators swarmed the field. There had been violent clashes between demonstrators and police in Australia before the Springboks New Zealand tour. The protests began on the Springboks' arrival in Auckland on 21 July and escalated during the 56 day, 15 match tour. The worst violence occurred in Auckland at the last game in September, when protesters cut television cables to prevent the game's transmission. While a plane buzzed the crowd, demonstrators and police took part in a bloody melee. Hundreds were arrested.

2004: Tour de Lance

Although four cyclists have won the 101-year-old Tour de France five times each, American Lance Armstrong became the first cyclist to win it six times. He won by the huge margin of over six minutes. The three-week race is more than 3000km-long, winds through tiny French villages, across the Alps and the Pyrenees and ends in Paris. His victory was even more amazing because Armstrong was given a 50:50 chance of survival in 1996, after testicular cancer spread to his brain. No one thought Armstrong would ever race again. He attributed his recovery to his determination and his willingness to try experimental drugs.

1928: Francis Birtles arrived in Melbourne in a Bean car, after driving from London, England, across Europe, the Middle East and Asia. The car had just 25-horsepower.

1909 Louis Bleriot made the first crossing of the English Channel by airplane and thus, also the world's first international air flight.

1943 The Italian Fascist Council convened two weeks after the Allied attack on Italy and voted to remove Benito Mussolini from power and to arrest him.

1955 Iman (Abdulmajid), the model and movie star was born in Mogadishu, Somalia.

1957 Tunisia was proclaimed a republic, independent of France. It is a national holiday.

1975 A Chorus Line opened on Broadway and ran for 15 years. Its composer Marvin Hamlisch won a Tony. Few have won 'the grand slam' of entertainment. Born in 1944, Hamlisch has won three Oscars, four Grammys, four Emmys and many other awards, including the Pulitzer Prize. He has composed music for more than 40 movies.

Lance Armstrong of the riding for the US Postal Service team during the Tour de France between Annemasse and Lons Le Saunier in 2004.

26 JULY

1875: Forever Jung

Carl Jung the Swiss psychoanalyst was born in Kesswill, Switzerland. He trained with Dr Sigmund Freud, the father of modern psychiatry. It was assumed that Jung would succeed Freud as the leader of the International Psychoanalytic Society. However, they had a falling out over Freud's theory that all neurosis could be traced to infantile sexual conflicts. Also counter to Freudian doctrine was Jung's belief that all people had a natural tendency toward religion and spirituality. Their split made Jung theorise how people could approach a problem differently with different conclusions and from it he formulated the idea of 'extrovert' and 'introvert.' He developed a theory of four basic mind functions: thinking, feeling, sensation and intuition, one of which is usually dominant in an individual. Jung's most significant contribution was his theory that individuals draw on mankind's collective experiences, 'the collective unconscious,' accessible through mythology and dreams. When he died at Küsnacht in 1961 he was mourned as one of the most original thinkers of his generation.

1894: Brave New Visions

The boundary pushing author Aldous Huxley was born in Surrey, England. He was a precocious writer who was widely published in his early twenties. He is best remembered as the author of *Brave New World*, *Antic Hay* and *Eyeless in Gaza*. He wrote about 30 other novels, poetry, satire and collections of essays. Huxley was also a mystic, parapsychologist and a philosopher and spent many years in the America where he died in 1963. He wrote, 'Most human beings have an almost infinite capacity for taking things for granted.' To avoid that capacity in himself, he tried mescalin and LSD.

2004: Triathlon

Britain's Simon Lessing and Australia's Kate Major took the men's and women's titles respectively at the 2004 Ironman America Lake Placid triathlon. The gruelling event consists of a 3.8km swim, a 180km bicycle ride and a 42km marathon run. Each received a prize of $20 000. Lessing posted a time of eight hours, 23 minutes and 12 seconds. Australians Luke Bell came in second and Courtney Ogden third. Kate Major took 15 minutes off the bicycling course record, to win with an overall time of nine hours, 24 minutes and 42 seconds. The win was her first. America's Heather Fuhr was second and Joanna Lawn, a two-time Ironman New Zealand champion, came third.

1847 Liberia, Africa celebrated its independence with a national holiday. It was a homeland for former American slaves.

1946 Helen Mirren was born in London. She is best known for her role as Detective Jane Tennison in the *Prime Suspects* series.

1952 Bob Mathias won his second decathlon, shattering his own world record to achieve 7887 points.

1953 Fidel Castro's '26th of July Movement' anniversary. The revolutionary Communist Castro had attacked a barracks, was captured and served two years in jail in Cuba.

1965 The Maldives in the Pacific Ocean near India became independent from Great Britain. It is a national holiday. It was hard hit in the 2004 tsunami.

Swiss pioneer of psychology Dr Carl Gustav Jung (1875 - 1961) portrait photo from about 1960.

27 JULY

1940: Bugs Bunny

The Looney Tunes' street-smart, grey rabbit was 'born'. His signature line, spoken by Mel Blanc, was 'Eh, what's up, doc?' pronounced with a New York City accent. His major co-stars were Elmer Fudd, Yosemite Sam, Daffy Duck, Wile E. Coyote and Road Runner. In 2002 Bugs appeared in the number one spot of the Fifty Greatest Cartoon Characters of All Time, compiled by *TV Guide*. Bugs Bunny was the first cartoon character to have his own American postage stamp.

2003: Bob Hope

The comic Bob Hope died, aged 100. He was born 29 May, 1903 in London to a stonemason father and a Welsh concert singer. His birth-name was Leslie Townes Hope. The family immigrated to Ohio, America when he was four-years-old. Hope was one of the most enduring entertainers ever. He began in vaudeville, made a successful transition to radio, then television and the movies. He unfailingly performed for the 'boys in uniform' as a morale booster every Christmas Day. His theme song was *Thanks for the Memory*. Hope received both an honorary knighthood from Queen Elizabeth II and the Congressional Medal of Honour, but never won an Oscar for his acting, although he received four honorary ones for his contributions to show business.

2002: Helen Clark PM

New Zealand's Prime Minister Helen Clark faced a big challenge when she called a general election for this day. Her Labour Party was under pressure from both ends of the political spectrum. Although her party won, it was without the absolute majority she wanted. Her coalition with the Green Party was threatened by the possibility of their withdrawal if she approved the release of genetically modified organisms in 2003. Before she became leader of the Opposition in 1993, she had held various Cabinet appointments. She was elected Prime Minister on 27 November 1999. Her special areas of interest are social policy and international relations.

1866 A telegraph cable was successfully laid under the Atlantic Ocean, linking the America and Europe.

1921 Insulin was first isolated from a dog's pancreas by Dr. Frederick Banting and Charles Best at the University of Toronto Medical School, Canada.

1942 Kim Fowley, rock musician, producer and manager, was born in Los Angeles. He worked with a wide variety of artists, including The Beach Boys, The Byrds, Frank Zappa and Cat Stevens.

1946 Gertrude Stein, writer and arts patron, died in Paris. She wrote 40 novels and is best known for *The Autobiography of Alice B. Toklas*. She held a famous salon in Paris during the 1920s and encouraged writers such as Ernest Hemingway.

1953 Korean War armistice was signed. Both North Korea and South Korea claimed victory. The war lasted three years; the truce took two years to negotiate.

1984 James Mason, the stiff upper lipped British actor died aged 75. He played heroes and sophisticates. He appeared in *Madame Bovary*, *Lolita* and *Julius Caesar*.

Deborah Kerr and James Mason star in the film 'Julius Caesar', directed by Joseph L Mankiewicz in 1953.

28 JULY

1864: Bush Balladeer

Adam Lindsay Gordon was born in the Azores, to an English army officer and came to Australia as a young man. An outstanding steeplechase rider, he made a famous leap on horseback at Blue Lake, Mount Gambier, South Australia on this day. The leap was over a fence onto a tiny lip on the edge of Gambier's bowl-like crater. He was Australia's first true bush poet and was published to critical acclaim. He wrote *Bush Ballads and Galloping Rhymes* and *Sea Spray and Smoke Drift*. Saddened at the loss of his daughter and bankrupted by a fire, he killed himself in 1870 aged 36. A statue commemorating his leap was erected in Melbourne in 1932 and he is the only Australian poet honoured with a bust in Westminster Abbey's Poet's Corner.

1903: 100 Mile March

'Hear the wail of the children, who never have a chance to go to school, but work ten to eleven hours a day in the textile mills,' said Mother Jones, in a march she led on this day. The 100-mile march to US President Theodore Roosevelt's home in New York, was to call attention to the plight of child labourers. Approximately 1.7 million children under 16 years of age were working in appaling conditions in mines, mills and factories. The President was 'unavailable,' but the march led to some improvements. Mary Harris Jones, who called herself Mother Jones and intentionally dressed like an old woman, so that she would be treated more respectfully, lost her husband and four children to yellow fever in 1867. When she lost her home and business in the Great Chicago Fire, a union helped her and she devoted her life to union activism. Her task, she said, was to 'raise hell' which she did until she died, aged 100.

1936: Garfield Sobers

Sir Garfield Sobers was born in Barbados. He is considered the world's greatest all-round cricketer. He played in his first Test match at age 17 against England. Three years later, on the West Indies tour of Pakistan, Sobers scored 365 not out, the highest Test score of the time. He played for teams in England and Australia, then captained the West Indies team for 39 Tests, between 1965 and 1972. He retired from cricket in 1974 with 8032 runs.

1866 Beatrix Potter, who wrote and illustrated the classic *Peter Rabbit* children's stories, was born in London. She died in 1943.

1901 Rudy Vallee, crooner, saxophone player and radio idol to millions, was born in Vermont. He died in 1986.

1914 Austria-Hungary declared war on Serbia, leading to World War I. Archduke Ferdinand of Austria-Hungary and his wife had been assassinated in Sarajevo, Bosnia by a Serbian nationalist on 28 June.

1920 Pancho Villa, the revolutionary leader of raids in northern Mexico, surrendered to Mexican government officials, on condition that his life was spared. He was assassinated three years later.

1945 Rick Wright, keyboard player with *Pink Floyd*, was born in London.

Caroline Blackwood, the daughter of the Marchioness of Dufferin, reading a book by Beatrix Potter in her pram in 1934.

Inset: Portrait of British children's author Beatrix Potter in the 1890s.

29 JULY

1979: Marcuse for a Free Mind

The German-American Marxist philosopher, Herbert Marcuse, died, aged 81. Urban African-American radicals and intellectuals embraced him for his opposition to American imperialism and oppression. He was an influential and brilliant academic who wrote *One Dimensional Man* and *Eros and Civilization*. One of his best-known students was Angela Davis, the iconic Black Panther who is remembered for being on the FBI's most wanted list when she was alleged to have smuggled a gun into prison for an escape attempt. Her childhood was clouded by constant fear of the Klu Klux Klan in Alabama, but she studied in New York, France, Germany and under Marcuse in California. Davis is a respected Black intellectual and continues her struggle today as a professor at Santa Cruz University and a social activist.

1996: Sprinter Johnson

One of the all-time best sprinters is the American Michael Johnson. At the Atlanta Olympics he blazed down the track in his gold running shoes to win the 400m. This was his 55th straight 400-metre victory. He set an Olympic record of 43.49 seconds. His victory margin of 0.92 seconds was the largest since 1896, the first modern Olympiad. Three days later he made Olympic history when he won the 200m final. Timekeepers couldn't believe their eyes at his 19.32 seconds in the 200 metres. Johnson also became the first man to win both the 200 metre and 400 metre. Johnson rewrote the World Championship record books when he won nine gold medals in 1999, the most by any athlete. The African-American track star was born in Dallas, Texas in 1967.

2004: Masingita Masunga - Miss Confident

As part of South Africa's National Women's Day, Masingita Masunga's company staged the first beauty pageant for the disabled, called Miss Confidence South Africa. Masunaga copes with cerebral palsy herself. Always a fighter, after twice failing her high school final examinations because of her poor writing skills, she convinced the Department of Education to provide her with a writer. After graduation in 1998, she formed a company, Tinyungubyiseni Talent Promotions, to give physically disabled South Africans the opportunity to contribute to society and to be part of the mainstream culture. Masunaga's goals are to raise public awareness that 'a disability is not an inability.' Her company promotes *Nyeliti—Star Beyond Limits* for musicians with physical disabilities and soccer tournaments and motivational talks to school children. Masunga was selected as one of South Africa's Women of the Year in 2004.

1030 Viking King St. Olav died in the Battle of Stiklestad near Trondheim, Norway. He is the patron saint of Norway

1881 The first shipload of Russian Jews arrived in New York City escaping the ruthless Russian pogroms. They had an immediate impact on American music, literature and culture that continues today.

1895 The Land of the Moa, New Zealand's first melodrama, was staged at the Opera House, Wellington. It was set in New Zealand and showed a Maori tribe disputing land ownership.

1966 Miles Hunt of the English 1980s and '90s grunge rock group The Wonder Stuff was born in Birmingham. Their *Eight Legged Groove Machine* and *Never Loved Elvis* did well. The band dissolved in 1994.

1968 Pope Paul VI announced the Roman Catholic Church's opposition to birth control, despite recommendations for change.

Left: American militant, Angela Davis, gives a press conference in 1972 in Moscow, Russia.

Below: Herbert Marcuse (1898 - 1979), German-born American philosopher and political theorist.

30 JULY

1945: Schoolboy demands Justice

Just after midnight a Japanese submarine torpedoed the *USS Indianapolis* causing the American Navy's worst disaster. The ship sank in less than 15 minutes, killing 350 sailors and leaving 900 more flailing in the dark ocean. Its surface was on fire and many died excruciating deaths. The *USS Indianapolis* had just delivered an atomic bomb to Tinian Island and was headed for Okinawa to train for the American invasion of Japan. The American Navy was unaware of the sinking as the ship's top-secret mission required a communication blackout. For four days sailors succumbed to the sharks, hunger and thirst. By the time an aircraft spotted the survivors only 318 sailors remained alive. The Navy court-martialled the *Indianapolis'* captain, Charles Butler McVay, despite the fact that the surviving crewmembers considered him blameless. McVay was held responsible, stripped of his rank and committed suicide. For fifty years the survivors tried to clear McVay's name. Incredibly, it took the efforts of an eleven-year-old boy, Hunter Scott, to succeed. Scott, working on a school history project, became fascinated by the lack of information on the tragedy and began interviewing *Indianapolis* survivors, who told him of the horrific incident and of McVay's innocence. After years of lobbying both the House and the Senate Scott finally appeared before the Senate Armed Services Committee, chaired by John Warner. Warner said Scott, now 14-years-old, was the youngest person to appear before them. He was given 15 minutes to testify, but it became a three-hour session. Warner said he had gone into the meeting supporting the Navy's position in the court-martial, but he changed his mind. Many of the survivors told Scott that they could now die in peace.

1974 Hilary Swank

The American film star was born in Bellingham, Washington, of Spanish and Native American extraction. Here acting career began with a role in the television series *Buffy Vampire Slayer*. She won Oscars for *Boys Don't Cry* and *Million Dollar Baby*. Apart from acting she is passionate about anything that involves the outdoors, including: sky diving, river rafting and skiing.

1818 Emily Bronte, one of the writing Bronte sisters, was born at Thornton, Yorkshire. She wrote *Wuthering Heights*.

1935 The first Penguin paperback was published in London. The title was *Ariel*, about Percy Bysshe Shelley, by Andre Maurois. It cost sixpence.

1947 Arnold Schwarzenegger, body-builder, movie actor and Governor of California, was born in Thal, Austria.

1966 A home crowd of 97 000 at London's Wembley Stadium watched England win its first soccer World Cup victory since 1930. The game was won by the 'Wingless Wonders', in overtime against West Germany, by a score of 4:2.

1980 Vanuatu became an independent republic from France and Britain. It is a national holiday. It was formerly called the New Hebrides.

Actors Hilary Swank and Morgan Freeman pose for a photo backstage during the 77th Annual Academy Awards on 27 February, 2005 at the Kodak Theatre in Hollywood, California. Both won Oscars for their roles in Clint Eastwood's sentimental, old-fashioned boxing movie "Million Dollar Baby".

31 JULY

1944: Antoine de Saint-Exupery,

The French aviator and author, died, aged 44, when his plane crashed. He wrote the classic *Le Petit Prince; Wind, Sand and Stars and Night Flight*. In *Le Petit Prince*, he wrote, 'Grown-ups never understand anything for themselves and it is tiresome for children to be always and forever explaining things to them.'

1951: Dreamtime at Wimbledon

Australian Evonne Goolagong-Cawley won the Wimbledon singles tennis championship when she was only 19-years-old. She defeated the two outstanding players of the time, Australia's Margaret Court-Smith and America's Billie Jean King. Born in Griffith, New South Wales on this day, she was the first Aboriginal to win major tennis title. Tennis coach, Vic Edwards, spotted the teenager's athleticism and became her legal guardian and coach. She was runner-up in three Wimbledons, losing to King twice and Chris Evert Lloyd in 1976. In 1980, she turned the tables on Lloyd and beat her in a thrilling final. Goolagong-Cawley won the Australian Open four times, Wimbledon twice (1971 and 1980) and the French Open in 1971.

1975: Bob Hawke - Teetotaller

The flamboyant Bob Hawke said on this day that if he were elected Australian Prime Minister, he would give up beer drinking. He earned notoriety when he attended Oxford University in the 1960s on a Rhodes scholarship. He drank 2.5 pints of beer in 11 seconds for a mention in Guinness World Records. He wrote, 'This feat endeared me to some of my fellow Australians more than anything else I ever achieved.' He worked for the Australian Council of Trade Unions and was elected to Parliament in 1980. Three years later he led the Labor Party to victory. As Prime Minister he won four general elections between 1983-90. In 1983, when Australia II won the America's Cup, he exuberantly declared that, 'Anyone who sacks a bloke today, because he doesn't turn up for work, is a bum.' By 1990 he was the Labor Party's longest-serving Prime Minister but narrowly lost a party ballot to Paul Keating, who replaced him as Prime Minister. Hawke retired from politics in 1992. Hawke caused a controversy in 1995 when he divorced his wife Hazel of 39 years, to marry his biographer, Blanch d'Alpuget later that year.

1703 Daniel Defoe was placed in the village stocks for the crime of libel, after writing a political pamphlet. The public pelted him with flowers.

1954 K2, the world's second highest mountain located in the Pakistani Karakoram, was conquered for the first time by an Italian team.

1971 The Lunar Rover was used for the first time for exploring the Moon's surface.

2004 Gary Lewis became the first Maori member of the British Royal Family when he married Lady Davina Windsor. His wife is twentieth in line to the throne. He is a former champion sheep-shearer and now a builder.

Evonne Goolagong Cawley on court at Wimbledon in 1978:

British guitarist Eric Clapton performs at the 10th edition of the Pavarotti and Friends 2003 benefit concert in Modena, Italy. The concert raised funds to help Iraqi refugees.

On 1 August 1971 Clapton performed in George Harrison's Concert for Bangladesh at Madison Square Garden, New York. Clapton, Ringo Starr, Billy Preston, Leon Russell, Bob Dylan, Ravi Shankar and others played, not as individual acts, but as part of a revue with Harrison remaining onstage throughout the evening. His presence cemented the impression of a group musicians coming together to support a worthy purpose.

'Concert for Bangladesh was George's moment. He put it together and he pulled it off. For that he deserves the admiration of all of us.' - Jon Landau, *Rolling Stone* 1972.

1 AUGUST

1882: Native Australian Poet

Australian poet Henry Kendall died on this day, aged 43. His first published poem was about the wreck of the ship the *Dunbar* and he signed it 'Henry Kendall N.A.P'. His publisher asked him to explain. Kendall told him it meant 'Native Australian Poet', which was apt because he was one of the first to write about Australian scenery and themes. Kendall was born near Milton on the far south coast of NSW and his widowed mother encouraged him to write and publish his poetry. His first collection was *Poems and Songs*. When his daughter's death plunged him into alcoholism, his wife left him and he spent long periods of time in a Sydney asylum. His later years were relatively happy and he was reunited with his wife. Poems in his collection *Leaves From Australian Forests* include the melancholic 'The Last of His Tribe' about a dying Aboriginal and the description of bell birds as the 'silver-voiced' birds.

1944: Anne Frank

Anne Frank, aged 15, wrote her last diary entry, which read: 'I keep trying to find a way to become what I'd like to be and what I could be if ... if only there were no other people in the world.' Anne's father, Otto, a prosperous German–Jewish businessman, had thought his wife and two daughters would be safe in the Netherlands, but the Nazi invasion forced the Franks into hiding. Four others hid with the Frank family in a factory annex for about two years. Anne's diary records her fears, hopes and dreams. The Franks were betrayed and the Gestapo arrested them. Anne and her sister died in early 1945 of typhus in Bergen-Berlsen Camp. Their bodies were probably dumped in a mass grave. Her mother perished in the Auschwitz Camp. Two of Otto's employees found the diary and gave it to Otto, the only survivor. He spent the next 40 years until his death, promoting *The Diary of Anne Frank*, a testament of hope to all who read it. It has been translated into about 40 languages.

1999: Nirad C Chaudhuri

The Indian–English writer died in Oxford, aged 101. He was born in what is now Bangladesh and educated at Calcutta. A brilliant student, he failed to graduate because he did not take his Master's exams. he was a prolific writer, publishing his last book when he was 99. Always a Victorian-style gentleman in manners and taste, he is best known for *The Autobiography of an Unknown Indian* and its sequel, *Thy Hand, Great Anarch!* published posthumously.

1715 The oldest boat race: took place in England. It was established by Thomas Doggett, and called the Doggett, Coat and Badge Race.

1774 Carl Wilhelm and Joseph Priestley discovered the element oxygen.

1834 Slavery was abolished in the British Empire.

1957 Bruce Mason's *The Pohutukawa Tree* premiered in Wellington. The tale about culture clash was a milestone in New Zealand theatre.

1971 George Harrison's New York Concert for Bangladesh featured Eric Clapton, Ringo Starr, Leon Russell and others.

2000 *The Steel Dragon,* the world's longest full circuit roller-coaster, opened in Japan.

Jewish diarist Anne Frank (1929–1945) sitting at a desk with an open book in 1942.

2 AUGUST

1975: Joan Baez Day

Fans of folksinger/peace activist and the 'mother of all the female singer/songwriters who followed her' honour Joan Baez in Atlanta Georgia. Baez went from coffee shop performances and relative obscurity to megastar status after the Newport Folk Festival in 1959, with her 1960 album *Joan Baez*. Among the earliest singers to urge social protest and an advocate of non-violence, she became a symbol of the anti-Vietnam War movement, with songs like 'We Shall Overcome'. She was voted best female vocalist in 1972 and racked up eight gold albums, including the soulful *Blessed Are*, along with a gold single, 'The Night They Drove Old Dixie Down'. In 1975 she toured with Bob Dylan on his Rolling Thunder Revue. She was the founder of the Institute for the Study of Nonviolence in 1965 and was the founding president of Humanitas International Human Rights Committee, 1979-92. She is the recipient of honourary degrees, the Thomas Merton Award and France's Chevalier d'Honneur. Baez was born in 1941 in Staten Island, New York.

1992: Jackie Joyner-Kersey

The 30-year-old American became the first person to win two consecutive Olympic gold medals in the gruelling two-day heptathlon at the Barcelona Olympics. The competition consists of seven events for women (male Olympians compete in a ten-event decathlon): javelin, long jump, an 800 m run, 200 m sprint, 100 m hurdles, shot put and the high jump. She won by a margin of 199 points. Joyner-Kersey was born in East St Louis, Missouri in 1962. She was named after Jackie Kennedy and came from a family of talented athletes. The two-time world champion heptahlete went on to win three other Olympic medals, one gold, one silver and one bronze. *Sports Illustrated* voted Joyner-Kersey voted the greatest athlete of the 20th Century. She is considered to be one of the best female athletes in history,

1997: Thredbo Mudslide

The only survivor of one of Australia's worst man-made disasters was detected after a frantic search by rescuers in the debris of a ski-lodge. Rescuers hailed it as miraculous. Four days earlier mud and earth engulfed a ski lodge in picturesque Thredbo one of Australia's oldest and most popular skiing villages. Eighteen people lost their lives. Official enquiry findings three years later determined that leaking water mains were responsible for undermining a poorly designed road embankment on the hillside. The resulting landslide swept down the slope into a ski lodge below, collapsing the concrete floors like a pack of cards, and trapping the sleeping residents inside.

1610 Henry Hudson, Dutch navigator employed by the English, entered Canada's Northwest Territories at what is now called Hudson Bay. He thought it was the Pacific Ocean.

1870 Tower Subway, the world's first underground tube railway, opened in London.

1892 Jack Warner was born in London, Ontario, Canada. He was the youngest of twelve children of Jewish–Polish immigrants. He and two brothers built Warner Brothers studio, Hollywood's most powerful movie studio.

1903 Macedonia's national holiday commemorates the nationalist uprising against the Ottoman Empire. It is called Illenden, the Prophet Elias Day.

1933 Actor Peter O'Toole, forever associated with his role in *Lawrence of Arabia*, was born in Conemara, Ireland.

1990 Saddam Hussein's Iraq invaded Kuwait.

Bucharest, Romania: American folk singer Joan Baez speaks during a press conference about her concert in Bucharest on 11 July 2004 .

3 AUGUST

1492: Columbus Sails

Christopher Columbus set sail for the spice lands of the Far East that Marco Polo had opened up by the overland route from Europe. Columbus believed that the earth was spherical. He convinced Spanish royalty to underwrite his exploratory trip. After five weeks at sea, he landed in San Salvador. He thought that he had reached Asia, not realising that he had reached a different continent, America, the so-called 'New World.' Assuming he was in India, he called the natives Indians, hence the name 'American Indians.' Columbus's name lives on worldwide—the District of Columbia (America), Columbus (Ohio), Colombo (Sri Lanka), Archipelago de Colon, (Galapagos), Colon (Panama Canal) and Colombia, (Central America.) and many more.

1964: Lucky Dube

The first black musician aired on a white South African radio show, Lucky's song was the powerful 'Together as One'. He was born in Johannesburg on this day and named Lucky because his mother thought that she could not have children. Dube started his career singing in bars and churches. His band could not afford instruments, so they wrote and performed a play, which earned enough money for him to buy a guitar. His first two albums, *Slave* and *Prisoner*, sold over 500 000 disks, making him South Africa's top seller.

1977: Archbishop Makarios

The powerful Archbishop of the Orthodox Church of Cyprus and Cypriot President for seventeen years died. Makarios supported the political unification of Cyprus and Greece. Cyprus was a British protectorate with a population of 500 000, with two major ethnicities, Turks and Greeks. Turks were outnumbered 8:1 and there was a long-standing enmity between them. The Greeks wanted union with Greece and the Turkish–Cypriots wanted partition. The British exiled Makarios in 1956 to restore stability. When he returned in March 1959 he predictably defeated his Turkish–Cypriot opponent 2:1 in the election. Both the Greek and Turkish governments met and approved the British plan for Cyprus. Foremost on Makarios' agenda in the new republic was a new constitution. Britain demanded the protection of the minority Turkish–Cypriots' rights, along with British rights to strategic military sites. Turkish–Cypriots rioted against the new constitution, leading to United Nations intervention in 1964. A ceasefire was achieved in 1965.

1460 Scotland's King James II was accidentally killed by one of his own cannons, while waiting for Queen Mary.

1920 PD James, considered one of the greatest mystery novelists, was born in Oxford, England. Her books include *Devices and Desires* and *Innocent Blood*.

1926 Tony Bennett was born in New York City. His signature song is 'I Left My Heart in San Francisco'.

1937 Steven Berkoff actor/director/producer was born in London. His movies include *Children of Dune, A Clockwork Orange* and *Beverly Hills Cop*.

1984 Mary Lou Retton was the first American to win an Olympic medal of any kind in gymnastics when she won gold in Los Angeles.

17 July 1974: Archbishop Makarios III (Mihail Christodoulou Mouskos, 1913–1977), (left), first president of the republic of Cyprus, with British prime minister Harold Wilson in London, during Makarios' brief removal from leadership. He was reinstated in 1975.

4 AUGUST

1792: Shelley

'If Winter comes, can Spring be far behind?' wrote English poet Percy Bysshe Shelley in 'Ode to the West Wind'. He was born on this day in Sussex into a wealthy family. He never outgrew a rebellious streak that was first exhibited at Oxford University when he privately published horror novels. He became anti-establishment, anti-royalty, anti-meat-eating, anti-marriage and anti-religion. At nineteen, Shelley eloped and married 16-year-old Harriet Westbrook. He abandoned her and lived in a ménage à trois with Mary Godwin (who wrote *Frankenstein*) and her 15-year-old stepsister Claire. They moved to Italy and from 1819–20 he wrote his major works, including 'Prometheus Unbound' and the lyrical poems 'To a Skylark' and 'The Cloud'. Shelley translated Greek, Latin, Spanish, German, Italian and Arabic classics. When Harriet killed herself, he married Mary. His personal and domestic entanglements marred his reputation during his life, but he is now considered one of the great Romantics.

1901: Satchmo

Louis Armstrong was born on this day into extreme poverty in New Orleans, Louisiana. His father abandoned the family. His 15-year-old mother probably prostituted herself and Armstrong often foraged for food in rubbish bins. Armstrong learned the trumpet at a school for truants and went on to play it like no-one else ever has. Armstrong's perfect pitch and perfect rhythm made him a worldwide influence on music. He was nicknamed Satchmo (Satchelmouth). He said, 'If you gotta ask what [jazz] is, man you'll never know' and 'My life has been my music'. Some of Satchmo's best-known songs are 'Ain't misbehavin', 'What a wonderful world' and 'Hello Dolly'. Armstrong refused to play in his hometown until its clubs were integrated in 1964.

1936: Jesse Owens

The standout performer at the 1936 Berlin Olympics was the African–American Jesse Owens, The Nazi dictator Adolf Hitler preached the superiority of white skinned blue-eyed Aryans over all others, especially Jews and dark-skinned people. Owens won four gold medals, in the 100 m, 200 m sprints, the 4 x 100 m relay and on this day, the long jump.

1693 Champagne invented by Charles Perignon.

1805 Sir William Rowan Hamilton, brilliant Irish mathematician was born. He also knew fourteen languages by age 12.

1906 'Central', the magnificent Central Railway Station, opened in Sydney, Australia.

1921 Vladimir Lenin, Russia's revolutionary leader, appealed to the world for help. Poverty was so extreme that eighteen million peasants were starving, with grass soup their staple.

1962 Jamaica achieved independence from Britain. It is a national holiday.

Athlete Jesse Owens (1913–1980) flies through the air during the long jump event at the 1936 Olympic Games in Berlin. He won four gold medals and Hitler left the stadium to avoid having to congratulate a black competitor.

5 AUGUST

1912: Raoul Wallenberg

Born on this day at Stockholm, Sweden, Wallenberg saved up to 100 000 Jews from Nazi concentration camps. He became an honourary Citizen of Canada, of Israel and of America, and has a statue in his likeness in Great Cumberland Place, London. An architect by profession, he became a Swedish diplomat assigned to Budapest, Hungary during the Second World War. Wallenberg used his diplomatic status for the issuance of 'protective passports' that identified the Hungarian–Jewish bearer as Swedish. He also used Embassy funds to acquire 'safe houses' to hide Jews and directly intervened with Nazi officials on some occasions. Wallenberg was arrested by the Soviet Army at the end of the War and charged with being an American spy. He is presumed dead, possibly dying in a Soviet prison in 1947, but his disappearance remains unsolved and mysterious.

1962: Blonde Bombshell

Marilyn Monroe died, aged 36, from an apparent overdose of sleeping pills. Norma Jean Mortensen (later Baker) was named 'Norma' after the movie star Norma Talmadge. The beautiful, busty, blonde bombshell lived a rags-to-riches story without a happy ending. Her first marriage was to her neighbour Jimmy Dougherty in 1942. By 1946 she signed her first movie contract with 20th Century Fox and changed her name to Marilyn Monroe. By 1954 Monroe was the world's biggest movie star. She starred in 29 movies, including *Some Like It Hot*, *All About Eve*, *Asphalt Jungle*, *Seven Year Itch* and *Bus Stop*. Her marriage to baseball giant Joe DiMaggio was tempestuous but the two were thinking of remarrying before her death. Her marriage to fledgling playwright Arthur Miller was also disastrous, marred by two miscarriages. Two other marriages were unhappy. Twenty years after her death, rumours still abound about the cause of her death—was she murdered for having an affair with President John Kennedy? A formal investigation by coroner Thomas Noguchi ruled her death a 'probable suicide'.

1905 Albert Einstein fled from Germany in fears of his life from the Rathenau killers.

1975 Kim Fowley formed The Runaways, the first all-woman rock band.

1984 Welsh actor Richard Burton, known for his mellifluent voice, died age 58, in Geneva, Switzerland.

1986 Princess Anne won her first race as a jockey, riding Gulfland at Redcar.

1994 Bill Cosby American iconic comedian was found guilty of assaulting a bothersome photographer. He was fined 20 cents.

2000 Sir Alec Guinness died. He appeared in over 60 movies, including *Star Wars* and *The Bridge Over the River Kwai*. He was 86.

2002 Undertakers reported a trend away from hymns at funerals to songs such as Bette Midler's 'Wind beneath my wings'.

Swedish diplomat Raoul Wallenberg.in 1937.

6 AUGUST

1914: Kiwis Sting Nazis

The first defeat that Germany would suffer in World War 1 began on this day when a telegram from the British Secretary for the Colonies arrived for the New Zealand Governor. It asked him to arrange for New Zealand military to seize the strategic wireless station at Apia, Samoa. The cable was sent just two days after Britain had declared war against Germany. Germany had colonies throughout the Pacific Ocean, including part of New Guinea, the Mariana Islands and the Caroline Islands. From their bases, the Germans communicated news on shipping activity with Berlin and their harbours could also provide haven for German naval vessels if necessary. Under a cloak of secrecy 1430 New Zealand men and women shipped out of Wellington Harbour, on two troopships, accompanied by two cruisers. The destination was unknown. A third cruiser joined the convoy, then two Australian ships and one French ship. The only excitement was when one of the troopships ran aground at Noumea. The convoy reached Apia on 29 August, the radio was secured and the German flag hauled down. The next day, Samoa became a British possession under New Zealand jurisdiction and the German military officers were imprisoned in Wellington. The *New Zealand Observer*, disappointed at the relative lack of action, wrote a satirical piece about the 'horrible carnage' and how the fighting involved 'biting off Hun ears'.

1926: Channel Swim

New Yorker Gertrude Ederle became the first woman to swim the 35 km English Channel. Lloyd's of London had placed bets of 7:1 against the 19-year-old finishing the gruelling swim. At stake was a sporty Roadster that she was determined to win, she said. Her time was the best in the 51-year history of Channel swimming. She started in France. When Ederle waded ashore, she was surprised that English customs officials delayed her; it was hardly likely that she was smuggling something illegal in her swimsuit! She broke the record by two hours and her record stood for 35 years.

1766 **William Hyde Wollaston,** British optical scientist and chemist was born. His polarising beam splitter is used in today's CD players.

1775 **Daniel O'Connell** achieved his fight for Roman Catholic rights to sit in Parliament.

1922 **Sir Freddie Laker,** one of the pioneers in low-cost airfares was born in Kent, England.

1971 **Chay Blyth,** English sailor, 31, set a record of 292 days for his non-stop 'wrong way' sail around the world, east to west, against prevailing winds and currents.

1986 **Timothy Dalton** selected to portray the suave and deadly James Bond in movies, ending intense speculation. He is the fifth in an elite line: Sean Connery, Roger Moore, George Lazenby and Pierce Brosnan.

1996 **NASA** announced evidence of a primitive life form on Mars from exhaustive tests on a meteorite found in the Antarctica.

American Olympic gold medallist swimmer Gertrude Ederle enters the water for her cross-Channel swim in 1926. She plastered herself with olive oil, lanolin, Vaseline and lard to keep warm.

7 AUGUST

1858: Aussie Rules

A new game, Australian Rules Football was born, when Scotch College played Church of England Grammar in Melbourne, Australia. A plaque commemorates the event. However, *The Oxford Companion to Australian Sport* disputes this story, attributing the game to a group of Englishmen who created it by combining game rules the colleges they had attended in England—Rugby, Winchester and Harrow. Aussie Rules is played with two teams of eighteen players each. Fans call it the world's best spectator sport because players move the ball by throws or kicks, forward, backward or sideways. There is no offside rule like soccer, so the whole field is used. To play well requires speed, agility and strength. It is hard for players and for spectators to predict where the ball will go, adding to the excitement. Aussie Rules has a strong following throughout the Pacific, Britain, Ireland and Canada.

1908: Slow Train

A steam train chugged out of Wellington railway station in New Zealand for the first non-stop trip to Auckland. Actually, the railroad was incomplete by 29 km so how could it be a non-stop journey? The engineer surprised the passenger, including Member of Parliament, by laying temporary track, which the train slowly crept across, arriving in Auckland in 19 hours. Aucklanders cheered as the engine severed a commemorative ribbon. The 29 km section required the construction of three viaducts, a tunnel and four bridges, took three months to build and was completed 6 November. Previously, the journey took three days, with three changes and two overnight stops.

1959: Spaceship Earth

The American Explorer VI satellite sent back the first photograph of our planet from space. People were amazed at how small, compact and fragile Earth looked compared to the vastness of space. All the continents seemed to be connected and the national boundaries that appear on world maps were nowhere to be seen..

1941 Rabindranath Tagore, Nobel laureate in literature, mystic, educator and poet, died in his birthplace, Calcutta, India.

1974 Philippe Petit caused a major traffic jam in Wall Street, New York City, when he walked a tightrope between the World Trade Centre Twin Towers.

1987 Lynne Cox, American swimmer, took two hours and six minutes to cross the 4.3 km Bering Strait from Alaska to Siberia, in just a bathing suit, in the 5°C water. Her high body fat count contributed to her success.

1992 Buckingham Palace, Queen Elizabeth's London home, was open to the public for the first time. Ticket sales were used to repair extensive fire damage at Windsor Castle.

1997 Russian space crew arrived to repair the orbiting space station Mir. It was a major accomplishment to repair the propulsion system fuel lines in space.

Spaceship Earth: our planet as seen from space, showing Africa and Antarctica.

8 AUGUST

1576: Tycho Brahe

The cornerstone for an astronomical observatory was laid in the island of Hven, near Copenhagen, Denmark. There Tycho Brahe would continue to revolutionise astronomy, designing and building instruments and observing orbits, not just positions, proving the 'heavens are changeable'. The 1560 solar eclipse had fascinated the teenaged Brahe and he began secretly studying astronomy despite his family's desire for him to pursue law. When he found that written accounts and his observations did not match, he knew he needed an observatory. The King had heard about his work and offered Brahe both money and the site to establish his observatory. He relocated to Bohemia and while conditions were not nearly as favourable, one of his assistants was Johannes Kepler. Kepler's laws of planetary motion, derived largely from Brahe's work, became the foundation of modern astronomy.

1588: Drake Bowls, Faces Armarda

A fleet of 130 Spanish ships was sighted off Plymouth. Sir Francis Drake, known for his intense hatred of the Spanish, supposedly was in the middle of a lawn bowls game and said, 'There is plenty of time to finish my game of bowls and thrash the Spaniards too.' The British ships were smaller, more manoeuvrable, able to weave in and out of the Armada, firing their cannon. The fleeing Spanish encountered a fierce storm that sank more ships. Drake chased others into Calais harbour and destroyed them. Only about half the Armada returned home.

1974: Bye Bye Tricky Dicky

The first American President ever to resign from office appears on television. Richard M. Nixon had won a landslide re-election just two years before, faced impeachment before the US Congress for his part in the Republican Party's burglary of the Democratic National Committee's headquarters at the Watergate Building in Washington, DC and for his prolonged attempts to conceal the misdeed. Editor Norman Cousins said that Nixon's motto was, 'If two wrongs don't make a right, try three.' Realising that he did not have enough votes to avoid impeachment, Nixon resigned to put 'the interests of America first'. As President, Nixon had ended the Vietnam War and had reached out in friendship to China, but the Watergate affair overshadowed his successes. The next day, Vice President Gerald R. Ford became president. One of his first acts was to pardon Nixon.

1471 Thomas à Kempis, Dutch mystic and author died. His devotional *Imitation of Christ* is still popular today.

1786 Michel-Gabriel Paccard and Jacques Balmat made the first ascent of Europe's famed Mont Blanc.

1918 The Battle of Amiens: known as a 'black day of the German Army', the British launched their second major offensive and captured 16 000 German prisoners in two hours. It was a major turning point in World War 1.

1948 Svetlana Savitskaya was born. She was a Russian cosmonaut and second woman in space, on Soyuz T-7 and T-12.

1961 The Edge, birth name David Evans, was born in London. He performs with U2.

The Edge of U2 performs on stage on the first London night of their Vertigo/2005 World Tour at Twickenham Rugby Stadium on 18 June 2005 in London, England. The tour's opening leg covered 13 cities in North America before arriving in Brussels on June 10 for two months of open air European shows, finishing up in Lisbon in the middle of August.

9 AUGUST

1890: Big Organ Recital

The Sydney Town Hall's magnificent Grand Organ was unveiled before an audience of 4 000. Mr William Thomas Best, visiting from Great Britain, 'best by name and best by ability', played. The Grand Organ was the world's largest. It was constructed, tested and built by William Hill and son in England. The Westminster Cathedral organist proclaimed it 'the world's grandest'. It was dismantled and shipped to Australia, where it was reassembled. It has 150 stops, five keyboards for the hands and one for the feet. There are nearly 9 000 pipes that range in length from a few centimetres to almost 20 metres. The playing is tubular-pneumatic. The Grand Organ is breath taking to see and to hear.

1908: Great White Fleet

In one of the biggest naval shows ever, thousands of Aucklanders crowded the Harbour foreshores to see the American Great White Fleet arrive. The sixteen ships were ostensibly on a goodwill mission around the Pacific Ocean but were perhaps also demonstrating America's naval strength to Japan. It was called the Great White Fleet because of the ships' white painted hulls. In Auckland, the sailors were welcomed with banners, flags and streamers. Aucklanders had worried what the impact of 14 000 sailors would have on their sedate city so hockey, lacrosse, soccer, Aussie Rules football matches, dinners, concerts, horse race meetings and even a pantomime at the theatre were organised. Everyone had a fabulous time, although no-one was quite sure what it was all about.

1922: Larkin, Not Larrakin

One of England's most controversial poets Philip Larkin was born. Generally perceived as right wing, woman-hating and as a morose university librarian, he also wrote popular poetry such as this from 'This Be The Verse':

They f--k you up, your mum and dad,
They may not mean to, but they do.
They fill you with the faults they had
And add some extra, just for you.

His poems reflect jazz and speech rhythms. He was also a novelist, essayist and editor. His collections include *The Less Deceived* and *High Windows*.

1593 Izaak Walton, English fisherman, was born in Stafford. He wrote the classic *The Compleat Angler* in 1653. He lived until he was 90.

1899 P.L. Travers, pseudonym of Helen Goff, was born in Maryborough, Queensland. She wrote the Mary Poppins series of books from 1934. Travers said Walt Disney ruined her characters. An eccentric and reclusive woman, she died in 1996.

1930 Betty Boop 'born': first starred in Max Fleischer's animated cartoon *Dizzy Dishes*. She was created by Grim Natwick, originally as a dog, but was later given a human form.

1938 Rod Laver, tennis legend, was born in Rockhampton, Australia. He was the first Australian to win tennis' Grand Slam and repeated it in 1969. He became the first player to pass $1 million in career earnings when he turned professional in 1974.

1945 Nuclear bombs Three days after an atomic bomb was dropped on Hiroshima, Nagasaki was bombed on 9 August. About 200 000 people were killed in the bombings and an unkown number were injured. The bombings led to Japan's surrender.

Actress Betty Boop attends the 70th Anniversary Hollywood Christmas Parade on 25 November 2001 in Los Angeles, CA.

10 AUGUST

1999: No Oasis

Rock guitarist Paul 'Bonehead' Arthurs quit the band Oasis. The English band rose from obscurity to international acclaim in the 1990s. One reviewer said, 'With the Beatles gone, they are the future of rock'. Their first single, 'Supersonic' was released in 1994. The Manchester group consisted of schoolmates Liam Gallagher (vocals), Paul 'Bonehead' Arthurs (guitar,) Pail McGuigan (bass), Tony McCaroll (drums) and was later joined by Liam's brother Noel, who took over as manager and songwriter. Oasis' second album *(What's the Story) Morning Glory?* (with its strange punctuation) was the second fastest UK seller of all time, a global bestseller and was certified quintuple platinum in America. While the public loved the harmonies Oasis created, all was not harmonious. The Gallagher brothers frequently fought. McCaroll quit the band in 1995. Andy Bell and Gem Archer replaced them. 'Standing on the shoulders of giants', 'Be here now' and 'Familiar to millions' are some of their best known works.

2004: Helpmann Awards

At the annual Sir Robert Helpmann Awards in Sydney, New Zealand's Teddy Mahu Rhodes was named Best Male Performer for his role in *Dead Man Walking*, produced by the South Australian State Opera. Ross McCormack won Best Male Dancer in ballet for his part in the Australian Dance Theatre's production of *Held*. The awards were established by the Australian Entertainment Industry Association in 2001 to 'recognise distinguished artistic achievement and excellence' and were named in honour of Sir Robert Helpmann. Helpmann was the principal dancer for seventeen years at the famed Sadler's Wells Ballet and partnered Dame Margot Fonteyn. He was co-director of the Australian Ballet and helped inspire a generation of male ballet dancers. His choreography was based on his philosophy that all art should be entertaining.

1675 The Royal Observatory of Greenwich, in south London: King Charles II laid the foundation stone and John Flamsteed was the first Astronomer Royal.

1889 Dan Rylands patented a screw cap for bottles, while employed at the Hope Glass Works in Barnsley, Yorkshire, England.

1901 Ghosts at Versailles: Two English school teachers claimed to have come across a chateau at Versailles Palace that no longer existed. They saw Marie Antoinette and her court. They stuck by their story until their deaths.

1911 The House of Lords' power in the British Parliament was reduced to only a veto, making the House of Commons the centre of governance.

1985 Madonna's album *Like a Virgin* was the first solo album by a female to sell more than five million copies.

A character from Madonna's book poses for a photo with singer Madonna at a party in celebration of her latest children's book *Lotsa De Casha* at Bergdorf Goodman on 7 June 2005 in New York City. *Lotsa de Casha* is the latest of five children's books by Madonna. A portion of the money raised from the evening's book sales benefited UNICEF.

11 AUGUST

1897: Enid Blyton

The prolific English children's writer was born in London. She always had 'her nose in a book' as a child and loved writing. Blyton was widely published as a novelist and poet from her teenage years on. During her forty-year career she published over 600 books that were translated into 70 languages and sold 60 million copies. Her best known books were about Noddy, the Famous Five series and the Secret Seven series. The latter were set in rural England and the plots involved problem solving. Girls were avid Blyton fans because her series featured them doing exciting things when most other children's writers portrayed them as passive. Blyton died in 1968.

1921: Alex Haley

The African–American author of *Roots* was born in Ithaca, New York. Although American academics pursued genealogical research, the general public's interest was not ignited until 1976 when Alex Haley published his book. He had grown up listening to his grandmother's stories about 'Kin-tay' an ancestor who had been enslaved in Gambia, Africa and shipped to the American colonies. Haley went to Gambia, hoping to glean more information. Amazingly, in Juffure village where Kinte had been captured, a relative whose responsibility it was to memorise stories recited Kunta Kinte's story to Haley. Kinte was Haley's great-great-great-great-grandfather. It took Haley twelve years to research and to reconstruct the story. He established that Kinte had arrived in America in 1767. When his book was made into an eight-part television series, an estimated 130 million viewers watched *Roots*.

1956: Jackson Pollock

One of the 20th centuries more controversial artists, Pollock died, age 44, when he overturned his convertible on Long Island, New York. He used a unique 'spatter-and-drip' technique that opened up abstract expressionism and shifted the focus of painting from Europe to America. His partner, painter Lee Krasner, spent her life promoting his work until they separated. She returned to his studio to paint after his death. Australia's National Gallery of Art's first purchase in 1982 was Pollock's *Blue Poles*, which caused a furore for its world record price for modern art of $1.35 million. It is now appraised at more than $25 million.

1947 Ian Anderson, Jethro Tull's lead singer, Ian Anderson, was born in Blackpool, England. The band was named after the 18th century agricultural seed drill inventor. Their *Roots to Branches* was a best selling album.

1962 New Zealand links the North and South islands with a commercial rail–ferry service, the Aramoana. It was so successful that a second and third were added by 1966.

1998 The biggest merger of all time took place when British Petroleum merged with the American Amoco Corporation for US$110 billion.

1999 KISS received a star on the Hollywood Walk of Fame. Their thirty albums had sold eighty million records. The foursome was known for their garish face paint and stage extravaganzas, such as fire breathing and blood-spitting.

2000 Richard Carrasco completed the most number of 360-degree continuous skateboard revolutions.

Noddy and Big Ears in the television programme *The Adventures Of Noddy*, which was broadcast on the first night of Independent Television in 1955.

Inset: English children's author Enid Blyton with 15-year-old Gloria Johnson, who played Silky in the Christmas production of Noddy in Toyland at the Princes Theatre, London in 1957

12 AUGUST

1911: Swim Sensation

A 21-year-old full-blooded Hawaiian dived into the water of Honolulu Harbour in a 100 yard freestyle race and created a sensation. His name was Duke Paoa Kahanamoku. He beat the world record by 4.6 seconds, by such a huge margin that the Amateur Athletic Union officials in New York City disbelieved it. However, the Duke (a given name, not a title) proved his ability in the 1912 Olympics where he won gold for the American team. In a remarkable Olympic career spanning twenty years, he won three gold, two silver and one bronze medal. He joked that it took Tarzan (Johnny Weissmuller) to beat him. Kahanamoku is world famous for excelling in all water sports, ranging from surfing, paddle-boarding, canoeing, sailing, yachting, diving and water polo. The US Postal Service on issuing a commemorative postage stamp in his honour in 2002 described Duke as 'the greatest aquatic athlete the world has ever seen'. He is revered worldwide as the Father of International Surfing and as the Ambassador of Aloha for his quiet, unassuming ways and his humility.

1912: Mexican Laugh

Cantinflas was born in Mexico City. Cantinflas was a stage name chosen by Mario Moreno Reyes to hide a shameful secret from his disapproving parents—that he was a comedian and vaudevillian. Keeping the single moniker name, he became Mexico's most popular, successful and beloved comedian. He became an international star in *Around the World in 80 Days*.

2004: Black Grace

The all-male Maori and South Pacific dance troupe made their North American debut in Boston, at the Jacob's Pillow Dance Festival. A *New York Times* review said that Black Grace 'was startlingly fresh and full of invention, humour and infectious exuberance'. The dance, *Objects*, was described as 'one of the most haunting evocations of cultural displacement that I have ever seen'. Black Grace made its European debut in 2003 in Holland. Samoan-born Neil Ieremia founded the dance troupe in New Zealand. When he resigned from his bank traineeship to found the modern dance company, his father stopped speaking to him and his mother cried.

1881 Cecil B. de Mille, pioneer movie director was born in Massachusetts. He made more than seventy movies, noted for their extravagant costumes and dance sequences. He died in 1959.

1952 Anti-Yiddish purge. The Stalinist regime executed twenty-four leading Yiddish writers, including David Bergelson, Itzik Fefer and Perez Markish.

1962 Canada's Loch Ness: Two fishermen took a photograph of a 'Loch Ness' type monster in Lake Manitoba in Canada, apparently confirming Indian legends. It might have been a sturgeon, which range up to 3m and can live to fifty years.

1981 IBM unveiled their first PC (personal computer). It had 16 kilobytes of memory and one or two 160k floppy disk drives. It was created in secret in Boca Raton, Florida.

1985 Kyu Sakamoto, the first Japanese singer to have an American and British number one single with Sukiyaki, died in a plane crash.

1992 America, Mexico and Canada agreed to form a free-trade zone called the North American Free Trade Agreement (NAFTA). It would be the world's largest single trading bloc, worth about US$1.8 every day.

Duke Paoa Kahanamoku (1890–1968) playing a Native Chief in the film *Mister Roberts in* 1955. Kahanamoku was an Olympic swimming champion before his acting career and went on to serve as Honolulu's sheriff for 26 years.

13 AUGUST

1912: Nancy Wake

Code named The White Mouse, the most decorated servicewoman in the Second World War and top of the Gestapo's list of most-wanted Resistance fighters was born in Wellington, New Zealand on this day. She was raised in Australia. For many years, she was caught between her allegiance to both Australia and New Zealand, but in 2004, finally accepted Australia's highest honour, The Companion Order of Australia and financial help.

1995: Alison Hargreaves

The world's foremost female alpinist, and probably the best in history, died on K2 in Pakistan, the world's second highest mountain. Just three months before Hargreaves had climbed Mount Everest without support and without bottled oxygen, a feat that few have ever done. She was hailed as a national hero when she returned home to Scotland. This was the first step in her goal to be the first woman to climb the other two highest mountains, K2 and then Kanchenjungas without bottled oxygen. The 33-year-old climber and six other climbers had waited out adverse weather on K2 for six weeks and, when 13 August dawned incredibly clear, her group set off for the summit and reached it. A jubilant Hargreaves radioed that it was not snowing and that the conditions were splendid. However, a freak storm, even huge by Himalayan standards, with 224 km/h winds swallowed the seven climbers on their descent. Their bodies have never been found. Instead of the press eulogising Hargreaves, she was vilified. She was accused of being selfish and of being an irresponsible parent for pursuing such a risky passion. Male climbers—many of whom are parents—have never been subject to such controversy.

2004: John Psathas

The New Zealand musician headed for the Athens Olympics on this day and the biggest musical moment yet in his extraordinary life of achievement. Psathas was commissioned to compose most of the music used in the opening and closing ceremonies, including the spine-tingling moment when the Olympic flame was lit. He was born in 1966 and grew up in Taumaranui and Napier. He studied piano and composition at Wellington's Victoria University, supporting himself with gigs in a jazz band. His 1991 highly original 'Matre's Dance' for percussion and piano attracted international attention when it was performed by the world famous Scottish percussionist Evelyn Glennie. Drum Dances, Spike and Happy Tachyons followed. He was chosen to write the music for the Olympics after a worldwide search. He initially thought it was because of his Greek parents who immigrated to New Zealand.

1946 H.G. Wells, English author, historian and politician, died in London, aged 79. He is best remembered for his science fiction, *The Time Machine* and *The First Men in the Moon*.

1966 Nguyen Cao Ky, South Vietnamese Premier, predicts 'in two or three years, or even before, the Communists will accept defeat'. His forecast was off target. The war did not end until 1975.

1979 The Fastnet Race. A savage storm in the Irish Sea caused fifteen deaths in the yacht race—six because safety harnesses failed.

1994 Clifton Clowers in the ballad 'Wolverton Mountain', was actually a real person who died on this day, aged 102.

2003 Libya agreed on £1.7 billion compensation for the victims' families of the 1988 Lockerbie Pan Am 103 disaster.

Nancy Wake, an Australian who joined the French Resistance during World War II. Known to the Gestapo by the code name 'The White Mouse', she was eventually forced to escape to Britain, where she was trained as a spy and parachuted back into France. For the remainder of the war she distributed weapons to resistance fighters. This picture is dated 1951.

14 AUGUST

1924: Cobb and Co

Australia's horse and carriage line finished its last run in Queensland, replaced by motor vehicles and aeroplanes. It was founded during the 1850 gold rush and at its peak in the 1870s had 6 000 horses in use each day. Cobb and Co. coaches were often held up by bandits who stole gold, passengers' property and the mail.

1939: Bryce Courtenay

The author was born in Johannesburg, South Africa and moved to Sydney when he was 19 years old. He enjoyed a successful career in advertising for thirty-five years before publishing his first book, *The Power of One*, which became an international bestseller. Set in South Africa, it is probably his best novel and was made into a major motion picture. His *April Fool's Day* is an extraordinary memoir of the life and death of his gifted son who was born with haemophilia and received a transfusion infected with AIDS. Courtenay successfully led a campaign to change the Red Cross blood donor screening procedures.

1963: Great Train Robbery

At 3.10 a.m., the Glasgow-to-London train was held up. As it approached London, signals flashed 'slow' and the driver braked. The signal changed to red, so he stopped the train. One of the crew went to telephone the central office, but found the lines cut. A robber pushed a gun into the man and ordered him back into the engine where the driver lay unconscious. The thieves uncoupled the engine and the first two cars from the train and forced the crewman to move the train to a siding where a getaway gang was waiting with a truck. They stole about £10 million. Police were able to identify ten suspects from fingerprints. One, Ronald Biggs, was later sprung from a top security prison in 1965 and escaped overseas. He returned to England after 35 years in Brazil and surrendered to police.

1863 The schooner *Don Juan* arrived in Brisbane with sixty-seven indentured 'kanakas' from South Pacific Islands. They were bribed to work in Queensland, but treated no better than slaves. More than 1500 were imported before the year's end.

1880 Germany's Cologne Cathedral was completed, 632 years after construction began.

1900 The Boxer Rebellion was squashed in Beijing by British, French, German and other soldiers. The Boxers were trying to drive the 'foreign devils' out of China.

1908 The world's first international beauty pageant was held in Folkestone, Kent, England.

1997 Fiona Beales motorcycle jumped, from a ramp over twelve trucks, for a distance of 57.9 m. A native of Derby, England, she set the record there.

Ronnie's nicked: Great train robber, Ronnie Biggs, being escorted by three police officers in 1963.

Inset: Ronnie Biggs, who escaped from Wandsworth Prison in 1965, found refuge in Brazil but returned to Britain and jail in 2001.

15 AUGUST

1939: The Wizard of Oz

Young Dorothy and her little dog Toto are whirled away by a frightening tornado and land in a magical technicolour world, somewhere over the rainbow. She meets characters like the Tinman, the Scarecrow, the Cowardly Lion and the Wicked Witch of the West. *The Wizard of Oz*, one of the most popular movies of all times had its Hollywood movie premiere at Grauman's Chinese Theatre on this day. It was based on L. Frank Baum's children's classic *The Wonderful Wizard of Oz*, published in 1900.

1967: David 'Long John' McNamara

The Australian Rules legend and the greatest distance kicker of all time, died, aged 80. McNamara specialised in the place kick. He played for various Victorian teams and, in eighteen years, scored 187 goals in 122 games. McNamara was inducted into the inaugural Aussie Rules Hall of Fame in 2003.

2004: South African Gold

In one of the most thrilling races of the Athens Olympics, South Africa's swimming team won their country's first Olympic gold medal in the pool, in the 4 x 100 m freestyle relay. The swimmers, Roland Schoeman, Lyndon Ferns, Darian Townsend and Ryk Neethling were not favoured to win against the likes of the world-record holding Aussie team, which included crowd-pleaser Ian Thorpe and the American team, which included newcomer Michael Phelps. The South Africans set a world record of 3:13.17 seconds. Coming in under the record was Holland in second place and America third. Neethling said, 'We knew we were fast, but we didn't know how fast and we surprised even ourselves with that world record.'

1057 Macbeth, immortalised in William Shakespeare's play, was killed by Malcolm, in revenge for Macbeth's attempts to further his claim to the Scottish throne.

1903 New Zealand visited Australia to play in their first international rugby match in Sydney. They won 23-3.

1933 Maude Bonney left on a flight to try to be the first female to fly around Australia. She succeeded, arriving on 27 September.

1947 India and Pakistan won independence from Britain, at the stroke of midnight. It was followed by widespread celebration, violence and bloodshed.

1969 Three Dog Night. Popular from 1967 to 1977, went gold with their album of the same name.

Roland Schoeman (top) and Ryk Neethling of South Africa celebrate winning the Mens 4 x 100m relay and setting a new world record during the Athens 2004 Olympic Games in the Main Pool of the Olympic Sports Complex Aquatic Centre on 15 August 2004 in Athens, Greece.

16 AUGUST

1958: Madonna

Madonna Louise Ciccone, singer, actor and entrepreneur was born in Michigan. It is also the day she was married for the first time, in 1985, to the actor, Sean Penn. Their four-year marriage was turbulent and Penn was once jailed for firing a pistol at a hovering paparazzi helicopter. Madonna was a film and music icon of the 1980s and 1990s. She is known for her ability to 'reinvent herself', her relentless self-promotion, her trained dancing and her outrageous costumes. She has two children and is now married to Guy Ritchie.

1977: Elvis Presley

The American rocker died at his Graceland Mansion in Memphis, Tennessee, aged 42. His first hit was 'Heartbreak Hotel' in 1956 and his last hit, released after his death, was 'Guitar Man'. He was known as 'Elvis the Pelvis' for the way he rotated his hips. Tame by today's standards, his wiggles were considered obscene by some television stations that would only show him from the waist up. Some of his enduring classics include 'Love me tender', 'Love me tonight' and 'Blue suede shoes'. Graceland, decorated in the 1970s style as it was at Elvis' death, is a major tourist attraction. There are thousands of Elvis impersonators of all shapes, sizes and colours. His daughter, Lisa-Marie, who was left with his multi-million dollar inheritance, and her mother Priscilla run Graceland.

1996: Binti Jua

A female gorilla at Chicago's Brookfield Zoo, climbed into a 5.4 m moat to rescue a toddler who had fallen in. What amazed animal behaviour experts was how calmly Binti Jua reacted, sensing that the unconscious child needed help. She cradled the toddler and kept the other gorillas away. When zookeepers approached, she handed the toddler over to them. It is only in the past decade that anthropomorphism, describing animal behaviour in human terms, is not a dirty word. A professional working group called Animal Social Complexity and Intelligence, studies incidents such as Binti Jua and builds on the work of Jane Goodall's chimpanzee studies. Until now, that work had been considered 'anecdotal' and unscientific.

1819 The Peterloo Massacre. Police charged an unarmed crowd of 50 000 people protesting low wages and unemployment in Manchester. In a ten-minute skirmish, 500 were injured and some killed.

1865 Dame Mary Gilmore, newspaper editor and columnist, human rights advocate and literary giant, was born in rural Goulburn, Australia. She is featured on the Australia $10 note. She died aged 97.

1896 Gold was discovered in Rabbit Creek, a tributary of the Klondike River, in Canada's Yukon Territory. It led to the Klondike Gold Rush.

1954 James Cameron, movie director, was born in Kapuskasing, Ontario, Canada. His 1997 blockbuster movie **Titanic,** won him an Oscar.

1960 Joseph Kittinger set a world free-fall record of about sixteen miles (84 700 feet) before deploying his parachute.

A new baby gorilla rests in the arms of its mother, a 17-year-old western lowland gorilla named Binti Jua, after nursing at Brookfield Zoo on 9 May 2005 in Brookfield, Illinois. Binti Jua was named one of *People* magazine's 25 'Most Intriguing People' in 1996 after she rescued a 3-year-old boy who had fallen into the gorilla exhibit.

17 AUGUST

1979: Pythonesque

Monty Python's Life of Brian is released. The thought-provoking and satirical movie, in which a man named Brian is mistaken for Jesus Christ, was a huge success for British comedy. The Monty Python comic troupe (Graham Chapman, John Cleese, Terry Gilliam, Eric Idle, Terry Jones and Michael Palin) gave their name to the programming language Python and the word Spam for junk e-mail. In 1985 a giant fossil snake was discovered and named for them, Montypythonoides riversleighensis. The Monty Python humour draws on the talents of The Goons and Spike Milligan. Their final and probably most successful movie, *Monty Python's The Meaning of Life*, was released in 1983 and won the Jury Prize at the Cannes Film Festival. The group disbanded with Chapman's death from cancer in 1989. The *Chamber's Dictionary of the English Language* defines 'Pythonesque, adj. of humour, bizarre, surreal, as in the BBC television comedy programme Monty Python's Flying Circus.' A reconstituted Monty Python troupe opened *Spamalot* on Broadway in March 2005. It was created by Eric idle and stars Tim Curry, David Hyde Pierce, Hank Azaria and Sara Ramirez.

2004: Mariel Zagunis

Ranked 11th in sabre fencing in the world, the American surprised everyone when she won the gold medal at the 2004 Athens Olympics. It was the first fencing gold medal that America had earned in a century. Zagunis beat a former world champion Tan Xue of China 15-9 in the final. Tan out-fenced America's Sada Jacobson, ranked number 1 for the silver. Jacobson took the bronze. Zagunis did not even earn her spot on the American team until June. Women's sabre is a fairly new sport and was established as a world championship in 1999. Saber is the fastest form of fencing and the whole body above the hips is the target, including the head. Unlike foil and epee fencing, a fencer can score with the tip or the edge of the blade.

All six members of the Monty Python team on location in Tunisia to film *Monty Python's Life of Brian* in 1978. From left to right they are John Cleese, Terry Gilliam, Terry Jones, Graham Chapman (1941–1989), Michael Palin and Eric Idle.

1920 Maureen O'Hara was born in Dublin, Ireland. The actress appeared in *The Hunchback of Notre Dame* and inspired schoolmate Vivien Leigh to become an actress.

1945 President Akmed Sukarno, after hearing of the Japanese surrender in the WWII and, after 350 years of Dutch presence, declared that Indonesia was independent. The Netherlands refused to grant it until 1949.

1952 Nelson Piquet, racing car driver, was born in Brasilia, Brazil.

1953 Dexy's Midnight Runners' vocalist/guitarist Kevin Rowland was born in Wolverhampton England to Irish parents. Many of his songs protested anti-Irish prejudice. When the band folded in 1987, Rowland went solo.

1979 Gillian Anderson's acclaimed movie *My Brilliant Career* opened. It won the Australian Best Film of the Year Award and received wide international acclaim.

18 AUGUST

1920: Women's Suffrage

The Nineteenth Amendment to the United States Constitution was ratified and gave women the right to vote. It reads: 'The right of citizens of the United States to vote shall not be denied or abridged by the United States or by any state on account of sex. Congress shall have power to enforce this article by appropriate legislation'. The Amendment was first introduced in 1878. Like all amendments, it required three-quarters of American State legislatures to pass it. Few early supporters had lived to see the Amendment's passage, nor were any women present when the ratification was signed. America was not the first country to grant women the vote. This belongs to New Zealand, which enfranchised women in 1889.

2004: Major Martin Outfoxes Nazis

Bill Jewell, WWII submarine skipper, died in London. Jewell pulled off a top-secret assignment—he planted a decoy body with 'official' documents to mislead the Nazis. The corpse was that of an unidentified man from a mortuary. First he was given an identity: 'Major William Martin'. Then he was dressed in a British major's uniform. A military briefcase was chained to his wrist. Inside the briefcase were the documents about a planned 'invasion' signed by high-ranking military, a love letter from his 'fiancee' and two theatre ticket stubs. The 'invasion' plans for Sardinia and southern Greece were bogus. The Allies' real plan was to invade Sicily and then Italy. Jewell confided in a handful of his crew and the rest were told he was launching a meteorological device. With help, Jewell put 'Major Martin' in the water off the southwest coast of Spain, along with a life vest and a capsized aeroplane raft. An obituary even ran in the newspapers, reporting that Martin had died in a plane crash. A Spanish fisherman netted the body. He returned the briefcase to the British, after first giving copies of the documents to the occupying Germans. As hoped, the Germans fortified the wrong coast. Jewell's exploits were made into a movie, *The Man Who Never Was*.

1825 Scottish explorer Alexander Gordon Laing was the first European to reach Timbuktu. He was murdered soon after by natives.

1925 Arkady Strugatski, Russian science fiction writer, was born in Batumi, Georgia. Collaborating with his brother Boris, many of his books were written in code to avoid censorship. Arkady died in 1991. His books include *Far Rainbow* and *The Second Invasion from Mars*.

1932 Luc Montagnier, the French virologist, was born. He was the first to isolate the AIDS virus, in 1983.

1982 The English city of Liverpool named four streets after its native sons The Beatles: John Lennon Drive, Paul McCartney Way, George Harrison Close and Ringo Starr Drive. They are popular tourist destinations.

1987 New Zealand's Philip Rush triple-crossed the English Channel. His time of 28 hours, 21 minutes, was ten hours faster than the previous swimmer's feat.

A young Beatle, George Harrison (1943–2001,) with his guitar tucked under his arm, taking a break from playing at the Cavern, Liverpool in 1960.

19 AUGUST

1884: Jenolan Caves

Australia's major cave system, the beautiful Jenolan Caves, was first gazetted. Aborigines had frequented them and the name is derived from Jen-o-lan, meaning 'High Mountain'. Bushrangers since the 1830s had taken refuge in them and rumours persist of hidden treasure they left behind. Jenolan consists of several hundred caves, of which nine are open to tourists. The caves are 182 km west of Sydney and are one of NSW's most popular tourist attractions.

1953: The Dionne Quintuplets

Marie, Cecile, Yvonne, Emilie and Annette announced to the media that they intended living separate lives. They were born near Callander, Ontario, to a poor family. Since they were the first quintuplets known to have lived for more than a few hours after birth, they attracted enormous international interest. They had lived in the media glare since they were born in 1934, displayed behind a glass wall to an eager, paying public who waited patiently in line to see them.

1960: Noah's Ark Aloft

The USSR launched its *Sputnik 5*, which included a 'Noah's Ark': two dogs named Belka and Strelka, mice, houseflies, rats and plants. When the satellite returned to Earth the next day they were the first living organisms recovered from an orbit. The purpose was to experiment on animals first before sending a person into space.

1977: Groucho

The most famous of the comic Marx Brothers, Groucho Marx, died. His other brothers were Chico, Harpo, Gummo and Zeppo. Their first success was *I'll Say She Is*, a musical and theatrical 'hodge-podge', followed by the ever popular movies *The Cocoanuts* and *Animal Crackers*. Groucho had a zany sense of humour and a quick wit. He famously said when he resigned from a Hollywood club, 'Please accept my resignation. I don't want to belong to any club that will accept me as a member' and 'I never forget a face, but I'll make an exception in your case'. He hosted the radio show *You Bet Your Life* and later a successful television show. Groucho was known for his outspoken criticism of American political policy and was investigated by the FBI. At the 1972 Cannes Festival he was awarded a Commandeur des Arts et Lettres and received a Special Academy Award for the Marx Brothers.

1909 Indianapolis Speedway, which became one of the world's most famous auto racetracks, opened as a dirt track for testing local manufacturers' cars.

1914 The Australian Red Cross Society was formed to help cope with WWI casualties.

1919 Afghanistan gained its independence from Great Britain. It is a national holiday.

1953 England won cricket's 'Ashes' Test for the first time in twenty years,

1991 Communist hard-liners tried to stage a coup in the USSR against President Mikhail Gorbachev while he was on holiday. As tanks thundered into Moscow, thousands of protesters under the wily leadership of Boris Yeltsin diffused the coup attempt.

Julius 'Groucho' Marx (1895–1977), one of the Marx Brothers, an American comic group.

20 AUGUST

1857: *Duncan Dunbar* Wrecked

One of Australia's worst peacetime maritime disasters occurred at the entrance to Sydney Harbour. The clipper ship the *Duncan Dunbar* (usually called the *Dunbar*) was bringing 121 passengers and crew from England to Sydney. For many of the families aboard, they were relocating to Australia for a new life and others were returning home. After 81 days at sea and with their destination just an hour or two away, the *Dunbar* ran into a winter storm off South Head. Instead of riding out the storm overnight, Captain James Green chose to attempt a night time arrival. The *Dunbar* headed into a sheer cliff face and was wrecked. Only one person survived, seaman James Johnson, who managed to cling to a rocky ledge for about three days. Sydneysiders were devastated at the magnitude of the disaster. It has been speculated that the captain and lookout crew were confused by on-shore lights.

1869: Klondike Kate

Katherine Ryan, a Canadian-Northwest frontier heroine, was born in New Brunswick. She moved west to pursue a nursing career. When she heard about the Klondike Gold Rush, she decided to participate and became one of the few single women in the rush. In the remote Yukon wilderness, Klondike Kate staked and worked three claims and opened a restaurant. She was appointed the first female 'Mountie' (the Northwest Mounted Police) and was the first female gold inspector, earning royalties on gold taken from the Yukon. Klondike Kate also used her nursing skills to sew miners' wounds.

1975: Mars

NASA launched the *Viking 1* in 1975 as a first step toward trying to ascertain more data on whether there was life on Mars. Its sister, Viking 2 was launched 9 September 1975. Viking 1's lander touched down on Mars in July 1976 and Viking 2 in September 1976. The public was thrilled at the high quality photographs transmitted back to Earth. Scientists were pleased with the weather information and analysis of the Martian atmosphere and surface that were transmitted.

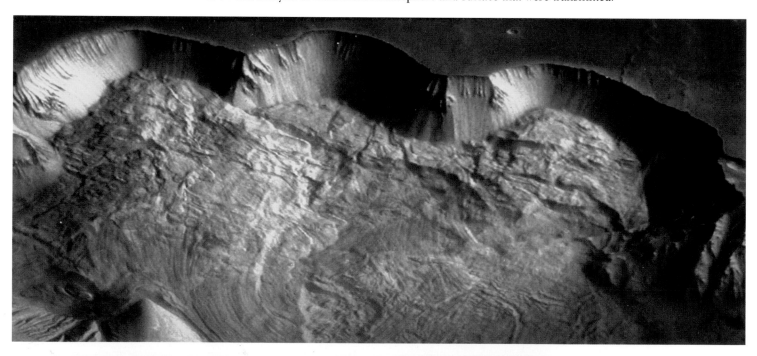

1778 Bernardo O'Higgins, 'The Liberator of Chile', was born in Chilian, Chile. He became its first ruler after independence. He died in 1842.
1882 The 1812 Overture by Pytor Ilyitch Tchaikovsky premiered in Moscow.
1980 Reinhard Messner, probably the greatest climber of all time, in an astonishing feat of mountaineering made the first successful solo summit of Mount Everest.
2003 UN Heritage Sites Protected. After pressure from environmentalists and governments of fifteen of the world's largest mining companies and metal producers agreed: United Nations World Heritage sites were off limits.
2003 Madame Tussauds in London unveiled an interactive wax model of Pop Idol judge Simon Cowell. It made statements typical of Cowell's, such as 'Extraordinarily bad'.

Cliff-like features in the Ophir Chasm, part of the Valles Marineris canyon system near the equator of Mars, taken by Viking during its mission to study the red planet in 1976.

21 AUGUST

1959: Sandwich Islands No More

American President Dwight Eisenhower proclaimed the Territory of Hawaii the fiftieth State of the United States. The statehood bill had passed Congress the previous March, after a petition weighing 113 kg and over 1.6 km long, containing over 120,000 Hawaiian residents' signatures was submitted in favour of statehood. Newsprint rolls were spread on a downtown Honolulu street and held in place by stones. Signers walked across the stones to find a place to add their signature. The official referendum in Hawaii in June was passed by a huge margin. On 21 August Statehood was celebrated with fireworks and partying. For many, it was the end of a 110-year struggle. For others, it was a day of sorrow and concern that Americanisation would inevitably destroy Hawaii's unique culture and traditions.

2004: Gold Haul

The final day of the 2004 Athens Olympics swimming events was one of the Games' highlights. Jenny Thompson, aged 31, became the most decorated athlete in American Olympic participation, when she won her 12th medal, breaking a tie between swimmers Mark Spitz, Matt Biondi and shooter Carl Osburn. Inge de Bruijn of the Netherlands, one of the Sydney Olympic stars, where she had won three gold medals, had won silver and two bronze medals in Athens, but the gold had eluded her. On the last day, de Bruijn won a gold medal and retained her 50 m freestyle title. Aussie Grant Hackett became the fourth man to win the gruelling 1500 m freestyle in two Olympics and broke the Olympic record. He turned in an amazing sprint in the last 100 m against his American challenger Larsen Jensen who had been offered $1 million if he could beat Hackett. One of the big upsets of the Games was the Aussie women's 4 x 100 m medley relay defeat of the American team, which had won eight of the previous eleven Olympics. The Aussie team of Giaan Rooney, Liesel Jones, Petria Thomas and Jodie Henry set a world record of 3:58:30. It was Thomas' eighth Olympic medal—equal to the best ever by Aussies Dawn Fraser and Susie O'Neill—just one behind Ian Thorpe. The much-hyped Michael Phelps failed to equal Mark Spitz's 1972 haul of seven gold medals, but won four gold and four other medals.

1930 Princess Margaret Rose was born in Glamis Castle, Scotland. She was the first princess born in Scotland in 300 years. She was Queen Elizabeth II's sister.

1944 Peter Weir, the acclaimed Australian movie director, was born in Sydney. He directed *Witness, Gallipoli* and *The Truman Show.*

1947 Ettore Bugatti, the French car manufacturer died, aged 65.

1976 Renee Richards launched a career as a female tennis player by winning her first match. It immediately caused controversy, as she was a transgendered man.

1983 Benigno S. Aquino Jr, the Filipino Opposition leader, was assassinated when he returned after three years of self-exile in America. It contributed to toppling President Ferdinand Marcos. Aquino's widow, Corazon, became President in 1986.

Athens, Greece: Australia's women relay team celebrates after winning the women's 4 x 100 medley relay final on 21 August 2004, at the Olympic Aquatic Center at the 2004 Olympic Games in Athens. Australia 's team : Giaan Rooney, Liesel Jones, Petria Thomas and Jodie Henry.

Petria Thomas of Australia competes in the women's swimming 200 m butterfly.

22 AUGUST

1770: Cook claims Oz

Captain James Cook wrote in his journal on this day: 'I now once more hoisted English Coulers and in the Name of His Majesty King George the Third, took possession of the whole Eastern Coast (of New Holland) from the above Latitude down to this place by the name of New South Wales'. New Holland was the name given to Australia by the Dutch and Cook laid claim to the parts that the Dutch explorers had not mapped. Cook was one of the world's greatest explorers, circumnavigating the world twice and on his three voyages sailing as far south as the unknown Antarctica and as far north as the Bering Strait in the Arctic.

1908: Snap

France's Henri Cartier-Bresson described as the greatest photographer of the 20th century was born on this day. Trained as an artist, he was especially influenced by his friend Max Ernst and took up photography when he was saw the work of the gifted photographer Martin Munkacsi. Cartier-Bresson believed that the best photographs were decisive and he waited for hours for just the right shot. He also thought that the best shots were achieved when the photographer was unobtrusive and melted into the background. Cartier-Bresson was never very interested in the mechanics of photography and approached it from the aesthetic point of view. He died in 2004, three weeks before his 96th birthday, in his homeland.

1911: Missing Mona

Leonardo da Vinci's *Mona Lisa* was stolen from Paris' Louvre Museum. Considered by many people to be the world's most famous painting, the 16th century painting was a French national treasure for 400 years. Investigators decided that it could not be the work of professionals because the work was too well known and decided a 'madman' was responsible for the night-time theft. The painting was not tracked down until 1913. It was found in the possession of an Italian painter, who had tried to sell it to an art dealer.

1862 Claude Debussy, French composer and musician, was born. He wrote 'Prelude a l'après-midi d'un faune' and the captivating 'Claire de lune'. He died in 1918 in Paris.

1920 Ray Bradbury, science fiction writer, was born in Waukegan, Illinois. He wrote *Fahrenheit 451*, *The Martian Chronicles* and *Illustrated Man*.

1922 Michael Collins, chief of Ireland's Provisional Free State and its army, was killed in an ambush. Leader of the guerrilla campaign against Britain, he was frequently attacked. He was 31.

1926 Honor Blackman, British actress, was born in London. As a teenager she was offered a bicycle or elocution classes for a gift — she chose the classes. She appeared in *The Avengers* and *Bridget Jones' Diary*.

1953 Last prisoners released from Devil's Island, French Guinea. Its famous political prisoners had included Alfred Dreyfus and Henri Charriere, better known as Papillon.

Photographer Henri Cartier-Bresson wearing hat and holding camera up to his face.

23 AUGUST

1305: Drawn and Quartered

The English executed Sir William Wallace, the Scottish military leader and loyalist. As was customary with 'traitors', Wallace was hung, drawn and quartered. His head was placed on a spike on Tower Bridge. His limbs were displayed in various northern and Scottish cities to show rebels what the English had in store for miscreants. In 1995, Mel Gibson, the director and actor made a fictional account of Wallace's life in *Braveheart*. Wallace lived during a time when Scotland and England were separate monarchies and being in such close proximity constantly found reasons for going into battle, over fish rights, boundaries, forest ownership and so on. Wallace's exploits as a soldier stood out with his 1297 win against the English as part of the Wars of Independence when the outnumbered Scots won a decisive victory at the Battle of Stirling Bridge. As the English surged forward across the narrow bridge, the waiting Scots killed them. A flank of Scots approached from the rear and thousands of Englishmen drowned when the bridge collapsed. The next year, the English successfully invaded Scotland and seized castles near Falkirk. Wallace eluded capture until 1305.

1926: Rudolph Valentino

The movie star was adored by millions of women worldwide and there was widespread hysteria when he died prematurely at age 31 on this day. Slender, lithe and exotic looking, he was for a long time panned by critics, but now his work has received a more positive appraisal. He starred in black and white silent movies, such as *The Horsemen of the Apocalypse* and *The Sheik*. He died from a perforated ulcer. More than 100 000 fans stormed the mortuary for one last glimpse of their idol.

1939: Robin Hyde

The major New Zealand novelist committed suicide, aged 33. Hyde was a pseudonym for Iris Wilkinson. She was born in South Africa to an Indian father and an Australian mother. The family emigrated to Wellington, New Zealand where she became a well-known poet, publishing her first collection at 23, called *The Desolate Star*. She became a journalist and wrote several novels, including the classic *The Godwits Fly*. Hyde was largely forgotten as a writer, until the publication of *Houses by the Sea* in 1952. She is now regarded as one of New Zealand's major novelists and a role model for feminists.

1617 London's first one-way street was designated.

1949 Rick Springfield, Australian singer, was born in Sydney. His songs include 'Don't talk to strangers' and 'I'm your superman'.

1969 Taiwan began its domination of the all-American sport, Little League Baseball World Series.

1979 David Ryan broke the eight-hour sheep shearing record in Australia by shearing 500 sheep. Sheep shearing is a hotly contested sport in and between Australia and New Zealand.

1989 Over one million people held hands across the Baltic states in a show of resistance to the USSR. The line stretched 643 km across Estonia, Latvia and Lithuania.

Vilma Banky (1902–1991) and Rudolph Valentino (1895–1926) embrace each other in the desert adventure *Son of the Sheik*, directed by George Fitzmaurice for United Artists in 1926. Original Publication: *Picture Post*, 7002, 'What Women Think About British Men', published 1954.

24 AUGUST

79AD: Pompeii Preserved

On this day Roman writer Pliny the Younger witnessed the eruption of Mount Vesuvius that destroyed the two cities of Pompeii and Herculaneum. He wrote that the ash 'spread over the earth like a flood'. People were entombed by ash or lava as they ate or slept; a dog was 'frozen' in time by boiling mud as it scratched itself. The violent eruption was followed by a tsunami that revealed the seabed. About 20 000 people perished. The cities were abandoned as uninhabitable. Pompeii was rediscovered in 1748.

1875: Channel Crossing One

More people have successfully climbed Mount Everest than have completed the Channel swim. There's the danger of hypothermia, huge tides and unexpected storms on the 35-km crossing. England's Captain Matthew Webb was the first person to swim the Channel successfully. He became an immediate celebrity. On this day in 1875, he set out from Dover with three accompanying boats. Webb was stung by jellyfish, but persevered. He sipped brandy, coffee and beer and ate steak. He was caught in a cross-tide and in all, swam 38 miles. His time was 21 hours. Another 36 years passed, with seventy attempts before someone duplicated Webb's success. The record has now been lowered to 7 hours and 17 minutes.

1901 Clara Maass died in Havana, Cuba. She worked in yellow fever experiments and died of the disease at age 25.

1957 Actor Stephen Fry was born in Hampstead, England. He appeared in *Jeeves and Wooster*.

1959 Hawaii's Hiram L. Fong was sworn in as the first Chinese–American Senator and Daniel K. Inouye was sworn in as the first Japanese–American US Representative.

1965 Marlee Matlin, pioneering deaf actress, was born in Morton Grove, Illinois. She won an Oscar for *Children of a Lesser God*.

2003 David Kelly, Britain's weapons expert warned 'if he disappeared, look for him in the woods' because of his opposition to Tony Blair's Iraq policy. Kelly committed suicide. Blair's standing was shaken in public opinion polls.

2004 Morocco's Hicham El Guerrouj became the first man to win both the 1500 m and the 500 m races at the 2004 Athens Olympics.

Cast of Pompeiian victim trying to free a foot from the rain of lava that buried the town.

25 AUGUST

1883: First Carnegie Library

Officially opened in Dunfermline, Scotland. Andrew Carnegie, born in Dunfermline in 1835, sought a better life in America and became one the world's richest industrialists. He was passionate about public libraries because he was self-educated. More than 2500 Carnegie libraries were built—in America, Fiji, Australia, New Zealand and the UK. South Africa's Sydney Brenner acknowledged in his 2002 Nobel Prize acceptance speech the role that the Carnegie Library had played in his life. Carnegie also established the Carnegie Hall, the Carnegie Foundation and the Carnegie Endowment for World Peace. Carnegie said, 'The man who dies … rich, dies disgraced'.

1982: A Girl Wrote a Letter

Dear Mr Andropov,

My name is Samanatha Smith. I am ten years old. Congratulations on your new job. I have been worrying about Russia and the United States getting into a nuclear war. Are you going to vote to have a war or not? If you aren't please tell me how you are going to help to not have a war. This question you do not have to answer, but I would like to know why you want to conquer the world or at least our country. God made the world for us to live in together in peace and not to fight.

Sincerely, Samantha Smith

Andropov wrote to Samantha saying that he was 'trying to do everything so that there will not be war between our countries'. He invited her to visit the USSR. She made friends with children there and discovered they too wanted peace. Samantha became known worldwide as the Ambassador of Peace. Andropov's reply was a hint that the Cold War might be ending. Sadly, Samantha died two years later in a plane crash.

1918 Leonard Bernstein, one of the greatest and most charismatic conductors in American history, was born in Lawrence, Massachusetts. He first conducted the New York Philharmonic Orchestra at age 25 and was its director from 1959 to 1969. He composed 'Requiem' and the hit musical *West Side Story*.

1925 Neville Reid Westwood and G.L. Davies set out to drive around Australia's perimeter. They succeeded on 30 December.

1951 Singer Rob Halford of the popular heavy metal quartet Judas Priest was born in Birmingham, England. He would appear on stage on a Harley Davidson, wearing studded leather, carrying a whip.

1984 Truman Capote, the writer, died at 59. His work ranged from the light *Breakfast at Tiffany's* to the chilling *In Cold Blood*.

1996 Tiger Woods, aged 20, ended his amateur golfing career in grand style by becoming the first to win three American amateur championships. He then became professional.

British schoolgirl Samantha Smith (1972–1985) (second right) is greeted by Russian Young Pioneers at the airport, Crimean Peninsula, Russia, 9 July 1972. Smith had written a letter to Soviet leader Yuri Andropov after learning about the threat posed by nuclear weapons and, in response, received an invitation to visit the Soviet Union.

26 AUGUST

1781: Thayendanegea

The controversial chief of Canada's Mohawk people led a raid of Whites and Indian loyalists against Americans. The chief commonly went by the name of Joseph Brant. He was born on the banks of the Ohio River in 1742. Educated at an American Indian school, Brant went on to become a scholar, statesman, soldier, interpreter and leader of six Indian nations. He sided with the British in the Seven Years War. In the American Revolutionary War he became a captain in the British Army. As a dedicated Christian, he spent part of his life helping to build an Anglican church for his people. He translated parts of the bible into Mohawk. Because he fought against the Americans, he won land from the British for a reservation for his people in Canada. In 1775, he travelled to England and wore full Native American regalia. He died at the age of 64 in 1807. The city of Brantford Ontario, where a monument stands in his honour, is named after the chief.

1883: Krakatoa

The Indonesian volcanic island of Krakatoa (Krakatau) blew up causing tsunamis that killed 36 000 people, up to 16 km inland along the Javan and Sumatran Coasts. The whole northern part of Krakatoa subsided into the ocean. The sound of the eruption was heard 4828 km away and earthquake instruments 14 484 km away in California registered the shock. Volcanic dust infiltrated the atmosphere and for years caused brilliant sunrises and sunsets. The volcano still has active vents. A new island of lava, called the 'Child of Krakatoa' has formed.

1945: Aung San Suu Kyi

Burma's 1991 Nobel Peace Prize winner, an advocate for civil rights, was born in Rangoon. Her father, the national leader, was assassinated when she was two years old. On this day in 1988, Kyi addressed a massive rally of 500 000 people calling for democratic government and free elections in Burma. The military government warned her against delivering more speeches. She persisted and was placed under house arrest in 1989. The government told Kyi she was ineligible to run as a candidate for the National League for Democracy, which she heads. She ran and won by a landslide.

55BC Roman forces under Julius Caesar invaded Britain. They built roads, canals, aqueducts and bridges, many of which survive today.

1845 J.C. Williamson, an American actor who revolutionised Australian and New Zealand theatre by recruiting foreign stage talent, was born in 1845. He died in 1913.

1935 Geraldine Ferraro, the first female vice-presidential candidate for a major American political party, was born in Newburgh, New York. She was running mate to Democrat Walter Mondale in 1984.

1938 Joseph Goebbels, Nazi propaganda minister, passed a law requiring all Jews to change their names to Israel or Sarah.

1976 Legionnaire's disease was identified in America after the deaths of twenty-eight people who attended an American Legion meeting in Philadelphia. It was a transmuted viral pneumonia.

Myanmar democracy leader Aung San Suu Kyi makes her way through a large crowd of supporters and well-wishers after being freed from 19 months under house arrest on 6 May 2002, making a triumphant return to her party's headquarters in Yangon where she declared her release was unconditional. More than 300 jubilant National League for Democracy (NLD) members let out a great roar as her car approached the building and in the crush it took several minutes for her to be able to alight from the vehicle. The charismatic 56-year-old Nobel peace laureate told reporters her release from house arrest was unconditional and that the military junta would allow her to travel wherever she wishes.

27 AUGUST

1910: Mother Teresa

The Macedonian nun was born. She started working at age 18 in a Calcutta convent, but felt called to ministering to the very poorest of the poor. She said, 'The poor are our brothers and sisters'. She founded the Order of the Missionaries of Charity, which became a model for 700 clinics and shelters worldwide. Her inspiration was Father Damien, who worked with Hansen's disease (leprosy) patients at Molokai, Hawaii. Mother Teresa was a tiny, indefatigable, persuasive and strong-minded woman, who was instantly recognisable in her blue-trimmed white sari. She received the Nobel Peace Prize in 1979. Mother Teresa died in 1997 and is under consideration for sainthood.

1955: First World Records

The first copy of the *Guinness World Records* (GWR) was published. It was an immediate success. In 2003 the 100-millionth copy of the book was published, making it the biggest-selling copyright book ever. The title bears Guinness brewery's name because when Guinness chairman Sir Hugh Beaver was trying to settle a bet, he found that no popular records book existed. Twin brothers Norris and Ross McWhirter were recommended to him as record enthusiasts. GWR is no longer connected to the brewery. Its 50th anniversary issue in 2005 was dedicated to Norris, who was murdered in 2004.

1986: George Nepia, Invincible

One of the greatest Rugby players died, aged 81. He was only 19 years old when he played internationally for New Zealand as a member of the 'Invincibles'. In his thirty-nine consecutive games, he was known for his superb fielding, kicking and tackling. Rugby has brought New Zealand some of its proudest and most controversial moments, especially involving rival South Africa's apartheid policy. In 1921, a Maori team defeated the visiting all-white Springboks 9:8. A South African journalist cabled his paper: '... spectacle of thousands Europeans cheering on band of coloured men to defeat members of (whites) was too much for Springboks who (were) disgusted'. Nepia said, 'It provoked a reaction and bitterness which ... Maoris have neither forgotten nor forgiven'. When New Zealand sent the All-Blacks to South Africa without Maori players, or when Springboks toured New Zealand, there were violent demonstrations. By 1981, New Zealand was fully behind its Maori players discrimination was no longer tolerated.

1858 Guiseppe Peano, Italian mathematician who reduced the greater part of mathematics to strict symbolic form without words, was born. He died in 1932.

1899 Eduardo Torroja y Miret, Spanish architect, was born. He pioneered concrete-shell structures and reinforced concrete, such as the Madrid Hippodrome with its 22-km cantilevered roof.

1908 Lyndon Baines Johnson was born near Stonewall, Texas. He became 36th American President following the assassination of John Kennedy. A complex individual, he ushered in important civil rights legislation and the 'Great Society' but escalated the Vietnam War. He served from 1963 to 1969. He died in 1973.

1988 Singer George Michael achieved his eighth American number one single with 'Monkey', a record only surpassed by Michael Jackson for the decade.

1991 Moldavia declared its independence from the Soviet Union and became a republic.

New Zealand rugby player George Nepia (1905–1986).

28 AUGUST

1913: Robertson Davies

The Canadian writer was born in a small Ontario town in Canada. He studied literature at Oxford University. On his return to Canada, his first interest was in drama. Davies started the Dominion Drama Festival and the Stratford Shakespeare Festival. He produced his first successful play, *Fortune, My Foe* in 1948. He wrote several successful plays, but after a New York theatre flop, he turned to novels. His best known work is his trilogy: *Fifth Business*, *The Manticore* and *World of Wonders*, about semi-rural Ontario. In 1961 he was appointed Master of Massey College at the University of Toronto. Although he died in 1995, his influence is still felt by Canadian writers.

1963: I Have a Dream

At the conclusion of the civil rights march on the Lincoln Memorial in Washington, Rev. Martin Luther King Jr. turned a summer stroll in support of civil rights into a defining moment. Standing in front of the Lincoln Memorial, he delivered his 'I Have a Dream' speech to a crowd of 200 000 African–Americans and whites. His galvanising speech is one of the best known in history. With his voice rising and falling like a biblical orator, King said, 'I have a dream, that one day on the red hills of Georgia the sons of former slaves and the sons of former slave-owners will be able to sit down together at the table of brotherhood. I have a dream that my four children will one day live in a nation where they will not be judged by the colour of their skin but by the content of their character...' At the end of each thought, he would pause and say, 'I Have a Dream'. He concluded his speech with the prophetic words that his people would be 'free at last, free at last, thank God Almighty free at last'. Remarkably, King gave the unrehearsed speech without notes and his voice never faltered. It marked a turning point for the American civil rights movement. That year, he was chosen Man of the Year by *Time* magazine and the next year was awarded the Nobel Peace Prize. King led a 80-km non-violent march in Alabama, from Selma to Montgomery to allow African–Americans to register to vote and helped with the enactment of the federal Voting Rights Act. He was assassinated in 1966.

1889 Charles Boyer, philosopher turned movie actor, was born at Figeac, France. He starred in about eighty movies, including *Gaslight* and *The Madwoman of Chaillot.* Boyer died in 1978.

1907 Fitzgerald Edwards, a runner of British Guyana, was the first black man to win a gold medal at the British Empire Games. He also won three bronze medals at the 1932 Olympics. In 1936, then a resident of Canada, won the first-ever Lou Marsh Award.

1922 The Miss America beauty pageant banned the use of perfumes that might 'seduce' the judges in their voting.

1947 Manolete, Spain's legendary bullfighter, was critically gored by a bull in a fight in Linares and died the next day.

1988 Three Italian stunt planes collided during an air show in Ramstein, West Germany. Debris killed seventy spectators.

A crowd of over 200 000 Americans gathered on the Washington Monument Mall on August 28, 1963, at the end of the march on Washington for jobs and freedom, during which Martin Luther King delivered his famous 'I have a dream' speech.

29 AUGUST

1915: Ingrid Bergman

The Swedish movie star was born in Stockholm, Sweden. She died on her 67th birthday after a seven-year battle with cancer in 1982. She was a three-time Oscar winner, for *Gaslight*, *Anastasia* and *Murder on the Orient Express*. Orphaned as a child, she was taken in by an aunt, who died two months later. Bergman's serene and disingenuous exterior never showed her internal pain. She is also remembered for her role in *Casablanca* opposite Humphrey Bogart and distinguished herself in *Joan of Arc*. Unfortunately, she said, the public assumed that when she convincingly portrayed a saint in a movie that she was a real-life saint. When her marriage to dentist Peter Lindstrom unraveled after thirteen years and she became pregnant to Roberto Rosselli, her director in Stromboli in 1949, her fans and the press ostracised her.

1923: Lord Richard Attenborough

The great movie director was born in Cambridge, England. He began his acting career at 12 years old and made his professional stage debut six years later after attending the Royal Academy of Dramatic Art. He became a movie director in 1969, with his satirical *Oh! What a Lovely War*. His philosophy is to be true to the content and sincerity of the work before stylism . It was his life's ambition to bring *Gandhi* to the screen, which he made in 1982, starring Ben Kingsley. Attenborough received an Oscar as Best Director. Other movies include *The Great Escape*, *In Which We Serve* and *Chaplin*, which starred Robert Downey, Jr. His daughter, her mother-in-law and his granddaughter died in the 2004 tsunami in Phuket, Thailand.

1947: Temple Grandin

The professor of animal science and inventor was born in Boston, Massachusetts. The equipment Dr Grandin has designed for humanely handling cattle, to eliminate fear in the slaughterhouse, is used in at least half of all countries. She was born with autism and is hypersensitive to sound and touch, which helps her relate intuitively to animals, she has said. She has authored over 300 professional articles in her area of expertise. Grandin is probably one of the first autists to achieve a doctorate and she is an inspiration to many coping with the serious brain disorder. She has written about her challenging life in *Emergence: Labeled Autistic* (1986) and *Thinking in Pictures and Other Reports From My Life with Autism* (1995).

1792 The British battleship *Royal George* sank in a freak accident while it was being repaired at Spithead, London. It was tilted too far to the port side and a wind gust tilted it further. Water rushed in, drowning 900 navy personnel.

1957 Strom Thurmond, the American Senator from South Carolina, set a filibuster record by speaking for 24 hours and 18 minutes.

1975 Astronomers observed how a star in Cygnus became a nova. It became the fourth brightest in the sky.

1986 Britain's identical twins May and Marjorie Chavasse beat the 700-million to 1 odds by turning 100 years old.

2000 Australian Government announced it would restrict inspections by United Nations human rights officials because of criticism of Australian treatment of Aborigines.

Richard Attenborough and his wife Sheila Sim bring in the new year in style, January 1955.

30 AUGUST

1871: Ernest Rutherford

The pioneering physicist was born near Nelson, in rural New Zealand. He was the fourth of twelve children and although he was competitive he was also compassionate. His mother taught school and his father ran a mill and farmed. Rutherford liked to build machines and to take things apart; he was a born experimenter and had uncanny intuition. He said of himself: 'I am a simple man and I want a simple answer'. He studied at Cambridge University and set up a laboratory at McGill University in Canada. He had a knack for choosing brilliant colleagues to work with him. Later he set up a lab at the University of Manchester and at the University of Cambridge's famous Cavendish laboratory. Rutherford was awarded New Zealand's first Nobel Prize for his work in radioactivity. He dissected the atom and showed that most of its mass is concentrated in its dense nucleus. He was elevated to the peerage and chose his birthplace as his name, Lord Rutherford of Nelson. He was outraged by the treatment of non-Aryan scientists in Nazi Germany and founded the Academic Assistance Council. Rutherford died in a freak gardening accident, age 56. He was buried in Westminster Abbey near Sir Isaac Newton. At his death, in the many tributes that were paid to him, a friend wrote, 'It can be truthfully said of him, as of very few people, that he had no enemies.'

1882: Cricket Is Dead

The *Sporting Times* ran a mock obituary lamenting English cricket's death, following Australia's successful win over England by seven runs, the day before. The obituary said, 'The body will be cremated and the ashes taken to Australia'. This is the origin of the name of the cricket series The Ashes that is used today. The two countries had begun their first-class Test series against each other in 1878.

1979: Earl Mountbatten of Burma

The last British Viceroy of India and a hero in WWII in Burma was blown up by the Irish Republican Army (IRA) while fishing. The IRA said that their motive was to drive British intruders from their land. Two others were killed and four seriously injured. Mountbatten, who had encouraged the romance between Prince Philip and Queen Elizabeth II was very close to the Royal family. He was godfather to Prince Charles.

1891 Physician Claire Straith was born in Michigan. He specialised in reconstructive surgery and developed new techniques and instruments. He convinced automakers to use safety glass in automobiles.

1922 Turkish War for Independence Victory Day. It is a national holiday, with fireworks.

1927 Geoffrey Beene, American fashion designer, was born in Louisiana. He quit medical school to study fashion and launched Geoffrey Beene, Inc with a line of women's sportswear. He died in 2004.

1943 Jean-Claude Killy, Olympic gold medallist alpine skier, was born in Saint Cloud, France.

1963 A 'Hot Line' Teletype (a typewriter keyboard that sends and receives messages) was set up between Moscow and Washington to reduce the risk of accidental nuclear war. Messages would be encoded to prevent interception. It was a result of the Cuban missile crisis.

Chamrousse, France, 9 February 1968: French skier Jean-Claude Killy, salutes the crowd in Chamrousse, near Grenoble (French Alps), after winning the gold medal in the downhill in front of his teammate during the Winter Olympic Games.

31 AUGUST

1986: Henry Moore

The internationally acclaimed sculptor died age 88 in Hertfordshire, England. He was born in 1898 in Castleford, Yorkshire. The painter Paul Cézanne and sculptor Alberto Giacometti influenced him. His flowing evocative shapes, often of the female human form, such as his 1946 *Draped Reclining Figure* and his 1949 *Three Standing Figures* were considered groundbreaking. His work is still very popular in America and in Europe and Australia, with many campuses and public areas featuring his work.

1992: Sydney Harbour Tunnel

As Sydney grew, the magnificent Harbour Bridge linking the North and South shore became increasingly jammed with traffic at peak hours. First, the tram tracks were changed into traffic lanes, but still the traffic grew, as the population topped three million. An innovative solution enabled a private construction company to design and to finance the construction of a tunnel beneath the Harbour. The A$2 billion Sydney Harbour Tunnel officially opened on this day. It is a 960-metre tube made up of eight prefabricated concrete sections, with large-scale modifications to the freeway approaches and exits at both ends. The tunnel has been built to withstand sinking ships in the busy harbour and earthquakes. The toll-based tunnel carries more than 75 000 cars a day. It will be handed over to the NSW Government in 2022.

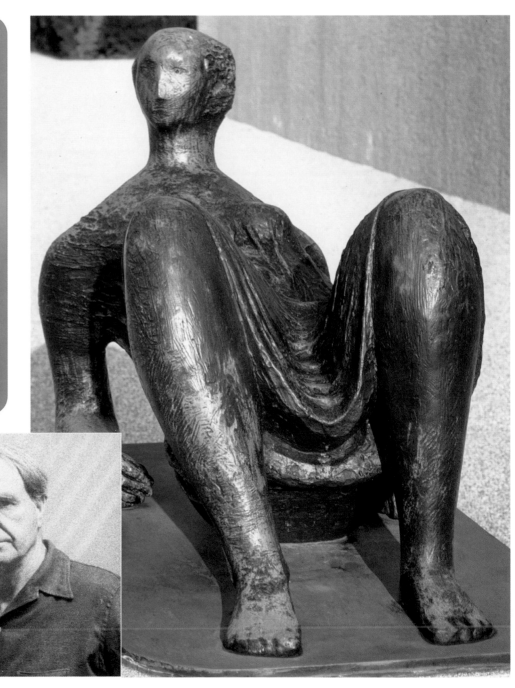

1913 Sir Bernard Lovell, radio astronomer, was born in Oldham Common, Gloucestershire, England. He headed the 1957 team that built the 76-m Jodrell Bank Radio Telescope near Manchester, just in time to track *Sputnik 1*.

1947 A United Nations Special Committee on troubled Palestine recommended its partition into two states, one Jewish and the other Arab. Arabs were disappointed. Jews were pleased. This was the first international recommendation for the creation of a Jewish state.

1947 Great Britain opened its first nuclear power plant at Harwell.

1963 Painter George Braque died in Paris, aged 81. He and Pablo Picasso launched Cubism, using geometric shapes. He focused on birds, beach scenes and still life.

1995 Sterling Morrison, guitarist, died at 53 from cancer. He was a founding member of experimental rock group The Velvet Underground.

Draped Reclining Figure: bronze sculpture by Henry Moore in the Sculpture Garden, Hirshhorn Museum in Washington, DC America.

Inset: English sculptor Henry Spencer Moore (1898–1986) in his Hertfordshire studio in 1959.

1 SEPTEMBER

1 SEPTEMBER

1912: Healy Refuses Easy Gold

The International Swimming Hall of Fame says, 'one of the most underrated Australian Olympians of all time would have to be swimmer Cecil Healy. Not only is he a gold medallist but he is also responsible for one of the greatest acts of sportsmanship in the history of the Games.' At Stockholm in 1912 on this day, Healy, an Australian surf lifesaver, won a gold medal for the 4 x 200 m freestyle relay. When it was time to swim in the 100 m semi-final freestyle, the three American contenders did not show. They were automatically disqualified. Healy said that he had no intention of swimming unless they had a chance to swim. After much debate, the judges relented. The Americans swam in a special semi-final with the top two eligible for the final. In the final, America's Duke Kahanamoku came in first and Healy second. Kahanamoku never forgot the Australian's kindness and visited Australia in 1914–15 to teach his freestyle stroke and also taught surfing. Lieutenant Cecil Healy from Manly near Sydney died in WWI in the battle for Mont St. Quentin, France, just 74 days before the Armistice was signed. Healy epitomised the Australian surf lifesaver—brave, fair and unafraid to take an ethical stand. Highly knowledgeable on world events as a journalist, he had predicted the Great War and wrote about it as early as 1913.

1943: Sir Arthur Streeton

Known as 'Smike' to his Aussie mates, Streeton died on this day in Olinda, Victoria. Australia's most famous native-born landscape painter, he was a member of the Heidelberg School of Australian artists. Their artworks were considered to be the first western art to realistically depict the Australian landscape with its harsh sunlight, earthy colours and distinct vegetation.

1984: Tina Turner

The sexy 66-year-old American released her signature song 'What's love got to do with it'. Raised in Nutbush, Tennessee, she was a gospel singer as a child. When she was 17 years old she met Ike Turner who was touring with his R&B band. He invited her to join his band. Later, she married Ike and changed her name from Anna Mae Bullock to Tina Turner. Turner has enormous charisma, with a growling/gospel voice. She is known as the most dynamic female soul singer in the history of music.

1557 Jacques Cartier, French navigator and explorer, died in St. Malo, France. In search of a northwest passage from Europe to Asia, he discovered the St Lawrence River and his exploration was the basis for France's claim to Canada.

1890 Sir Arthur Upfield was born in Hampshire, England. He is the greatest Australian detective writer. His twenty-nine novels about the half-caste Inspector Bonaparte are still popular forty years after his death. His descriptions of the Outback are superb.

1951 Australia, New Zealand and the USA signed the ANZUS Pact. This was Australia's first defence treaty with a foreign country.

1957 Gloria Estefan, Latin music's biggest singing success was born in Havana, Cuba. She records in both English and Spanish and with the Miami Sound Machine is a global superstar.

1983 Korean Airlines, Flight 007 from New York City to Seoul, South Korea, strayed off course, flying into Soviet air space. It was shot down by a Soviets fighter plane and all 269 people on board died.

Tina Turner performs live on stage at Wembley Stadium, London in 1990.

2 SEPTEMBER

1922: Henry Lawson

Australia's 'bush poet' and author died at age 55. He was born in northern New South Wales and wrote bush ballads such as *Andy's Gone with Cattle* and *The Roaring Days*. Both widely acclaimed and widely criticised, some critics called him an alcoholic drifter with few literary skills. His social reform politics were also controversial, but his work has stood the test of time. Lawson's collected poems and prose includes *While the Billy Boils*, *Joe Wilson and His Mates* and *In the Days When the World was Wide*. Lawson, the first writer given a state funeral was eulogised by Prime Minister WM Hughes: 'The nation has lost one of its foremost poets and short story writers; a man of imagination, perception and literary genius.'

1964: Keanu Reeves

The actor was born in Beirut, Lebanon to a geologist father and a showgirl mother. His father was part Chinese, part Hawaiian and he was named for a great, great-uncle. After his parents divorced, he, his mother and sister moved to Toronto, Canada, where he still lives. Reeves has acted in over forty movies such as *River's Edge* in 1986 and *The Matrix* in 1999. He was ranked number 23 in *Empire* (UK) magazine's Top 100 Movie Stars of All Time in 1997. Reeves maintains a very low profile and pursues hockey, surfing, motorcycling and playing bass, while fans and critics try to decide who he is and how talented he is.

1966: Salma Hayek

The actress was born to Lebanese parents in Coatzacoalcos, Mexico. She decided at 5 years old that she wanted to be a movie star. Her first big break was as Teresa in the popular Mexican soap opera of the same name. Her dreams were bigger and, to the disappointment of her fans, she moved to Hollywood. There she quickly found that Mexican women were typecast as maids or prostitutes. When she vented on a talk show, a producer by chance heard her, was impressed and cast her opposite Antonio Banderas in *Desperado*. Her dream came true when she set up her own production company to co-produce *Frida*, about her fellow Mexican Frida Kahlo. She starred in the title role. *Frida* was nominated for six Oscars and won two.

1961 Carlos "El Pibe" Valderrama, the dread-locked soccer player, was born at Santa Marta, Colombia. He is considered a genius at setting up goals.

1964 WWI's Medal of Honor winner, infantryman Alvin C York, died in Nashville, Tennessee aged 76. Originally a pacifist, he became one of the Allied heroes when he led a group of eight soldiers who overcame a German machine-gun battalion and captured 32 prisoners.

1972 American Bobby Fischer won the World Chess Championship, defeating Russian Boris Spassky in the 21st game. Spassky protested his final move, so Fischer replayed it, and beat him again. Their game had started on 11 July.

1988 The Human Rights Now! tour kicked off at London's Wembley Stadium. It would travel to five continents .Stars included Sting, Tracy Chapman, Youssu N'Dour, Bruce Springsteen and Peter Gabriel.

1994 Roy Castle, the popular British entertainer and TV presenter died age 62 from lung cancer at Buckinghamshire. He was famous for combining his talents of comedy, singing, dancing and music, hosting the popular children's TV series *Record Breakers* in the 1980s and 90s.

Mexican actress Salma Hayek performs in a scene on the set of the film *Frida* on 12 April 2001 in Puebla, Mexico. Hayek plays the title role in the movie, which was filmed on location in Mexico City, Paris and New York.

3 SEPTEMBER

1901: Flag Down Under

When Australia became a Commonwealth in 1901, it needed a national flag. The public was invited to submit designs. An expert panel of judges assessed the 32 000 entries. Five people submitted almost identical designs and shared the prize offered by a magazine. Some of the flag's major features have interesting symbolism. The Federation Star, the big star beneath the Union Jack, has points representing the states and the combined territories. The Southern Cross Constellation is a prominent feature of the Australian sky and used by early navigators. It occupies the right-hand side of the flag. Interestingly, the flag design was never debated in Parliament and the flag was not formally adopted until 1953. Other famous Australian contests include a design for Canberra, the national capital and for the Opera House.

1954: Remote Fair Isle

The tiny island of Fair Isle, between Shetland and Orkney islands off the Scottish coast, became a National Trust property. About 70 residents live there. The island is famous for woollen sweaters hand-knitted with intricate patterns and for birds. The sweaters first became fashionable when the Prince of Wales wore one in the 1920s. Fair Isle has been famous as a migratory bird sanctuary since 1948, when George Waterston, an ornithologist, purchased it. Waterston 'hatched' the plan in a prisoner of war camp, along with a fellow ornithologist Ian Pitman. The Fair Isle Bird Observatory studies the origins of the spring and autumn migratory birds, their routes and feeding habits.

1966: Donovan

The songwriter and singer climbed to number 1 on the American singles chart, with 'Sunshine Superman'. It was described as one of the earliest and best examples of psychedelic pop. Donovan Philips Leitch was born near Glasgow, Scotland in 1946 and later moved to England. He incorporated folk music, jazz, rock, romantic, Medieval and pastoral themes. By 1970, he tired of being a celebrity and escaped with his wife and children to a Southern California desert. By the 1980s he stopped recording altogether. Donovan returned to music in 1996 when Tom Petty invited him to tour with him, with Donovan's new album, *Sutras*.

1752 The Gregorian Calendar was adopted by the British Empire and the American colonies, in one of the greatest technological advances in history, replacing the Julian. It required eliminating eleven days, from 3 September to 14 September, at which Britons protested: 'give us back our eleven days'. The calendar started in January, not March.

1939 New Zealand and The Allies declared war on Germany. 'Where she [Britain] goes, we go, where she stands, we stand,' said New Zealand Prime Minister Joseph Savage.

1953 Florence Horsbrugh became Minister for Education, the first British female Tory (Conservative) Cabinet Minister.

1967 Sweden changed from driving on the left side of the road, to driving on the right.

1992 Barbara McClintock, famed but largely ignored geneticist, died on 2 September aged 90. She was a Nobel Laureate in Medicine and Physiology in 1983. She said she 'knew by seeing, and saw by knowing', describing her intense relationship with the maize kernels she studied.

British folk rock singer Donovan poses with his ten-year-old daughter, Astella Dee. Astella performed at the San Remo Festival in Italy, in 1982.

4 SEPTEMBER

1907: Edvard Grieg

The Norwegian composer died. He studied music in Leipzig and Copenhagen. He later toured Europe as a pianist and as a conductor. He was always drawn to his Norwegian roots and, in his own compositions, he used the traditional folk music themes and rhythms of his country. He was a student of Scandinavian folklore and brought that richness to his compositions, for example *Peer Gynt Suites* is based on Henrik Ibsen play. He wrote over 200 songs. Grieg founded a musical society in Oslo and organised the first Norwegian music festival in Bergen, his hometown.

1999: East Timor Crisis

The United Nations announced the results of the East Timor referendum election, held on 30 August, on this day, in which a majority of East Timor citizens had voted for independence from Indonesia. It resulted in hundreds of East Timorese deaths with pro-Indonesian militants rampaging and killing in protest against the referendum result. East Timor has had a troubled history. It is a tiny, impoverished island in the Indonesian archipelago, about 643 km northwest of Australia. The Portuguese colonised it in the 16th century so Roman Catholicism is the main religion and Portuguese the language spoken. After the Portuguese withdrew in 1975, Indonesia, already governing West Timor, annexed East Timor against its will. A nationalist movement began immediately. More than 200 000 East Timorese have died because of the brutal repression. Indonesia's President BJ Habibie announced the 1999 referendum. Habibie invited United Nations troops, and Indonesia staged a phased withdrawal. Nationhood was declared on 20 May 2002, for the newest nation of the Millennium.

2000: Elephant Park

South Africa announced it would send some of its excess elephants to Angola. The Angolan wildlife parks had been decimated during a 25-year-long civil war. The first park to be rehabilitated was Quicama, where five different species, including rhinoceros and elephants were to be re-introduced. Animal welfare activists were concerned that poachers might kill the elephants for ivory, or food, or old Soviet landmines might detonate accidentally. Angola reassured the welfare activists that the animals would be released into a 20 000 hectare area, with a secure electric fence. South Africa had claimed that the only alternative was to kill the excess elephants.

1781 Los Angeles, California was founded. Its original name was El Pueblo Nuestra Senora de la Reina de Los Angeles de Porcuncula (the town of the queen of the angels).

1824 Anton Bruckner, Romantic Austrian composer, was born in Ansfelden. Known as a 'country bumpkin' he wrote mainly symphonies and was unappreciated in his lifetime. He died in Vienna in 1896.

1825 Dadabhai Naoroji, 'The Grand Old Man of India', was born in India. He was a professor of Mathematics and Natural Philosophy. He became a politician in both India and England. As president of the Indian National Congress, he mentored Mohandas (Mahatma) Gandhi. He was the first Indian elected to the British Parliament. He died in 1917.

1909 Boy Scouts held their first parade in England. Founded two years before, there were already two thousand members.

1936 Beryl Markham, English aviator, set out to fly the Atlantic, from the east to the west. She crash-landed the next day, in Canada, but was unhurt. She was the first person to fly solo across the Atlantic from east to west.

East Timorese anti-independence militia members brandish homemade gunsa and other crude weapons In Liquica, East Timor on 14 May 1999. After an andependence victory following the United Nations vote for the territory's future the Indonesian Government backed militiamen rampaged through East Timor terrorising residents and United Nations staff.

5 SEPTEMBER

1908: My Country

Australia's most celebrated poem, 'I love a sunburnt country', first appeared in print, in *The Spectator* magazine in London. Young Dorothea MacKellar wrote it when she was living in England and was homesick for Australia. She led a privileged childhood, as the only daughter of a prominent Sydney physician and Parliamentarian. Her family owned several country properties and she was a skilled rider. She never married, although she was deeply in love with in Englishman. She returned to Australia to ask for her family's blessing and wrote to her fiancée that they approved. Sadly, he never received the letter and he married someone else. She was widely published in Australia, America and Britain. A statue in her honour stands in Gunnedah. There is also a poetry contest in her name.

1972: Munich Kidnap

Palestinian guerrillas infiltrated the Munich Olympic Village at 5 a.m. and took nine Israeli athletes hostage. By 9 a.m., 12 000 sharpshooters and negotiators surrounded the village. In exchange for the Israelis, the kidnappers demanded the release of 234 imprisoned Palestinians. When negotiations stalemated, a helicopter transported the hostages and guerillas to Munich airport at midnight, ostensibly to acquire a plane to fly them to Egypt. Instead, waiting sharpshooters opened fire. All but three guerillas, along with all the hostages, were killed. In reprisal, Israel dropped bombs on Palestine for four days. In a still controversial decision, the Olympic events continued. Security has since escalated at all Games.

1982: Legless Air Ace

Sir Douglas 'Tin Legs' Bader died, aged 72. Bader was a Battle of Britain war hero. He was nicknamed 'Tin Legs' because he wore prostheses on both legs. He had been an outstanding athlete in school and was trained as a pilot at the Royal Air Force College. Bader was a show off and attempted an acrobatic manoeuvre that he was not trained for. He crashed and both his legs were amputated. After a desk job for several years, the 29-year-old Bader begged to return to flying in 1939, during the Battle of Britain. He created two fine Squadrons, who became known for their dog-fighting ability. He also promoted the 'Big Wing' formation and the four-plane formation, which became the English and American standard. In 1941 Bader was shot down and became a German POW. After the War, he spent his time visiting hospitalised veterans. His story was told in the bestseller *Reach for the Sky*, which was later made into a popular movie.

1666 The Great Fire of London ended after burning for three days. More than 13 000 buildings were lost. It probably started at a bakery. Many believe it led to today's fire insurance industry.

1883 Broken Hill in far western NSW. Charles Rasp discovered deposits of silver-lead-zinc. Rasp and associates established Broken Hill Pty Ltd two years later and it became Australia's largest mining and industrial consortium.

1902 Darryl Zanuck, controversial movie producer, was born in Nebraska. He co-founded what would become Twentieth Century Fox. His films include *Grapes of Wrath* and *Forever Amber*. He died in 1979.

1959 The first trunk telephone calls from a public pay phone, which did not require an operator's assistance, were made in the UK.

1966 Terry Ellis of the funky R&B En Vogue was born in Houston, Texas. The singing quartet included Cindy Herron, Maxine Jones and Dawn Robinson.

Standing on left, British fighter pilot hero Douglas Bader (1910–1982) with Air Chief Marshall Sir Keith Park from New Zealand (on right) in a 1947 photograph. The third officer is unidentified.

6 SEPTEMBER

1860: Jane Addams

The social reformer and feminist, was born in Cedarville, Illinois. Her mother died when she was a toddler. Her father, a Quaker and idealistic Illinois politician heavily influenced Addams. She founded Hull House for women in the Chicago slums, after visiting London's Toynbee Hall, a cultural and social centre in the East End slums, which provided an opportunity for theology students to live among the poor, to learn from each other and in turn change society for the better. Addams decided to establish a 'settlement house' for young women, to help them with job training. It was an immediate success and was imitated in many countries. She received the Nobel Peace Prize in 1931.

1907: Johnny Kelley

The inspirational Boston Marathon runner, was born. He ran the race 61 times and won twice. He ran his last marathon at age 84 and then became the race's grand marshal. There is a statue of Kelley in Boston, at the base of hill near Newton City Hall that runners call 'Heartbreak Hill'. *Runners* magazine named him its Runner of the Century. He died in 2004 at age 97.

1997: Diana

The Princess of Wales' funeral was held at Westminster Abbey. The 36-year-old princess and her friend Dodi Fayed, 42 and their chauffeur were killed in a car accident in Paris on 31 August. Preceding it, a million people had lined up to pay their last respects to her, as her body lay in state. The funeral began with a solemn procession through the streets of London, through sobbing crowds of mourners who threw flowers at the cortege. As 31.5 million Britons watched on television and billions watched worldwide, Diana's brother gave a eulogy in which he accused the press of making her the 'most hunted person of the modern age.' He blamed the paparazzi for his sister's death. Diana's friend, Elton John rewrote 'Candle in the wind' in her memory. She had been divorced from Charles, the heir apparent, the previous year. Diana was one of the most famous celebrity's of the century and was heavily involved in charity work. The Princess of Wales Memorial Fund continues her work.

1620 The first Pilgrims left England on board the *Mayflower* to settle in America. They were escaping religious persecution.

1915 The English military tested its first prototype tank.

1966 Hendrik Verwoerd, the architect of South Africa's apartheid policy, was fatally stabbed at a parliamentary session.

1972 Rick DeMent, American swimmer, forfeited his Olympic gold medal in the 400 m freestyle when he failed a routine drug test. The drug was prescription asthma medication. On the same day, the following year, he set a world record for the distance.

1975 Glen Campbell, country and western singer, hit number 1 on the Billboard pop music chart with the perennial favourite 'Rhinestone cowboy'. He is also known for his dedication to charity. He represented America as Bicentennial Ambassador of Goodwill.

A message where is written "Mummy" stands on the coffin of Diana, Princess of Wales, as the gun carriage carrying her remains makes its way to Westminster Abbey fot the funeral ceremony 06 September.

7 SEPTEMBER

1905: Martial Law in Tokyo

Tokyo, Japan was placed under martial law, after 300 demonstrators were injured over the treaty to end the Russian–Japanese War. The treaty was announced two days before. After centuries of isolation, Japan built up a military force and, like European powers, began Empire building. By 1894 Japan had invaded Mainland Asia and fought against China for control of Korea and Manchuria. Japan next launched an attack against Russia's Asian naval bases in 1904. It was an embarrassing defeat for Russia, with up to 250 000 deaths and the loss of about 20 of its ships. Russia was slow to deploy its Baltic Fleet, which had to sail halfway round the world. American President Theodore Roosevelt negotiated the peace treaty. Both countries promised to withdraw from Manchuria. Russia promised not to interfere with the Japanese occupation of Korea. The seeds for future wars were unwittingly sown.

1936: Tassie Tiger Extinct

The last Tasmanian Tiger died in captivity at Hobart Zoo in Tasmania. Its scientific name is Thylacine. It was a secretive, shy animal, like a large striped dog, with a pouch and was hunted to extinction because it preyed on fowl.

1978: Keith Moon

The drummer for rock band The Who died age 32. He was outrageously wild and some people would describe him as 'out-of-control' not only in his drumming style, but also in his life. He was known for trashing his drums and for destroying hotel rooms. In 1974 Moon released his only solo album, *Two Sides of the Moon*. He died in his sleep after overdosing on an anti-seizure medication that he was taking for alcoholism.

1998: Google

Launched by friends Larry Page and Sergey Brin in a garage, Google remains the most popular Internet search engine. The Stanford University doctoral students wanted to test their theory that a search engine which looked at the relationship between websites would produce better results than the search engines then in use. The system was originally called 'BackRub' because the search engine went back to web pages to determine their popularity and presumably, their relevance. Their hunch turned out to be correct. The name Google comes from the word 'googol', which is represented by the number 1 plus 100 zeroes. Google performs over 200 million Internet searches a day.

1822 Brazil declared its independence from Portugal. It is a national holiday.

1888 A 'hatching cradle', now called an incubator, was first used at New York's State Emigrant Hospital to nurture tiny Edith McLean. She was just 2 pounds, 7 ounces.

1892 'Gentleman Jim' Corbett and John Sullivan, famous boxers, slugged it out in the first fight under the Marquis of Queensberry rules in New Orleans, Louisiana. It was also the first fight where gloves were worn. Corbett won.

1975 Victory Day is celebrated with a national holiday in Mozambique. It became independent in June 1975. A Portuguese colony since the 16th century, both Portuguese, Bantu and other indigenous languages are spoken.

1913 Sir Anthony Quayle, actor/director was born in Ainsdale, Lancashire. He started in vaudeville, progressed to the Old Vic, helped found the Royal Shakespeare Company and also appeared in movies. He died in 1989.

A Tasmanian tiger (Thylacine), which was declared extinct in 1936, is displayed at the Australian Museum in Sydney, 25 May 2002.

8 SEPTEMBER

1925: Peter Sellers

The comic actor was born in Southsea, Hampshire, England. He made his stage debut when he was two days old, with his vaudevillian parents. The madcap comedian of the BBC's *The Goon Show* starred in the 1959 *Mouse that Roared*, the classic 1964 antiwar movie *Dr Strangelove* in which he played three roles and as the bumbling Inspector Clouseau in the Pink Panther movies. He had a wide and wild range of voices. One of his last movies was *Being There* in which he played a pudgy, retarded gardener. He died of a heart attack at age 54 in July 1980. He is considered one of the comic geniuses of the century.

1944: V Bomb Mark II

The Blitz, the incessant bombing by V-1 rockets of South England since 1940, was now intensified with V-2 rockets. The V-weapons were ground-to-ground rockets, called V for Vergeltungswaffe. The supersonic V-2 was more deadly than its predecessor, the V-1, as it was installed with the world's first ballistic guidance systems and had an operational rangle of 300 km and carried a 1000 kg warhead. About 42 000 Londoners were killed in the Blitz.

1966: Star Trek

Based on Gene Rodenberry's sci-fi epic the television show premiered in America. Montreal-born William Shatner starred as Captain Kirk of the space ship *Enterprise*. It launched a cult following of 'Trekkies', estimated at hundreds of thousands worldwide. Some of them speak Klingon, the fictional Star Trek language. Star Trek was cancelled in 1969.

1565 Saint Augustine, Florida. The first permanent European settlement in the United States was established. With access to the wealth of the Caribbean, the Spanish and British played tug-of-war over it for many years.

1760 Aaron Hart, a British military officer who took part in the French surrender at Montreal, was Canada's first known Jewish settler.

1841 Antonin Dvorak, Czech composer, was born. He is best known for his composition 'The New World' Symphony. He died in 1904.

2004 *The Genesis* spacecraft crashed after a parachute malfunctioned. It had been launched three years previously to orbit the moon and collect solar wind samples.

Peter Sellers (1925–1980) looking for clues as the mishap prone Parisian Inspector Jacques Clouseau in one of the Pink Panther films. circa 1980.

9 SEPTEMBER

1971: Gordie Howe

The ice hockey player retired—for the first time—but he returned to the game two years later. He was born in Floral, Saskatchewan, Canada. He is one of the finest ice hockey players, particularly adept in scoring goals. His career has spanned five decades and in a feat unsurpassed by any athlete in any sport, he finished in the top five in scoring in twenty straight seasons. He debuted professionally at age 18, for the Detroit Red Wings and led them to four Stanley Cups.

1975: Martina Navratilova

The 18-year-old tennis player defected from Czechoslovakia and was granted political asylum in America. She became the most successful female player in sports history, dominating the game in the 1970s and 1980s. She has won 167 single tournaments and a record nine Wimbledon singles titles.

1976: Mao Zedong

The Chinese revolutionary leader died at 82. He had risen from a guerrilla fighter with a small cadre of soldiers to become the Chinese Communist leader of 800 million people. Worshiped by many as a god, he intentionally built up a personality cult. Warlords and colonial powers had ruled China for generations and its peasants were some of the world's most oppressed people. Mao emerged as the unlikely victor of the four-year civil war against the Nationalists under Chiang Kai-shek in 1949. Through Mao's leadership, the Chinese once again became a proud people. Mao guided the huge, isolated, under-developed country, to a nuclear power with an expanding industrial base. He brutally purged one million rivals. He changed Marxist thinking that peasants were ignorant, 'like sacks of potatoes'. His *Little Red Book* included quotations such as 'Political power grows out of the barrel of a gun'. Just months before his death, he welcomed and American delegation led by President Nixon, in a step toward a new political future. His hand picked party functionary, Hua Kuo-feng, who was expected to steer a more moderate course, succeeded him. After Mao's death, his wife and three others called the Gang of Four were imprisoned by Hua Kuo-feng for allegedly plotting a revisionist coup.

1087 William the Conqueror, who had conquered England by defeating Harold at the Battle of Hastings in 1066, died at Rouen while waging war on France.

1828 Leo Tolstoy, Russian writer and philosopher was born at Tula Province in Russia. He wrote short stories, essays and plays. He is best known for his novels *Anna Karenina* and *War and Peace*. He died in 1910.

1923 Japanese earthquake: The horrifying devastation of the 1 September quake was revealed to the world. Tokyo and Yokohama were levelled, with over 100 000 people killed and 2.5 million left homeless.

1964 William Willis, a 71-year-old American author and adventurer, arrived in Queensland after intentionally drifting on his *Age Unlimited* raft from Peru via Samoa to Australia. He covered about 17 702 km in 204 days.

A group of Chinese children in uniform in front of a picture of Chairman Mao Zedong (1893–1976) holding Mao's *Little Red Book* during China's Cultural Revolution. circa 1968.

10 SEPTEMBER

1894: Percy Grainger

The Australian composer gave his first piano recital on his first concert tour. He was born in Brighton, Victoria, between 1901 and 1914 he lived in London and then Leipzig. He published his 'Colonial Song' and 'Mock Morris' during this time. Edvard Grieg encouraged the young man and inspired him to examine English folk tunes as sources of inspiration for compositions. He also studied with Grieg and produced the definitive annotated edition of Grieg's Piano Concerto in 1907. In 1914 Grainger moved to America where he lived the rest of his life, although he still thought of himself as an Australian. Some of Grainger's 1200 works include 'Country Gardens', 'The Warriors', 'Marching Song of Democracy' and 'Lincolnshire Posy'. Grainger also introduced his contemporaries' works on his frequent concert tours such as the music of Grieg, Delius and Cyril Scott. Working with the scientist Burnett Cross, he invented the forerunner of today's electronic synthesiser, the 'Free Music Machine'.

1962: Laver's First Grand Slam

Australia's Rod 'Rocket' Laver won the US Open singles title. The 24-year-old had defeated fellow countryman Roy Emerson, to win the first Grand Slam in men's tennis since American Don Budge in 1938. A Grand Slam is the winning of four major tennis titles, Australia, France, Wimbledon and the US Open. The left-handed Laver could play any type of shot. Laver was born in Rockhampton, Queensland. He is the only player to win the Grand Slam twice; he won again in 1969. When he turned professional he was the first tennis pro to earn more than US$1 million.

1962: Margaret Court

Margaret Court, from Australia, won the US Lawn Tennis Association's women's singles. With Rod Laver's win (above) these were the golden days of tennis for Australia. Court is considered the finest Australian female tennis player ever. In 1963 she was the first Australian to win at Wimbledon, aged 21. She was born in Albury, New South Wales and moved to Melbourne for training. In 1970 she won the Grand Slam at the relatively mature age of 28. She defeated Billie Jean King in an arduous contest, 14–12, 11–9. She retired twice, once on her marriage in 1966 and finally in 1976.

1892 The world's longest lacrosse throw of 488 feet 6 inches (148.91 m) by Barnet Quinn recorded in Guinness World Records.
1913 The Lincoln Highway, construction began on the first coast-to-coast road in America.
1938 Karl Lagerfeld, German fashion designer , was born in Hamburg.
1945 Jose Feliciano was born in Lares, Puerto Rico. Blind since birth, he sings in both Spanish and English and has earned six Grammy awards, plus platinum and gold worldwide.

Rod Laver on his way to claiming the Men's Australian Singles title by beating Roy Emerson in the final on 22 January 1962.

Australian tennis player Margaret Court in1962.

11 SEPTEMBER

1973: Chilean Coup d'Etat

General Pinochet, acting with the support of the American government, staged a military coup in Chile, overthrowing and murdering the democratically elected socialist president, Salvador Allende. Thousands of government supporters, students and unionists were rounded up, tortured and murdered. For 17 years the Chilean Junta ruled with an iron fist. Before Allende's election, the American Secretary of State, Henry Kissinger stated, 'I don't see why we need to stand by and watch a country go communist because of the irresponsibility of its own people'. In 2005 Gneral Pinochet was stripped of immunity from prosecution to face tax fraud charges related to millions of dollars he held in secret bank accounts.

1994: Jessica Tandy

Jessica Tandy died in Connecticut, USA on this day. She had an acclaimed stage career spanning 60 years and won many awards, including a Tony for *A Streetcar Named Desire*. She also starred in *Driving Miss Daisy*. Tandy was happily married for nearly fifty years to the actor Hume Cronyn. They appeared together in *Cocoon*, *To Dance With the White Dog*, *Camilla* and others. She died in 1994 age 85. She was born in 1909 in London, England.

2001: World Trade Centre Attack

Known in America as 9/11, the symbol of global capitalism, the World Trade Center, New York, was destroyed by two hijacked passenger planes. A plane hit each of the Twin Towers. A third plane struck the Pentagon, in Washington, DC. A fourth plane crashed in Pennsylvania, after passengers apparently attacked the hijackers. Over 3 000 civilians died. In 1993, a truck bomb in the Trade Center's underground garage killed six and injured 1 000, but nobody thought that the Twin Towers could collapse. On September 11 they collapsed in just one hour. Extraordinary heroism was displayed by firemen giving lives, a colleague staying to die with a worker in a wheelchair and people holding hands as they jumped from the inferno. On 30 May 2002 a symbolic ceremony was held at Ground Zero to cut down the last standing steel girder and to honour those who died.

1885 D.H. Lawrence, English novelist ,was born in Nottinghamshire. His *Lady Chatterley's Lover* was a cause celebre. He wrote about Australia in *Kangaroo*. He died in 1930.

1913 The 11th World Zionist Congress passed a resolution in favour of establishing a Hebrew University in Jerusalem. The outbreak of WWI prevented its immediate implementation.

1914 Australia's first WWI deaths were recorded in the storming of a German wireless station at Rabaul, Papua New Guinea.

1948 Mohammed Ali Jinnah, the first Governor General of Pakistan, died.

1955: Miss America Philco Corporation and the ABC network televised the first live Miss America broadcast. 27 million viewers watched California's Lee Meriwether capture the title.

1978 Georgi Markov, a Bulgarian defector, was killed on a London street when he was stabbed with an poison-tipped umbrella.

Above: Chilean Army troops firing on the La Moneda Palace in Santiago during Pinochet's American-backed coup against President Salvador Allende, who died in the attack on the palace on 11 September 1973.

Below: Guards watch out for attackers as Chilean president Salvador Allende leaves a building during the military coup in which he was overthrown and killed on 11 September..

Right: American Secretary of State, Henry Kissinger, faces the media in Brussels, where he attended a NATO meeting on September 11 1973, while the coup was in progress.

12 SEPTEMBER

1878: Cleopatra's Needle

The London landmark was erected on the Embankment on the Thamas on this day in. The ancient Egyptian obelisk, historically, has nothing to do with Cleopatra. It is one of a pair; the other is in New York. There were seven others that have been destroyed. They date from 1450 BC and various pharaohs inscribed their stories of conquest on them. The obelisks stand 21 m high. The Romans moved them to Alexandria in 12BC and they toppled sometime after that. Mehemet Ali, viceroy of Egypt, gave the Needle to England and Sir William Wilson donated the money for its transportation in 1877. It was moved in a specially built barge-like cylinder, towed behind a mother ship. The two separated in the Bay of Biscay and the obelisk was nearly lost. It arrived in London six months later. New York's obelisk stands in Central Park.

1940: Lascaux Caves

Four boys followed their dog through a narrow entrance in Southern France and discovered an amazing cave system. The walls were covered with prehistoric art, thought to be between 15 000 and 17 000 years old. The paintings were done in charcoal, ochre and iron oxides. They mainly depict animals and hunting and are read from left to right, like a comic strip. The Caves were closed in 1963 to protect the paintings, but a replica was opened nearby for visitors.

1977: Steve Biko

The 30-year-old civil rights South African activist died in police custody. His death stirred outrage worldwide. The story of his life: dropping out of medical school to found the Black Consciousness Movement in 1969, a group that was more militant than the African National Congress (ANC) and his anti-apartheid martyrdom was made into a movie called *Cry Freedom*. He rejected the ANC's more moderate philosophy of working with whites towards justice. His philosophy was that only when blacks stopped feeling inferior to white South Africans would they achieve political freedom. It is believed that he was murdered for starting to act in a more conciliatory manner towards the ANC, because of a threat of impending unity between the two groups. The white minority government feared that the resulting powerful coalition would overwhelm them.

1941 Walter Lindrum set a world record for the fastest billiards century, in 46 seconds. His father and brother were also billiards champions and he learned to play in the family saloons.

1944 Britain approved a Jewish fighting force, known as the Jewish Brigade, recruited from Palestinian Jews.

1958 Researcher Jack Kilby invented the 'chip' essential to electronics. His consisted of a transistor and other components on a slice of germanium. He called it the Integrated Circuit.

1993 Willie Mosconi, the world pocket billiards champion, died. He was champ from 1941 to 1956.

Photograph of South African activist, Steve Biko, murdered by police in 1977. The film, *Cry Freedom* is based on his life.

13 SEPTEMBER

1848: Phineas Gage

The foreman of a railway construction gang, Phineas Gage had a 1.09 m long metal tamping rod blown through his skull. He was preparing the bed for the Rutland and Burlington Rail Road near Cavendish, Vermont, tamping dynamite into a hole when the dynamite exploded. The 6 kg iron rod went through his brain and out the other side. Amazingly, he survived and did not lose consciousness. Doctors plugged the two holes and kept him under observation. Although Gage was not physically impaired, he went through marked personality changes, including irritability and swearing. Gage's accident helped physicians pinpoint some of the lobe functions of the brain.

1857: Milton Hershey

The famous American chocolatier and philanthropist was born. He apprenticed to a Pennsylvanian confectioner and then opened his own shop in Philadelphia. He started with caramels, sold that business and then focused on chocolates in 1900, with his own factory. His Hershey bar's tag line became 'The great American chocolate bar'. He built a company town surrounding his factory in Hershey, Pennsylvania, with shops, schools and parks. He opened a school for white boys from broken homes, which inherited his entire stake in the company.

1916: Roald Dahl

The Welsh children's writer was born to Norwegian parents. He started writing in 1942 after a skull fracture, which induced strange dreams. The cruelty he experienced at boarding school is a theme in some of his books, where virtue wins over vice and children fight against tyrannical adults, for example *Matilda*, *Witches* and *James and the Giant Peach*. His *Charlie and the Chocolate Factory* was made into the movie *Willie Wonka and the Chocolate Factory*. He also wrote short stories, novels and literary pieces for adults and won three Poe wards for his suspense fiction. In all, he wrote about 30 books. He died in 1990.

1900 The Australian Salvation Army screened two and a quarter hours of film, sermons and Christian music, called S*oldiers of the Cross*. The 'Salvos' were early film pioneers.

1903 Claudette Colbert, comedienne and actress, was born in Paris. She won an Oscar for *It Happened One Night*. She appeared in more than 60 movies and also on stage. Colbert received a Life Achievement Award from the Kennedy Center for Performing Arts. She died in 1996.

1985 The World Health Organization declared AIDS a global epidemic.

1996 Tupac Shakur, rapper/actor, was shot and later died, aged 25. Shakur was a member of hip-hop's Digital Underground, but went solo in 1992. His '2Pacalypse Now' made him a superstar of gangsta rap.

British children's author, playwright and short story writer Roald Dahl (1916–1995) in portrait taken around 1979.

14 SEPTEMBER

1927: Isadora Duncan

The 'mother of modern dance' died. The 45-year-old interpretive dance pioneer was killed in a bizarre accident in Nice, France, when a long scarf was caught in the rotating wheel of her sports car, strangling her. Millions worldwide mourned Duncan. She was born in San Francisco in 1877 and was trained in classical ballet as a child. She rejected its stylism and created her own unfettered style of 'modern dance.' Her family moved to Europe, where she set up Duncan dance schools. She performed worldwide to enormous acclaim, although some cities banned her on the grounds of lewdness, for her diaphanous Greek robes and bare feet. She thought a dancer should always reveal her soul and feelings. At the height of her success in 1913, her children Deirdre and Patrick drowned when her limousine rolled accidentally into the Seine River.

1933: Zoe Caldwell

The esteemed stage actress, was born in Melbourne, Australia. She has received four Tony awards for *Slapstick Tragedy*, *Medea*, *Master Class* and *The Prime of Miss Jean Brodie*. Her professional career was launched at age 9 in a production of *Peter Pan* and after private lessons she quit school at age 15 to perform on radio and teach speech. Caldwell toured widely as a dramatic and Shakespearean actress until her Broadway breakthrough in 1965. She has chosen to concentrate on the stage and has expanded to directing, rather than pursue movie roles.

1947: Sam Neill

The popular actor was born in Northern Ireland while his father was stationed there on military duty, but was rasied in New Zealand from the age of seven. He was nicknamed 'Sam' because several boys at school shared his birth name, Nigel. He is New Zealand's most outstanding movie actor, director and producer with over eighty movies to his credit. He is especially known for his roles in *My Brilliant Career*, *A Cry in the Dark*, *The Piano* and *Reilly: Ace of Spies*. Neill has an Otago vineyard where he grows Pinot Noir for his Two Paddocks label.

1321 Dante Alighieri, the brilliant Italian scholar who wrote *The Divine Comedy* died at Ravenna.

1914 In an unsolved mystery, Australia lost its first submarine *AE1* off the coast of New Britain, Papua New Guinea, the day after Germany surrendered New Britain.

1990 Ken Griffey Sr and Jr, the father and son duo, hit back-to-back major league baseball home runs that thrilled the crowd in their Seattle Mariners game against the California Angels.

1993 A public ceremony was held to celebrate the first major agreement signed by leaders of Israel Yitzhak Rabin and Palestine's Yasser Arafat, at the White House. Problems persist to this day.

Actor Sam Neil attends the PBS Summer 2003 TCA Press Tour at the Hollywood Renaissance Hotel, 11 July 2003 in Hollywood, California.

15 SEPTEMBER

1890: Agatha Christie

The author of over 100 books was born in Torquay, England. She had her heart set on becoming an opera star, but began writing with encouragement from her mother. She is best remembered for her highly readable, classic detective fiction, featuring the sleuths Hercule Poirot and Miss Jane Marple. Christie's second marraige was to Max Mallowan, a young archeologist she met on a trip to Mesopotamia. She often accompanied him on his Middle Eastern digs, leading to books such as *Death on the Nile*.

1940: Kiwi's Battle of Britain

The turning point in WWII's Battle of Britain occurred on this day when the German Luftwaffe began losing its air superiority. Few are aware that one of every twelve pilots who flew in the Battle was a Kiwi. One of the most distinguished of them was Denis (Denny) Sharp. Sharp was known as 'The Black Prince' because of his movie star looks, like an Errol Flynn or a Ronald Colman. Born in Dunedin in 1918, he was an expert marksman and hunter as a youth. He was recruited into the Royal Air Force (RAF) and into the famed 258 Squadron. Although the German Luftwaffe vastly outnumbered the RAF Hurricanes and Spitfires, Sharp and other legends like 'Tin Legs' Bader and Bernard Fergusson prevented the planned German invasion of Britain. He also saw action in Singapore, India and Burma, that included flying the last Allied plane out of Singapore before it fell to the Japanese and spending three months behind enemy lines. His war exploits read like a movie script. Later he retired to Australia, where he died in 2004.

2000: Nikki Webster Opens Sydney Games

Thirteen-year-old Nikki Webster soared above the arena in the Sydney Olympics Opening Ceremony and into everyone's heart. Her Aboriginal guide Djakapurra Munyarryun led her on a journey through Australia's long history. Webster has been performing since she was a small child. She has had a very successful music career since the Olympics. Her debut album, *Follow Your Heart*, produced a platinum hit 'Strawberry Kisses'. She also landed the role of Dorothy in *The Wizard of Oz* on a 13-month-long East Coast Australia tour.

1821 Guatemala, Honduras and Nicaragua all celebrate their independence from Spain. with national holidays.

1923 Martial law was declared in Oklahoma after the Ku Klux Klan, the dreaded white supremacy group, apparently mobilised to assassinate the governor and seize power.

1984 Prince Henry, better known as Harry, was born. He is third in line to the British throne after his father Charles and brother Prince William.

Nikki Webster appears during the segment 'Girl and Reef' of the opening ceremony of the 2000 Summer Olympics in Sydney on 15 September 2000.

16 SEPTEMBER

1975: Sir John Guise

The 70-year-old former politician was the first native-born Papuan to be appointed Governor-General of Papua New Guinea. The country was granted its independence from Australia in a ceremony attended by Sir Michael Somare, the Prime Minister of PNG, Australia's Prime Minister Gough Whitlam, Charles, the Prince of Wales and other dignitaries. The Australian flag was lowered and the Bird of Paradise flag was raised. PNG has had fluctuating stability since independence. It is a huge country, to the north of Australia, where more than 800 languages are spoken.

1980: Jean Piaget

The Swiss child psychologist died, aged 84. He had been interested in science from childhood and had his first scientific paper published when he was 11 years old, about an albino sparrow. Piaget was later influenced by anthropologist Claude Levi-Strauss and was interested in psychoanalysis and intelligence testing. His career intensified when he married and had three children: Jacqueline, Lucienne and Laurent, who fascinated him. Along with his wife, Valentine, a former fellow student, he observed and studied the children's development, from newborn to their acquisition of language. Piaget's contribution was his focus on how children channel experience into thought. He theorised that a child's elementary steps become increasingly sophisticated and are essential in helping a person towards an understanding of reality. He wrote three books about his observations that were landmarks in child psychology. .

1981: Big shops

On the prairie of wind-swept Alberta, Canada, is the world's largest shopping mall. The first section opened and other sections followed over the next seventeen years. The West Edmonton Mall (known to locals as 'West Ed') has over 800 shops, including six department stores. It has 21 movie theatres, 110 restaurants and a 354-room hotel. Some of its unusual features are: a submarine in the world's largest indoor lake, a shooting gallery, an ice skating rink, the world's largest indoor wave pool, an 18-hole miniature golf course, a casino, an indoor amusement park with rides and, of course, the world's largest car park. The mall cost $1.2 billion.

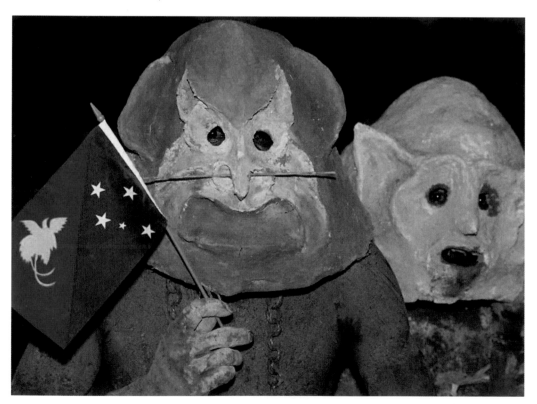

1886 Queensland introduced the payment of salaries to Members of Parliament. South Australia, Tasmania and NSW soon followed.

1901 The *Ronga* schooner capsised in New Zealand's Pelorus Sound. She did it again the next year, in nearly the same spot. She remained jinxed. Until she was destroyed by fire sixty years later, she had another thirteen incidents, including three collisions.

1954 Colin Newman, vocalist/guitarist for Wire was born in Salisbury, England. Along with drummer Robert Gotobed, guitarist Bruce Gilbert and bassist Graham Lewis the punk rockers deconstructed punk into experimental chaos.

1960 Amos Alonzo Stagg, 'grand old man of American football' retired after an astonishing coaching career, aged 98. He died four years later.

Goroka mudmen wave the national flag, featuring the bird-of-paradise and the Southern Cross at the 20th anniversary ceremony in Port Moresby. Tribal dancers from the highlands, islands and rivers of Papua New Guinea attended ceremonies across the country marking 20 years of independence from Australia.

17 SEPTEMBER

1900: Colonial Federation

Queen Victoria proclaimed that the six Australian colonies of Victoria, New South Wales (NSW), Queensland, Western Australia, South Australia and Tasmania 'shall be united in a Federal Commonwealth'. The population was nearing four million and Australia had served Victoria well in both the Boer War and Boxer Rebellion. Victoria appointed the Earl of Hopetoun as the first Governor-General. When Hopetoun arrived in Sydney he asked the NSW Premier, Sir William J. Lyne, to form the first Federal Ministry. Hopetoun had apparently not done his homework, because Lyne declined, as he was opposed to federation! Hopetoun then asked Edmund Barton to form a Ministry. Barton agreed and presented the Ministers' names on 30 December to Hopetoun. Two days later, on 1 January 1901, Australia became the Commonwealth of Australia. Queen Victoria died three weeks later. Hopetoun was Governor-General until 1902. Lord Tennyson, son of the poet, succeeded him.

1962: Baz Luhrmann

The award-winning Australian film-maker was born. One of his first movie successes was *Strictly Ballroom*. Other movies include *Moulin Rouge* (an updated La Boheme), which his friend Nicole Kidman starred in and William Shakespeare's *Romeo and Juliet*, a contemporary re-telling of the classic love story, starring Leonardo DiCaprio and Claire Danes. Luhrmann reached the top of the pop charts in 1999 with his spoken-word *Everybody's Free (To Wear Sunscreen.)*

1963: 'Let 'Em Have It'

Adolph 'Sailor' Gysbert Malan, an outstanding fighter pilot of WWII died. Born in South Africa, he became Commanding Officer of the Royal Air Force's 74th Squadron, the Tigers. When it was time to take off for combat, he would order his pilots,:'Let's cut some cake. Let 'em have it.' Between August and December 1940, the Tigers shot down at least 84 enemy planes. On 11 August, as wave after wave of Nazi bombers headed for Great Britain, the Tigers participated in four separate battles and downed 38 enemy planes. After the war, Sailor formed a protest group, the Torch Commando, an ex-servicemen's group to fight the South African National Party's plans to disenfranchise blacks.

1923 Hank Williams Sr., the iconic country and western singer was was born at Georgia, Alabama. His hits include 'Take these chains from my heart' and 'Your cheatin' heart. He died in 1953.

1934 Maureen 'Little Mo' Connolly, the celebrated tennis player of her time, was born at San Diego, California. She was seventeen when she won the US Open and was the first female to win the Grand Slam, in 1953. In 1954, she was injured in a horse riding accident and never played again. She died in 1969.

1974 American Ted Turner's *Courageous* decisively beat Australia's *Southern Cross* in the 23rd America's Cup Race, four races to nil.

1985 Laura Ashley, British designer, died aged 60 as a result of a fall. She combined Victorian prints wuth natural fabrics. She began working on scarves at home and expanded into an international fashion empire.

Director Baz Lurhman attends the Twentieth Century Fox Los Angeles premiere of the film *Master and Commander: The Far Side of the World* at the Samuel Goldwyn Theater, 11 November 2003 in Los Angeles, California.

18 SEPTEMBER

1709: Samuel Johnson

One of England's greatest writers was born in Lichfield, Staffordshire. He wrote novels, poems, essays, biographies, plays and founded magazines. He wrote the first English language dictionary, which took him nine years to complete. Johnson was often depressed, but could be playful—he defined a lexicographer in his cictionary: 'A writer of dictionaries, a harmless drudge.' He revealed in the company of the (Literary) Club, to which the major literary figures of his times belonged. Johnson wrote 'when a man is tired of London he is tired of life; for there is in London all that life can afford.' When he died in 1784 he was buried in Westminster Abbey.

1895: 'Dief'

John Diefenbaker was born in Ontario, Canada. His family later moved to Saskatchewan. As a child he read about a prime minister and decided that he would be one. He studied law and established a successful practice, but it took him 15 years of political election defeats before he was elected to a Commons' seat in the Opposition Conservative Party. Previous governments had identified Canadians as of either French or European ancestry; Dief felt that many ethnicities had been excluded and he fought vigorously for the inclusion of minorities. He even fought against his own party when necessary. He stood and lost twice for Party leadership, but was finally elected in 1957. Dief said, 'I am the first Prime Minister ... of neither altogether English or French origin. So I determined to bring about a Canadian citizenship that knew no hyphenated consideration...' He made many social changes in his five years as Prime Minister, including appointing the first woman Cabinet Minister and refusing to support American hostilities against Cuba. Dief was given a State funeral when he died in 1979.

Main photo: The Canadian designed and built CF-105 Avro Arrow was the most advanced jet interceptor of its time. Only three planes were completed before Prime Minister John Diefenbaker cancelled the project, for reasons that remain classified by the political intrigues of the Cold War. It is thought that American pressure to buy their arms lead to the scrapping of the Arrow. Diefenbaker certainly became frosty with American dignitaries from this time on.

Inset: Dwight D. Eisenhower (R) and John G. Diefenbaker at Canadian Parliament.

1860 Joseph Locke, English railway/civil engineer, died. He was chief engineer on the Grand Junction Railway. He pioneered double-headed rails secured onto wooden sleepers. His system was used worldwide.

1916 Rossano Brazzi, Italian movie director and screen idol, was born in Bologna. He appeared in more than two hundred movies, including *South Pacific, A Certain Smile* and *Summertime.*

1966 Nigel Clarke, vocalist/bass player, of the Dodgy trio was born at Birmingham, England. Other members were Andy Miller and Mathew Priest. The group was a fixture at music festivals with their melodic sixties sound.

1983 British adventurer George Meegan completed the longest walk ever from the tip of South America to Barrow, Alaska. It took six years to cover the 130608 km

19 SEPTEMBER

1846: Barrett and Browning

Elizabeth Barrett and Robert Browning, two English writers, eloped to Italy. Elizabeth and her adult siblings had been forbidden to marry by her father and she had lived her life as a semi-invalid recluse. Her father never spoke to her again. The couple had a tender marriage for fifteen years before Elizabeth died. Browning outlived her by 28 years. He was buried at Westminster Abbey. Elizabeth's best known poems include 'Aurora Leigh' and 'Sonnets from the Portuguese'. He was more prolific and his work includes 'The Ring and The Book' and 'The Pied Piper of Hamelin'. Their secret letters to each other before their elopement have also been published.

1893: First women to vote

New Zealand's women finally won the right to vote, when the Parliamentary Electoral Bill squeaked through by 20 votes to 18. They were the first women in the world to win universal suffrage. The major 'mover and shaker' behind the victory was British-born Kate Sheppard, a 21-year-old 1868 immigrant. Sheppard lived to see the first woman Member of Parliament take office in NZ in 1934, before her own death that year. She is featured on a New Zealand banknote. Sheppard had an immeasurable impact on women's rights worldwide.

1949: Rewi Alley

The New Zealander who was a 'Marco Polo in reverse' had his Chinese school for peasants 'liberated' by Mao Zedung's Red Army. This meant that he was no longer caught in China's bitter civil war. Alley spent 60 years in China, as a social reformer, educator and author, dedicated to helping the Chinese achieve a better life through industrial collectives. They considered him a Living Legend and his portrait hangs in Beijing's Great Hall.

1954: Miles Franklin

Stella Miles Franklin died, aged 75. Born in a country town, Franklin is considered one of Australia's greatest female writers. An early feminist and rebel, she was a freelance journalist and wrote under the names Old Bachelor and Vernacular. Franklin wrote novels such as the classic *My Brilliant Career* (later made into a movie), *Brent of Bin Bin* and *Back to Bool Bool*. She established the Miles Franklin Award for literature. Patrick White, who was Australia's first Nobel Laureate for Literature in 1957, won the inaugural award for his novel *Voss*.

1909 Ferdinand 'Ferry' Porsche was born in Wiener Neustadt, Austria. In 1947 he founded the Porsche AG Company known for its high performance sport cars.

1915 Elizabeth Stern, Canadian /American, was born. A pioneering pathologist in cervical cancer, she showed how cells went through 250 stages from normalcy to cancerous, which makes it an easily detectable cancer. She died in 1980.

1948 Jeremy Irons, English actor, was born on the Isle of Wight. He appeared in *Dead Ringers, Reversal of Fortune, Lolita* and was the voice for *The Lion King*.

1968 Physicist Charles F. Carlson invented photocopying, calling it xerography. He sold the rights to the Haloid Company, a photographic paper company, which later became the world giant Xerox.

English poet Elizabeth Barrett Browning (1806–1861), wife of Robert Browning.

English poet Robert Browning (1812–1889) published dramatic narrative poems, plays and tragedies. He married Elizabeth Barrett and lived with her for 15 years in Italy. 'The Ring and the Book' is considered his masterpiece.

20 SEPTEMBER

1957: Jean Sibelius

The Finish composer of symphonic poems died at age 91. His family had wanted him to study law. He went against their wishes and pursued a musical career in Vienna. After auditioning as a violinist for the Vienna Philharmonic, he realised his true calling was to compose. His music created a sensation. He was revered for his anthem *Finlandia*, for the *Lemminkainen Suite* and for his *Fifth* and *Seventh* symphonies. In 1897, the Finnish Government paid him a stipend to help him pursue his career and later made a lifetime grant. Sibelius was very popular abroad and was often invited to conduct his work. One of his last compositions was music for *The Tempest* written in 1925.

1967: Liz II Launches Liz 2

Queen Elizabeth II launched her name-ship, the luxurious liner *Queen Elizabeth II* on the Clydebank River. On the same day, *Queen Mary* made her last voyage. Known affectionately as the *QE2*, she is 293.5 m long and weighs 70 000 tons. It was the most extravagant trans-Atlantic cruiser of its time, with four swimming pools, nightclubs and theatres. In January 2004, Cunard's biggest ever cruise ship, the *Queen Mary II*, replaced her. The *Queen Victoria* will be launched in 2005.

1973: Battle of the Sexes

Reigning tennis queen Billie Jean King faced the male chauvinist Bobby Riggs. The 29-year-old King overwhelmed the 55-year-old Riggs before 30 500 spectators—the largest crowd to ever attend a tennis match. King won in straight sets. Riggs was a former Wimbledon and American National champion. He said, 'She was just too quick.' In the spirit of the battle of the sexes, King gave him a baby pig and he gave her a large lolly. King was thrilled that so many people became interested in tennis as a result of the contest.

1503 The first recorded use of a European word for a Canadian place name was Newfoundland.

1896 Charles Cavill, of Sydney's famous Cavill swimming family, was the first person to successfully swim across San Francisco's Golden Gate Channel.

1934 Sophia Loren, Italian actress, was born in Rome. she won an Oscar for Two Women. She also appearedin Black Orchid. Loren is married to director Carlo Ponti.

1946 The first Cannes Film Festival was held at the Grand Hotel on the French Riviera.

Billie Jean King returns a shot against Bobby Riggs during the Battle of the Sexes Challenge Match at the Astrodome on 20 September 20 1973 in Houston, Texas. Billie Jean King defeated Bobby Riggs.

21 SEPTEMBER

1904: Chief Joseph

The much-admired Chief of the Nez Perce Indians died. In early 1877 the Nez Perce's Wallowa Valley land in Idaho and Oregon was opened to white settlers. The Nez Perce resisted the American government's demand that the tribe move out within thirty days. For three months, Chief Joseph outmanoeuvred ten units of the American Army, over 1 600 miles, trying to reach Canada, to avoid his tribe being sent to an Indian reservation. He attracted worldwide sympathy. Finally, surrounded by the Army, just one day's march from the border, he surrendered with dignity. He made his famous speech. 'From where the sun now stands, I will fight no more forever.' This was the end of the Indian Wars. Chief Joseph died on a reservation.

1996: John Junior

John F. Kennedy Jr, the popular son of the late American President John F. Kennedy and Jackie Kennedy, broke women's hearts when he secretly married his long time girlfriend Carolyn Bessette. John-John, as the media called him, had been born in 1960 and was raised in the media spotlight. He became a lawyer and then a magazine publisher. Bessette, aged 31, was a fashion industry publicist. The two made a stunning couple. They managed to outsmart the press with their wedding, on Cumberland Island Georgia. They died in a single engine private plane along with Bessette's sister Lauren, when the plane Kennedy piloted went down off Martha's Vineyard, Massachusetts on 16 July 1999. Their bodies were recovered and they were buried at sea.

2003: Marsupial Life Saver

Lulu, a pet kangaroo, saved Len Richards' life when he alerted his family that he was lying unconscious in a paddock. The eastern grey kangaroo acted just like the TV kangaroo 'Skippy' when she gave a yipping kangaroo 'bark' and raised the alarm. The 10-year-old Lulu had been hand-raised by Richards' family after a truck killed her mother. Richards estimated that he was 'out' for 30 minutes before his family found him. All he remembered was walking along and then waking up in hospital. A tree branch had knocked him out. Lulu received an RSPCA Animal Valour Award in May 2004.

1348 Zurich, Switzerland: Jews were charged with perpetrating the Black Death epidemic. Some were executed and others expelled.

1909 Oceanographer Richard Fleming was born in Canada. His work focused especially on the Pacific coast currents off Central America. His co-authored 1942 text contained all that was known about oceanography in its time.

1915 Stonehenge was sold by auction. It was purchased £6 600 pounds. Three years later it was donated to the government.

1934 Leonard Cohen, songwriter/poet/novelist, was born in Montreal. He has written eight volumes of verse, including *Spice-Box of Earth*. His albums include *I'm Your Man*. He received the Governor-General's Performing Arts Award in 1993.

Chief Joseph of the Wallowa tribe of the Nez Perce, who tried to lead his people to Canada when the settlers drove them from their ancestral land in Oregon. Although they were captured at the border and forced to return to a reservation, the Americans respected his military leadership and dubbed him 'the Indian Napoleon'. Photo circa 1880.

22 SEPTEMBER

1828: Shaka Zulu

The warrior chief who created the Zulu Kingdom was murdered, aged 40. He rose to power during a time of famine and homelessness called the 'Mfecane'. He maintained good relationships with colonial administrators in Southern Africa; his own people increasingly hated him. His half-brother murdered him and seized the throne.

1862: Emancipation for Slaves

American President Abraham Lincoln issued the Emancipation Proclamation, which theoretically meant that all slaves were now free. In reality it only applied to states that were under Federal (Union) control. The Proclamation was a bold, largely symbolic gesture and had little immediate effect, because it was impossible to enforce. The Proclamation was issued in the second year of the bloody Civil War between the North and the South. Slaves in the five Southern were not affected; meaning that they stayed slaves until 1865, when the Confederacy surrendered and the Civil War ended. Their freedom was granted by the 13th Amendment to the American Constitution.

1989: Irving Berlin

One of America's most prolific songwriters, voted the greatest songwriter of the century, died aged 101. He wrote about 1 250 songs. His Russian family immigrated to New York when he was four years old. His father died and he sang on street corners for money. He could neither read nor write music. His patriotic song 'God Bless America' was premiered by Kate Smith on the evening of the WWI Armistice and became an instant classic. He gave the rights in perpetuity to the Boy Scouts and Girl Scouts of America. The song has earned them millions of dollars. Berlin fell in love with Ellin Mackay, whose father had serious reservations about Berlin's suitability as a spouse. Berlin wrote 'Always for Ellin' and established a trust for her to receive all the royalties. It is frequently played at weddings. Other well-known songs by Berlin include 'White Christmas' and 'There's No Business Like Show Business'.

1791 Michael Faraday, an early English pioneer in electricity, was born in Newington, Surrey. He died in 1867.

1955 The BBC monopoly on TV was broken after eighteen years, with the launch of a commercially funded Independent Television Authority. Its first advertisement was for toothpaste.

1981 France inaugurated its bullet-nose high-speed train, the TGV. Its maximum speed is 320 km/h and would eventually make the Paris—Lyon trip in two hours.

1989 *Baywatch* about California lifeguards debuted and became the most-watched television show on Earth, with an estimated one billion viewers.

2003 David Hempleman-Adams, English pilot, succeeded in his third attempt to become the first person to cross the Atlantic Ocean in an open wicker basket hot air balloon, travelling from Canada to Ireland.

Zulu warriors in the late 19th century with traditional wattle hut.

23 SEPTEMBER

1806: Lewis and Clark

The explorers returned to St Louis, Missouri, after two years trailblazing across America, to the Oregon Coast. After the Louisiana Purchase, American President Thomas Jefferson decided to send an exploratory team to find out more about the Purchase and beyond. He chose Captain Meriwether Lewis as leader and William Clark for his expertise with Native Americans. 'The Corps of Discovery' consisted of 33 people, including a Shoshone Indian interpreter Sacajawea, carrying an infant on her back. The Corps travelled along the Missouri River and then went by foot, via today's North Dakota, where they spent the winter in 1805. They continued on through Montana, to the Columbia River and to the Pacific Ocean. Their trip made valuable contributions to geography, geology and western tribes and was key to later settlement.

1930: Ray Charles

The 'Father of Soul' was born in Albany, Georgia. He was an outstanding singer, keyboard player, arranger and bandleader. Glaucoma blinded him at 6 years old. He attended a school where he learned to read and write music in Braille and play piano and organ. Orphaned at 15, he moved to Seattle and supported himself through music. Charles always said that he didn't want to be famous, 'just great'. He was that in jazz, gospel, pop and country and western. Some of his best known songs are Georgia on my mind', 'What'd I say', Hit the road Jack', 'Take these chains from my heart' and his patriotic and soulful 'America the Beautiful'. He died in 2004.

1997: The Rolling Stones

The legendary rock group kicked off their year-long Bridges to Babylon world tour in Soldier Field, Chicago. The enduring band started in 1961, with Mick Jagger (singer), Keith Richards (guitar) and Brian Jones (guitar), Ian Stewart (piano) Charlie Watts (drums) and Dick Taylor (bass). Taylor left soon after and was replaced by Bill Wyman. The Stones immediately attracted a following for their frenetic, high-energy performances, cultivating an contrasting image to The Beatles. Their lyrics were biting and full of protest. Three of their best-known albums are *Out of Our Heads*, *Through the Past Darkly* and *Sticky Fingers*.

490BC Pheidippides, an Athenian courier ran to Sparta to request help when the Persians landed at Marathon, Greece. He ran the 241 km in two days. After the battle, he ran 35 km back to Athens. He announced the Greek victory and died of exhaustion. Today's marathon run derives from this.

1846 German astronomer Gottfried Galle confirmed the existence of Neptune, the eighth planet of the solar system.

1949 Bruce 'The Boss' Springsteen, singer and guitarist was born in Freehold, New Jersey. His classics include 'Born to Run' and 'Born in the USA'.

1964 Marc Chagall's Paris Opera House ceiling was unveiled. It included operatic characters in his unique colourful, lyrical style.

Singer Mick Jagger and guitarist Keith Richards from The Rolling Stones in concert in 1997.

24 SEPTEMBER

1896: F. Scott Fitzgerald

Fitzgerald, who was born on this day, is known for his chronicling of the Jazz Age of the 1920s. His first novel, *This Side of Paradise*, made him instantly famous at the age of 24. He married the beautiful Zelda Sayre the same year and they lived a frivolous life of parties, more parties and extravagance. His two best novels are the classics *The Great Gatsby* and *Tender is the Night*. The latter is based on his wife's alcoholism and descent into schizophrenia and her eventual institutionalisation. He also wrote *The Beautiful and the Damned* and left his *Last Tycoon* unfinished. After his wife's hospitalisation, he lived with gossip columnist Sheilah Graham. He became so disabled by chronic alcoholism; people assumed that he was dead. He died aged 44 in 1940, thinking that he had not accomplished anything significant. Zelda died in a fire at the hospital where she lived in 1948.

1948: Phil Hartman

The comedian was born in Brantford, Ontario, but was raised in America. His childhood comedic hero was Jonathan Winters. He joined comedy troupe The Groundlings in the 1970s and met Paul Reubens 'Pee Wee Herman' who would become his lifelong comedian friend. He and Reubens wrote the hit *Pee-wee's Big Adventure* together. He performed on *Saturday Night Live* for eight seasons, where he was known for his deadpan antics and his impersonations of Bill Clinton, Barbara Bush, Jack Nicholson and Frank Sinatra. His wife, Brynn, who had alcohol and other problems, murdered him while he slept in 1998. She killed herself later that day.

1962: Nia Vardalos

The actor/scriptwriter was born in Winnipeg, Manitoba and became an overnight sensation when her one-act play was made into the movie *My Big Fat Greek Wedding*. Vardalos starred in the movie, with John Corbett as the male lead, based on her own background. Shot on a $3 million budget, the movie was a multi-million dollar box-office sensation. She next wrote and starred in *Connie and Carla*.

1879 America's first long distance bicycle race was held in Chicago. Great Britain's W. Cann won the six-mile race.

1917 Australia began driving licence tests. The first to pass was Herbert H. Klingberg.

1949 Trolley buses replaced trams in Auckland, the first New Zealand city to do so. By 1964, the last tram ran in Wellington.

1993 Cambodia's national holiday celebrates its new constitution.

Portrait of American author Francis Scott Fitzgerald (1896–1940). Photo circa 1935.

25 SEPTEMBER

1906: Dmitry Shostakovich

The brilliant composer was born in St Petersburg, Russia. His mother was a professional pianist and gave him his first lessons. His graduation exercise from the Leningrad Conservatory, his *First Symphony* was hailed as a masterpiece when he was just 19 years old. Although he was a committed Communist, his career was spent being in and out of favour with the Party. His 1936 opera, *The Lady Macbeth of the Mtsenk District* was violently attacked in *Pravda*, the Party newspaper and this affected his creativity. His music was described as 'bourgeois decadence'. However, during WWII his music found favour again, especially his *Seventh Symphony*. He wrote a wide range of music, including ballet, string quartets and choral pieces. He died aged 68 in Moscow in 1975.

1969: Catherine Zeta-Jones

Born in Swansea, Wales on this day, Zeta-Jones had always dreamed of being an actress and, at 11-years-old, had her first major role in *Annie*. At 15, she moved to London to pursue her career full time. At 17, she was cast in *42nd Street* and, the next year, was the lead. In 1991, she launched her successful television career in *Darling Buds of May*. Her film career did not take off until producer Steven Spielberg saw her in *Titanic* and she was cast in *The Mask of Zorro*, which was a success with audiences and critics. She won an Oscar for Best Supporting Actress for *Chicago*. She married actor Michael Douglas in 2000.

2003: Dog Barks at Bear

Shadow, a German-Shepherd mix dog, received America's National Hero Dog Award for saving his owner from a grizzly bear. Shadow's owner, Don Mobley, was collecting firewood on a sandbar of the Nakochna River, near Skwentna in Alaska, when he was caught between an angry grizzly and her cub. The bear charged at Mobley and was within three metres of him when Shadow charged out of the forest barking, frightening the sow and her cub away. Grizzly bears (also called brown bears) are notoriously territorial and protective of their cubs. Mobley, a backcountry wilderness guide, said that without Shadow he did not have a chance, as a grizzly can outrun a human, can swim and climb trees. The dog and owner were feted at a ceremony at Santa Monica.

1513 Vasco Nunez de Balboa, Spanish conquistador, trekked across the Isthmus of Panama to the Pacific Ocean.

1683 Jean-Philippe Rameau, French composer, was born. He wrote music for stage, including operas and religious music.

1844 New Zealand's first newspaper, the weekly *New Zealand Gazette* ceased operation. It was founded in 1840.

1897 William Faulkner, American literary giant, who changed the style of American writing was born at New Albany, Mississippi. He was a reclusive, but prolific writer and won the Nobel Prize in 1950. His best-known novel was T*he Sound and The Fury*. He died in 1962.

1944 Actor Michael Douglas was born in New Brunswick, New Hersey. He is married to Catherine Zeta-Jones and they share the same birthday. He has appeared in many movies inluding B*asic Instinct* and *Fatal Attraction*.

Academy Award winning Best Supporting Actress Catherine Zeta-Jones arrives for the 76th Academy Awards ceremony in 2004 at the Kodak Theater in Hollywood, CA.

26 SEPTEMBER

1948: Olivia Newton-John

The wholesome singer was born in Cambridge, England and raised in Australia. She won a talent show that returned her to England and joined Cliff Richards' popular TV show. Her breakthrough album in America was *If Not For You*. She moved to Malibu in California, where *Have You Never Been Mellow* and *Please Mr. Please* were hits. She starred in *Grease*, the popular musical in 1978. Newton-John is a breast cancer survivor and cancer awareness activist. She is a vintner with the label Koala Blue. She sang at the Opening Ceremony at the Sydney Olympics with Aussie star John Farnham.

1983: Australia II takes America's Cup

Australia won the America's Cup from the Americans; ending a 132-year winning streak, probably sport history's longest. The race was first held on 22 August in 1851 with a race around the Isle of Wight to and from Cowes. It was won by the *US America*, against fourteen English contenders. Ironically, the Royal Yacht Squadron offered the Cup to celebrate the British Empire's industrial might. The Cup was taken to the New York Yacht Club (NYYC), with a deed that stated that other yacht clubs could challenge for it and it acquired the 'America's Cup' name. For the next 132 years the NYYC retained it. Australians waited up at night to hear the news of the nail-biting seventh and last race. Business tycoon, Alan Bond's *Australia II* won by 41 seconds against Dennis Conner in *Liberty* and Australians celebrated as if it were a national holiday.

1986: Crocodile Dundee

Paul Hogan's hit comedy film was released. The screenplay was co-written by Hogan, the main star. Hogan stars as a laconic Aussie who can tackle the Australian Outback and take on New York City. It was an instant success, raking in over $328 million for Paramount Theatres and making Hogan, a former Sydney Harbour Bridge painter and Australian television actor, an instant household name. 'Hoges' was born in the 'real bush' at Lightning Ridge, in 1939. He also starred in *Crocodile Dundee II* and *Crocodile Dundee in Los Angeles*. Hogan was a spokesman for the Australian Tourist Commission, inviting people Down Under 'to slip another shrimp on the barbie'. He married his co-star, Linda Kozlowski.

Paul Hogan in a typical skit from his television show. He went on to claim Hollywood fame with movies including *Crocodile Dundee*.

1888 T.S. Eliot, poet and playwright, was born in St Louis Missouri, but lived most of his life in England. His works include *The Waste Land* and *Murder in the Cathedral*. He won the Nobel Prize for literature in 1948. He died aged 77.

1897 Pope Paul V1, birth name Giovanni Monini, was born at Concesio, Italy. He was elected the 262nd Roman Catholic Pope in 1963. He died in 1978.

1907 New Zealand became a Dominion, meaning that it was now self-governing.

1945 Smooth vocalist Bryan Ferry was born at Washington, Tyne and Wear, England. His timeless first album was the 1973 *These Foolish Things*. Even more melancholic was the 1978 *The Bride Stripped Bare*.

1947 Hugh Lofting, English/American children's author, died age 61. He was born in Maidenhead. He had a toy menagerie of animals as a child. He wrote fourteen highly popular Dr. Dolittle books.

27 SEPTEMBER

1956: Mildred 'Babe' Didrickson Zaharias

The outstanding female athlete died in her home state, Texas. She was nicknamed 'Babe' after the legendary baseball player Babe Ruth. She excelled in a vast variety of sports including track and field, baseball, swimming, billiards, tennis and football. Babe was also a national teenage basketball champion. She was the first American woman to win the British Open Golf tournament and won gold medals in javelin and hurdles at the 1932 Olympics. Babe died from cancer, aged 42.

1988: Shroud of Turin

After radiocarbon testing, scientists announced that the Shroud of Turin was not Jesus Christ's burial shroud. The 4.2 m long linen burial shroud is presently kept in the Cathedral of St John in Turin, Italy. The cloth, which from certain angles resembles a man's facial imprint, probably dates from 1260 to 1390 A.D. However, in 2005, Raymond Rogers, a Los Alamos National Laboratory scientist, said that the threads selected for testing in 1988 might have been contaminated. When Rogers examined the threads, he found that they do not contain vanillin, a flax fibre compound that gradually disappears over time. Rogers believes the shroud could indeed date from 1 300 to 3 000 years ago, but even if it is proven to date from the time of Jesus, science can never prove that it was Christ's.

1994: Under the Table and Dreaming

The Dave Matthews Band (DMB) album, which was certified platinum four times, was released on this day. DMB were one of the most successful rock bands of the 1990s. What makes them unique is that their concerts are rarely publicised, yet attract sell-out crowds, especially university students. DMB was formed by ex-pat South African Dave Matthews. Band members have changed, but as of 2005 they were Carter Beauford (drums), Stefan Lessard (bass) Dave Matthews (guitar, vocals), Leroie Moore (saxophone) and Boyd Tinsley (violin). The DMB started performing at university fraternity houses and by 1997 their *Live at Red Rocks,* debuted at number 3 on the charts. By 1998 they were at number 1 with *Before These Crowded Streets.*

1946 Post-war meat shortages in New York City led to increasing consumption of horsemeat. Poultry cost $1 a pound, compared to horsemeat at 21 cents.

1968 The American musical *Hair* opened in London, the day after censorship was lifted.

1998 Gerhard Schroder led his Social Democratic Party to victory in Germany's elections, ending Christian Democrat Chancellor Helmut Kohl's sixteen years of power.

A rehearsal of the hit musical *Hair* before it opens at the Shaftesbury Theatre in London's West End. The musical features a 'tribe' of liberated New York hippies.

28 SEPTEMBER

1953: Father of Observational Cosmology

Edwin Hubble died, aged 63. The Hubble Space Telescope was named after him. He attended Oxford University as a Rhodes scholar and studied law. After setting up a legal practice in Kentucky, Hubble decided to return to his first love, science and pursued a doctorate in astronomy. He developed Hubble's Law in 1929. It showed that the universe is expanding and that the speed at which galaxies are moving away from Earth are proportional to their distance from Earth. This helped theoreticians develop their Big Bang theory. Hubble also developed a classification system for galaxies, by content, distance, shape and brightness, which is still used.

1990: Bryan Adams

The singer and songwriter was awarded the member of the Order of Canada and in 1998 was promoted to Officer. He was born in Kingston, Ontario in 1959. He received his first guitar at age 10 and decided he wanted to be a musician. At fifteen, he left school to join a band and soon after, he signed a recording contract. Since then Adams has released fourteen albums. One of his most successful is *Waking Up The Neighbour*. It features the ballad '(Everything I do) I do for you'. His most recent album is *Room Service*. Adams has been nominated for three Academy Awards.

2004: Brian Wilson

An original member of the Beach Boys Wilson released his long awaited album *Smile* on the Nonesuch label. It received wide acclaim. It was vastly different from the Beach Boys' previous work such as 'Surf's up' and 'Help me, Rhonda'. A reviewer, Matthew Reed Baker, wrote: '[Fans] will find three suites comprising seventeen songs, each filled with trombones, strings, organs and whistles ... *Smile* is as bizarre as it is beautiful ... The open-minded listener will be rewarded by this feverish fantasia of sound, its inchoate joy and longing bursting through every note.' Reviewers were unanimous that it was worth the four-decade wait.

1867 Toronto became Ontario's capital.
1896 Salon Lumiere, Australia's first cinema, opened in Sydney by Marius Sestier.
1991 Miles Davis, the 'cool' jazz king died of a stroke and pneumonia, in Santa Monica, California, age d65. His impact on jazz is immeasurable. He began as a teenage trumpeter.
1996 Frankie Dettori won an incredible seven races at an Ascot meeting, the first jockey to do so. Bookmakers lost about £18 million.
1997 Fifteen-year-old LeAnn Rimes went to the top of the American album chart with her 'You light up my life'. She has been a star since she was 11, with her mix of inspirational country and Christian.

The Beach Boys (clockwise from top) Mike Love, Dennis Wilson, Brian Wilson, Carl Wilson and Al Jardine.

29 SEPTEMBER

1758: Admiral Lord Nelson

Nelson, considered Great Britain's greatest admiral, was born. He was a sickly child, but he was determined to be a sailor. At 12 years of age he joined the Navy and by 20 was a captain. He was a highly skilled commander and destroyed the French fleet in 1798 in the Battle of the Nile. He knew how to maintain morale and was a brilliant strategist. Nelson lost the sight in one eye and his right arm in battle. He became an admiral and coordinated the British victory over the Spanish and French, who outnumbered the Britons, at the Battle of Trafalgar off Spain, in 1805. He was killed during the battle, on his ship, the *Victory*.

1916: Trevor Howard

The British actor was born in Cliftonville, England. He was a consummate actor, who could play leading men and then switch to supporting minor roles. He studied at the Royal Academy of Dramatic Art and became a stage actor. WWII interrupted his career and Howard was wounded. He then pursued his movie career. Howard appeared in more than seventy movies, including the masterpieces *A Brief Encounter*, *The Third Man*, and *Mutiny on the Bounty*. Howard died 7 January 1988.

2004: Welsh Paralympic Glory

The Welsh Paralympic team returned home to a hero's reception after winning 27 medals at the Athens Olympic Games. The contingent won more medals per capita than any other country in the world. It won twelve gold, six silver, and nine bronze medals. This exceeded their Sydney 2000 Olympic haul of 26. In all, the United Kingdom won 94 Paralympic medals. The 'Golden Girl' of the team was Tanni Grey-Thompson, who was later voted the 2004 BBC Wales Sports Personality of the Year. It was the third time she had been selected. The 35-year-old Grey-Thompson has a lifetime record of 11 Olympic gold medals at five Paralympics, including two from the Athens Games. She is a wheelchair racer, in the T53 100m and T53 400 m events.

1952 John Cobb, the world water-speed record holder, was killed on Loch Ness, Scotland. His boat disintegrated after hitting waves at 240 mp/h.)

1958 America announced a policy that all measures to prevent contamination of the Moon would be taken on Lunar probes.

1967 Carson McCullers, American novelist, died aged 50. She was known for *The Heart is a Lonely Hunter* and *The Ballad of a Sad Café.*

1981 Siarhei Rutenka, handball player was born in Minsk, Belarus. He was the 2004 European Champion and the 2003–4 Slovenian Champion.

1988 Carolyn Waldo won two Olympic gold medals in synchronised swimming, becoming the first Canadian female to win two gold medals at a summer Games.

1990 Construction on the National Cathedral in Washington DC was completed after 83 years.

Portrait of English admiral Lord Horatio Nelson (1758–1805) and Nelson's Column in Trafalgar Square, London.

30 SEPTEMBER

1452: Gutenburg Press

The first section of the Gutenberg Bible was published in Mainz, Germany. Before Johann Gutenberg revolutionised communications, most books were handwritten. It was very slow and expensive, and few people could afford books. Gutenberg tinkered with grape pressing machines until he conceived the idea of a printing mould. He made metal stamps for each alphabet letter, and arranged the letters into words. Once ink was applied, paper could be laid on the words. Gutenberg created a printing press to hold the paper in place, and thus movable type printing was born. It took Gutenberg until 1456 to finish printing 180 copies of the Bible. During the decade after his invention, the number of books sold in Europe increased 20 times. Gutenberg abandoned printing in 1460, as he had made little money. He died in poverty in 1468.

1921: Deborah Kerr

The actress was born in Helensburgh, Scotland. Because she was a very shy teenager her aunt, who worked in radio, arranged for a stage job to help her become more confident. Kerr's talent was obvious and she was cast in her first movie, *Major Barbara* in 1941. Usually cast in prim character roles, she enjoyed a change of variety for her role in *From Here to Eternity*, in which she is famous for her love scene on a Hawaiian beach with Burt Lancaster. She also starred in *Black Narcissus*, *The King and I* and many more. She was nominated six times for an Oscar, but never won. She quit movies in 1968 saying that their violence and sex appalled her. She lives in Switzerland.

1935: Porgy and Bess

George Gershwin's opera opened for a 'dry run' in Boston, before its New York City stage debut. It was co-written with George's brother Ira, and novelist Dubose Heyward. It is considered the first true American opera. It closed after just 124 performances. When critics panned it, saying, 'How trite and feeble and conventional the tunes', George wrote a famous rebuttal saying, 'I am not ashamed' and pointed out that the opera *Carmen* had many songs. *Porgy and Bess* includes songs such as 'Ol Man River', 'Summertime' and 'It ain't necessarily so'. George Gershwin died less than two years later from a brain tumour, aged 38.

1207 Rumi the Sufi mystic and poet was born in Afghanistan. He founded the Whirling Dervishes, whose believers used mystical trance-like states from dancing and music to take themselves closer to God. He died in 1273.

1791 Wolfgang Amadeus Mozart's *The Magic Flute* premiered in Vienna.

1939 Len Cariou, Canadian TV/stage actor, singer was born in Winnipeg, Manitoba. He has acted on Broadway since 1970. In 1979 he won the Tony Award as Best Actor for *Sweeney Todd*.

1966 The former British African colony, the Bechuanaland Protectorate, became the independent Republic of Botswana.

1997 Ultima Online was released by the Austin, Texas-based Origin Systems. This was the first new type of role-playing game that can be played by 'massively multiple" players. Others included Doom and RPG: Age of Shadows.

Scottish actress Deborah Kerr, the star of numerous films of the 40s, 50s and 60s. Photo 1960.

Opposite page: Russian-born actor Yul Brynner (1915–1985), as King Mongkut of Siam and Scottish-born actress Deborah Kerr, as Anna Leonowens stand side-by-side, wearing formal royal costumes in a still from the film *The King and I* directed by Walter Lang in 1956.

1 OCTOBER

1 OCTOBER

1926: Mae West

The author and actress, with cast of her *Broadway Pleasure Man*, was arrested for indecency. The diminutive blonde, known for her tight fitting gowns and feather hats, had first attracted attention in 1927 when her play Sex was closed for indecency. This time, West pointed out that *Pleasure Man* had been running for a year with no problems, but the judge ruled she had added lewd gestures to it. She was gaoled for ten days. In 1938, the Federal Communications Commission reprimanded West for her radio script 'Adam and Eve'. The FCC found her 'offensive to the great mass of right-thinking, clean-minded American citizens'. In 1940, she starred in *My Little Chickadee*, her first movie with WC Fields. The public loved the unlikely duo. Off-screen, West could not tolerate his arrogance. West was famous for her purring one-liners: 'too much of a good thing is won-der-ful' and 'so many men, so little time'.

1935: Julie Andrews

The singer and actress, famous for her role as *Mary Poppins*, was born in Surrey, England. Her mother gave piano lessons and met a tenor in a variety show. Ted Andrews became Julie's step-father and began giving her singing lessons, discovering she had perfect pitch and a four-octave vocal range. The family toured as an act and Julie's career began at eight. She won an Academy Award for her role as the most famous nanny and went on to win her first Golden Globe for her portrayal of the singing nun Maria in *Sound of Music* in 1966. Golden Globes, BAFTA awards and Academy Award nominations have followed her film and theatre roles. In 2000 she was made a Dame and also underwent a disastrous operation to remove non-cancerous growths in her throat, which permanently damaged her singing voice but has not limited her film career.

1939 Buses began replacing trams in Sydney, Australia, and heralded the end of the tram network. Melbourne resisted and has kept its trams running.

1968 Cult horror movie *Night of the Living Dead* was released.

1971 Disneyworld Orlando Florida opened. It is the world's largest man-made tourist destination.

2003 Denmark's Estrid Geertsen set a world record, aged 99 years and 61 days, when she made a tandem parachute jump.

Screen siren Mae West: 'too much of a good thing is won-der-ful'.

Opposite page: British actors (from right) Robert Coote, Julie Andrews, Rex Harrison and a chorus perform 'You Did It' from the Broadway musical 'My Fair Lady' at the Mark Hellinger Theatre, New York, in 1956.

2 OCTOBER

1955: Juan Peron

The deposed Argentinian dictator left for exile in Paraguay. He spent 18 years there before returning to power in Argentina. Much of his power was based on Argentinians' adoration for his wife Eva—Evita. When she died in 1952, his power diminished. Evita had been born in poverty in 1919 and went to Buenos Aires to pursue acting. She was stunningly beautiful. Peron married him in 1945. When the wily Peron became President in 1946, he gave her extensive power to oversee health and labour and had her stifle the press. By 1947, over 100 newspapers or magazines were closed or banned. She also owned or controlled every radio station. Citizens, especially the poor, worshiped her. She was a gifted orator, who campaigned for women's rights. She died in 1952, aged 33, from cancer. While in exile, Peron married Isabel, who returned with him as Vice-President. On Peron's death in 1974, Isabel became President. When she resigned as head of the Peronist Party in 1985, Argentina was plunged into right-wing violence.

1951: Sting

The musician and movie star was born in Wallsend, England, as Gordon Sumner. Starting out as an English and music teacher in Newcastle, Sting began his career as a lyricist and singer with The Police before he launched his solo career. His first hit song was 'Spread a Little Happiness'. In 2000 Sting won the Grammy's Best Male Pop Vocalist Award for *Brand New Day*, which also won for Best Pop Album. His feature films include *Dune, Stormy Monday* and *The Grotesque*. He is a environmental activist and was the keynote speaker at Amnesty International's second annual Human Rights Awards ceremony in 1989.

1904: Graham Greene

The English writer was born in Berkhamsted. His father was the headmaster at Greene's school, which resulted in conflicting loyalties between his classmates and his father. Greene resolved the dilemma by running away to become a journalist. Conflict features in his books, such as *The Honorary Consul* and *Our Man in Havana* and love, salvation and politics take centre stage in *The Power and The Glory* and *The Third Man*. Many of Greene's books were made into powerful movies, such as *The End of the Affair* and *The Quiet American*. He died in 1991.

1925 London's red buses, with the roofed-in upper deck and jump-on entrance, went into service. They had already been used for fourteen years in Widnes, Cheshire.

1869 Mohandas Gandhi was born in Porbandar, India. The assassinated leader's birthday is a national holiday and sees thousands gathering in New Delhi where his body was cremated.

1946 Smoking might be dangerous say scientists at a New York conference when they discussed the possibility that it might cause cancer.

1985 Screen idol Rock Hudson died age 59. He was the first major star to reveal he had AIDS. He starred in *Magnificent Obsession, Giant* and *Pillow Talk*.

2002 English singer Robbie Williams signed the biggest deal in EMI Records' history when he signed an A$160 million deal.

Don't stand too close to me: Sting shot to fame with the band The Police and has maintained a successful solo career since then.

3 OCTOBER

1941: Chubby Checker

The musical entertainer was born in Philadelphia, with the birthname Ernest Evans. He enjoyed impersonating his musical heroes, such as Jerry Lee Lewis, Elvis Presley and Fats Domino. He was asked to record 'The Twist' as a single and developed a dance routine to go with it. The dance took off as it allowed a couple freedom to dance together, but apart. It was the first and only 45-rpm single to ever appear in the number 1 place in the charts in two different years.

1974: Pele

The world famous Brazilian soccer star played his last game at Meadowlands, New York before 75 000 spectators. Born in 1940, he is soccer's outstanding superstar. His birth name is Edson Arantes do Nascimento. Nicknamed Pele, from pelada, 'meaning rough and tumble street soccer,' he was only 16-years-old when he joined Brazil's national team. In 1958 he helped Brazil win the World Cup when he kicked two goals. His lucky number is 10 from his shirt number and from the letters of his last name. He always stays in hotel rooms numbered with a combination of 10. He played 110 games for Brazil, before he was recruited by the New York Cosmos in 1971, becoming the world's highest paid athlete. His playing was so extraordinary that scientists tested him and found superior reflexes and peripheral vision. He had an astonishing 1281 career goals in 1363 games.

1990: German Reunification

Two countries united to become the Federal Republic of Germany. Germany had been divided into two countries in 1949, the Federal Republic of Germany (West Germany) and the German Democratic Republic (Communist East Germany). After World War II Germany's capital, Berlin, had actually been divided into four zones, American, British, French and Soviet. The demarcation line was formalised between the West and the East in 1949. The two Germanys had competed as separate entities at international venues, like Olympic Games, and many families were involuntarily separated. The Federal Republic of Germany adopted the Constitution of the former West Germany. The 28-year-old the Berlin Wall, with its infamous 'Checkpoint Charlie' had been opened the previous November.

2333 BC Korea's Tangun Day is a national holiday to honour Tangun, who was the legendary founder of the Kingdom of Chosun.

1916 James Herriot, author of the books made into the BBC TV series *All Creatures Great and Small* was born as James Alfred Wight in Britian.

1944 The Polish Home Army in Warsaw, after struggling for 63 days against the German invaders, was outnumbered and forced to surrender. They had used supplies dropped by the British and USA and used the sewers for sending messages and for travel.

1951 Great Britain detonated its first H-bomb on Monte Bello Island, off the Western Australian coast.

1984 Tim McCartney-Snape and Greg Mortimer were the first Australians to climb Mount Everest. They were also the world's first to climb via the difficult North Face.

Let's twist again: Chubby Checker shows off the new routine that changed the way couples moved on the dance floor.

4 OCTOBER

1927: Faces in Stone

Gutzon Borglum began sculpturing the Mount Rushmore National Memorial in South Dakota. It is the world's largest sculpture, featuring 20-metre profiles of four American Presidents: George Washington, Thomas Jefferson, Abraham Lincoln and Theodore Roosevelt, carved into a granite cliff face. The Presidents were chosen because they represent America's founding, its political philosophy, its preservation and its expansion/conservation. Borglum died during the enormous project and his son Lincoln, completed it in1941. There was discussion about including the feminist Susan B Anthony, but the idea was rejected.

1957: Sputnik I

The USSR launched the first man-made object, an orbiting satellite, into space. The Space Race had begun. *Sputnik I*, just 22-inches in diameter, weighed 184 pounds. Its launch took the Americans by surprise, as it had plans for launching a satellite in 1958, which weighed eight times less than *Sputnik*. *Sputnik* orbited the earth and broadcast signals on two radio frequencies. It stopped transmitting after three weeks.

2004: SpaceShipOne

The first privately-funded spacecraft to successfully complete two space missions, within a two-week period, clinched the US $10-million Ansari X Prize. One of 24 competitors it paved the way for private space-tourism. The space-craft does not even look high-tech, looking more like a bi-plane, which would easily fit into a two-car garage at home. *SpaceShipOne 2004* also won *Time Magazine's* 'Coolest Invention of 2004' honour. Experimenters knew that getting a person into space was the easier mission; to get him back was more difficult. Its design came to experimental aircraft-maker Burt Rutan in a dream, that the craft would have wings that hinged at the highest altitude (about 65 miles) and acted like a feathered shuttlecock to allow it to float gently down. Microsoft co-founder Paul Allen financially backed Rutan. Visionary entrepreneur Richard Branson has ordered five larger *SpaceShipOne 2004* vehicles. Branson has more than 7000 eager space travellers signed up on his website for the $190 000 sub-orbital ride.

1935 Luna Park, underneath the Sydney Harbour Bridge was opened. Despite several attempts to close it down or move it, the iconic clown face remains.

1965 Pope Paul V1 arrived in New York City, the first Pope to visit the USA. In an address to the United Nations, he exonerated Jews of all blame in the death of Jesus Christ.

1966 Lesotho, formerly Basutoland, celebrates its independence from Great Britain with a national holiday. Lesotho is land-locked, situated within South Africa.

1982 Laurie Skreslet became the first Canadian to summit Mount Everest.

1986 The Oosterscheldedam, Netherland's most advanced sea barrier, was dedicated by Queen Beatrix.

Smithsonian Astrophysical Observatory scientists doctors J. Allen Hynek (1911-1986) (left) and Fred Whipple plotting the orbit of Sputnik I at the Harvard University campus, Cambridge, Massachusetts, October 1957.

5 OCTOBER

1958: Bungee Jumper

AJ Hackett, who popularised bungee jumping, was born in Auckland, New Zealand. His two childhood loves were carpentry and skiing/snowboarding and they found an outlet in bungee jumping. A bungee jumper gets an adrenaline rush by jumping with an elastic cord attached to their ankle. Hackett and a friend experimented with varieties of rubber and latex cords from a 60-foot high bridge, chosen because of the water below. Hackett has set records and made a fortune from bungee jumping. He jumped from Auckland's Sky Tower, 191 metres tall and recoiled 12 metres from the pavement. Hackett established the original bungee company, near Queenstown, on the South Island in 1988. It has facilitated over one million safe jumps.

1975: Kate Winslet

The actress was born into a two generational acting family in Reading England. Her career began at age seven in a television advertisement. Her first major movie was the critically acclaimed Heavenly Creatures, directed by New Zealander Peter Jackson where she played a real-life New Zealand teen murderer. Her career took off in *Sense and Sensibility*, *Jude* and *Hamlet*. She had major roles in *Titanic*, *Iris* and *Eternal Sunshine of the Spotless Mind*.

1993: Rwanda

The United Nations Assistance Mission for Rwanda (UNAMIR) was established. Its task was to assist Rwanda to peaceful multi-ethnic government. Canadian General Romeo Dallaire, a soldier, humanitarian and author was appointed its Force Commander. Six months later, the organisation's president was murdered. Dallaire assigned 12 Belgian soldiers to guard the new Prime Minister and when she and the soldiers were murdered, Belgium was incensed and withdrew its UN peacekeepers from its former colony. The situation escalated into genocide between the Tutsis and Hutus. Dallaire requested more peacekeepers and was denied. Eventually, after 1 million Rwandans had been slaughtered, the UN approved 5500 troops. Two million Rwandans were displaced. Dallaire was medically released from duty, suffering from post-traumatic stress disorder. Dallaire saved countless lives, but his experiences still haunt him. He has received many awards and was voted sixteenth on the list of The Greatest Canadians. In The 2004 movie *Hotel Rwanda* the Major, played by Nick Nolte, is loosely based on Dallaire.

1910 Portugal overthrew the monarchy and replaced it with a republic. It is a national holiday.

1936 The Jarrow Marchers set off for London to petition Parliament about the lack of jobs. After walking 280 miles (451 km) in one month, the Prime Minister Stanley Baldwin refused to see them.

1959 Canadian crooner Paul Anka scored a number 2 spot on the Billboard pop singles chart for one of the songs that defined the 1950s — 'Put Your Head on My Shoulder'.

1963 The British Nazi Party leader Colin Jordan and his bride were hit with 1000 eggs that protesters hurled at him after his wedding.

AJ Hackett breaks the world record for a 'bungee-jump from a building' with a 190 metre jump from the Sky Tower in Auckland, New Zealand, in 1998.

6 OCTOBER

1807: Sir Humphry Davy

The scientist made a groundbreaking discovery of a new metal, potassium. He created it by sending an electrical charge through wet potash. He wrote joyfully in his diary, 'Capital experiment today'. He kept building bigger batteries, until he built an arc that was even brighter than the Sun. The spin-off was the carbon-arc lamp, which was the most powerful source of light, until the laser 150 years later. Davy's work led to new discoveries of magnesium, calcium, strontium, boron and barium. He also invented a miner's safety lamp which alerted miners to gas. He completed his life's work by the age of 33 and he died aged 51.

1993: Air Jordan

Michael Jordan, known for defying gravity with his ability to leap to unbelievable heights in basketball, retired. He said, 'I don't have anything else to prove'. His record still stands at 32 292 points in 1072 games playing for the Chicago Bulls professional basketball team from 1984-98 and the Washington Wizards from 2001-03. He competed in the 1992 Barcelona Olympics on the gold medal winning American Dream Team.

2003: Hone Tuwhare

New Zealand's second Te Mata Poet Laureate was recognised with the Prime Minister's Award for Literary Achievement (ALA). He was born in 1922 and is of Nga Puhi descent. His first collection, *No Ordinary Sun*, was published in 1964 and he has since published several more. He is also a playwright. Two other writers were also honoured with the 2003 ALA—Janet Frame and Michael King. Frame, who died the following year, is best known for her lyrical autobiographical trilogy, made into the movie, *Angel at My Table.* King is a historian and biographer, best known for *Being Pakeha: An Encounter with New Zealand* and the *Maori Renaissance*. His thought-provoking book tackles the challenge of white people (pakeha) writing about Maori issues. His knowledge of Maori protocol has made Maori culture accessible to a wider audience.

1769 Captain James Cook on the *Endeavour* arrived off the New Zealand coast, signalling the end of Maori isolation.

1887 Charles-Edouard Jeanneret was born in northern Switzerland. He used the name 'Le Corbusier', his maternal grandfather name and reinvented architecture. His work was functional, with logical floor plans, cool beauty and an airy sense of space. He designed the United Nations building.

1911 Voting: it became compulsory for Australians to enroll on national electoral rolls, one of the few countries in the world which does this.

1939 Adolph Hitler announced that 'an experiment will be made with organising and regulating the Jewish problem' foreshadowing the Holocaust of the Second World War.

Dream player Michael Jordan shoots for the Washington Wizards.

7 OCTOBER

1952: Vladimir Putin

The Russian leader was born in St Petersburg, Russia. He was a brilliant student and a martial arts expert. The KGB (the Russian secret police) trained him in counterintelligence. He lived in Germany where it is likely he spied on NATO members and recruited informers and agents. He also gained deeper understanding of capitalism. After the collapse of Communism in East Germany and German reunification, Putin returned to Russia. He was elected as St Petersburg Deputy Mayor. He opened the city to foreign investment, to companies such as Credit Lyonnais, Coca Cola and electronic giants. Handpicked by the ailing President Boris Yeltsin to succeed him, few thought Putin would be a viable candidate, as he was well known for his iron hand in domestic and international affairs and his hard-line stance toward Chechen rebels. When Yeltsin stepped down before the end of his term, in Putin was elected Russia's second President March 2000.

1999: Adrienne Clarkson

Clarkson was sworn in as Canada's 26th Governor-General. She was born in Hong Kong in 1939 and was a wartime immigrant to Canada. She studied at the Sorbonne and is fluent in French. For nearly 30 years, she worked as a CBC host, writer and producer. She is popular for reaching out to Canadians in communities throughout the far-flung country, including hosting town-hall meetings. One of her major concerns is the Arctic region and its inhabitants.

2001: Empire Strikes Back

The first military response to the 11 September attacks in New York and Washington began. Cruise missiles and bombers targeted the airports of Kandahar and Kabul in Afghanistan and terrorist training camps near Jalalabad. The attacks were followed by a public broadcast from American President Bush who promised a 'sustained and relentless' campaign. Within three months, the Taleban were effectively ousted with help from the rebel Afghan factions, known as the Northern Alliance and allies including Great Britain and Australia. The Americans continue to hunt al-Qaeda militants, including leader Osama Bin Laden.

1916 American college football history went lopsided in a score of 222–0, when Georgia Tech walloped Cumberland, Tennessee.
1936 Charles Dutoit, one of the world's most acclaimed conductors, was born in Lausanne. He has been the music director of the Orchestre Symphonie de Montreal since 1977. In 1990 he also became music director with Orchestre National de France and, in 1996, Principal Conductor with the NHK Symphony Orchestra in Tokyo.
2004 Hang-gliding pioneer, Australia's William Bennett, died in a flying accident in Arizona, aged 73. He was nicknamed 'the Birdman' and introduced the controllable glider to the USA in 1969. He made hang-gliding a household word and held many records.

F-14 'Tomcat' and F/A-18 'Hornet' strike aircraft from the aircraft carrier *USS Enterprise* refuel during American attacks on Afghanistan.

8 OCTOBER

1984: Anne Murray
The Canadian singer won the country's Country Music Association's Album and Single of the Year Awards for *A Little Good News*. She was the first woman to win. She was born in Springhill, Nova Scotia and pursued careers in physical education and music. Trained as a soprano, Murray found her niche as an alto with a husky voice. Some of her hits are 'Snowbird', 'Could I Have This Dance' and 'Shadows in the Moonlight'. She has recorded more than 40 albums and sold over 22 million albums. Murray was made a Companion of the Order of Canada in 1984.

2004: Wangari Maathai
The Kenyan's selection for the Nobel Prize for Peace was announced, the first African woman to be chosen. She was honoured for founding Africa's largest community-based environmental organisation, for her work in fighting political oppression and for the empowerment of women. She started the Kenyan Green Party in 1987 to address the complex problems of deforestation and lack of sustainability. Dr Maathai has been tortured, beaten and imprisoned for her beliefs.

2004: Jacques Derrida
The controversial Algerian philosopher died in Paris. He invented 'deconstructionism'—the dismantling of texts and thoughts to reveal their contradictions. The result was 'just convoluted obscurity' his critics claimed, yet Derrida was one of the most cited of modern scholars. When Cambridge University proposed awarding Derrida an honorary degree, there was such an uproar, that the proposal had to be voted on—the first time that had happened in 30 years. He wrote more than 80 books, including *Of Grammatology* and *Writing and Difference*.

1885 Sweet Queensland sent its first direct shipment of sugar from Brisbane to London. Sugar became one of Queensland's major industries.

1899 Wowser: the distinctly Australian word was coined by John Norton to describe a puritanical person. It implies a person who dislikes partying and criticises anyone who does.

1945 US President Harry S Truman announced that the US would share the secrets for making an atomic bomb with the UK and Canada.

1985 Leon Klinghoffer and his wheelchair were thrown off the Italian cruise ship *Achille Lauro* into the Mediterranean by Palestinian hijackers, shocking the world.

1999 UK's National Farmers Union discovered egg production is increased when popular music is played. Why it works remains a mystery.

Kenyan activist Wangari Maathai, the first woman chosen to win the Nobel Prize for Peace.

9 OCTOBER

1967: Ernesto 'Che' Guevara

The idealistic South American revolutionary was murdered in Bolivia. He was 39-years-old. He trained as a doctor in Argentina. As portrayed in the 2004 movie, *The Motorcycle Diaries*, after travelling around South America, he became outraged at the suffering inflicted on poor people by foreign capitalists. He became a Cuban guerilla leader in Fidel Castro's 26th July Movement and a member of the Cuban government. Che then spent time in the Republic of Congo attempting to coordinate revolution. The CIA captured him in Bolivia and he was executed by the Bolivian military. He remains an iconic figure, especially in Third World countries, admired for his idealism and the hope for change he gave to poor people.

1970: Annika Sorenstam

The top female golfer was born in Stockholm. She enjoyed an outstanding amateur career as a member of the Swedish National Team from 1987-92 and was the World Amateur Champion in 1992. She racked up seven collegiate titles before turning professional. She joined the Ladies Professional Golf Association (LPGA) in 1993, winning in 1995 and 1996. By 2002, she was already an LPGA legend; the second player to win eleven LPGA events in one year, tying a 38-year-old record. She shattered the earnings record with nearly US$3 million. Sorenstam made history in 2003 when she played against male professionals in the Bank of America Colonial. Sorenstam has been compared to Tiger Woods for the renewed interest she has brought to the game and to tennis player Martina Navratilova for her skill and ability.

1978: Jacques Brel

The romantic singer died, age 49, in Paris, but is buried in the Marquesas Islands, near painter Paul Gauguin. He was born in Brussels in 1929. He was a singer, songwriter and guitarist. Brel was best known for his easy listening, thoughtful love songs, such as 'Tendresse', the poignant 'Ne Me Quitte Pas (If You Go Away)'. Singers ranging from Frank Sinatra, David Bowie, Dionne Warwick, to the Kingston Trio, performed translated songs. Brel made his debut at Carnegie Hall in 1965. The stage show, *Jacques Brel Is Alive and Well and Living in Paris*, opened off-Broadway in 1968—ironically when Brel was battling cancer. His last album, Brel, sold 650 000 on the first day of its release. Brel lived in self-imposed exile for a number of years in the Marquesas Islands. He returned to Paris for cancer treatment and died there. In life, Brel took aim at bigots and hypocrites, but he left three daughters, none by his wife.

1000 Leif Erikson Day is celebrated in Iceland, to commemorate the first known Norseman to land in North America.

1908 Jacques Tati (Tatischeff) was born in France. He starred in the classic *Mon Oncle* movies. He died in 1982.

1912 Baby bonus: The Australian Federal Government announced a maternity allowance for every white child born.

1974 Oskar Schindler died age 66. He is called a 'Righteous Gentile' by Israel for his heroic efforts to save 1200 Jewish employees during the World War II.

1985 A portion of Central Park, New York City was renamed 'Strawberry Fields,' in honour of murdered Beatle John Lennon's song.

1991 The first sumo-wrestling tournament ever held outside Japan was held in London's Albert Hall. It is Japan's national sport and is 1500 years old.

Che Guevara's image has become an icon, used to signify revolution and courage, especially among young people.

10 OCTOBER

1900: Helen Hayes,

The 'First Lady of the American Theatre' was born in Washington, DC. She was a child star from the age of 5. Her best remembered role was as Queen Victoria, in *Victoria Regina*. Hayes won a Best Actress Oscar in 1931 for *The Sin of Madelon Claudet* and a Best Supporting Actress Oscar for *Airport* in 1971. In her long career, Hayes was admired for her psychological strength and integrity, although she experienced tragedy in the deaths of her daughter and her husband. A theatre in New York City was named for her. Hayes died in 1993. Her husband was Charles MacArthur, the distinguished playwright and her son is actor and producer, James MacArthur, best known for his role as Danno in the TV cop hit, *Hawaii-5-0*.

1983: Sir Ralph Richardson

The esteemed British actor died in Marylebone, England age 80. He was born in Shakespeare country, in Gloucestershire and intended becoming a painter, until an inheritance made it possible for him to leave school and act. After his first role as Lorenzo in *The Merchant of Venice* he soon joined the Old Vic Theatre in London. His bulbous nose suited his comedy and tragic roles. Richardson was versatile on stage and starred in more than 70 movies. He was known for his noisy motorbikes and for the ever-present parrot on his shoulder. He raised mice and collected art. He told a *Time* reporter, 'Acting is merely the act of keeping a large group of people from coughing.'

2004: Christopher Reeve

The wheelchair-bound actor and activist died in a Westchester County, New York hospital, age 52. He had millions of fans worldwide for his role in *Superman* movies. He acquired even more fans after he became quadriplegic in a 1995 horse riding accident. Reeve established the Christopher Reeve Paralysis Foundation to research spinal cord injuries. which distributed more than $42-million for neuro-scientific research. He was a tireless advocate for the disabled worldwide. His widow, Dana, hopes that the Smithsonian Institution will choose to remember Reeve's life by his wheelchair, not by his Superman costume.

1813 Italian composer **Giuseppe Verdi** was born in Le Roncole. His 26 operas include some of the most popular ever written, including *Aida*, *Rigoletto* and *La Traviata*. He died in 1901.

1886 The first tuxedo was created when Griswold Lorillard of Tuxedo Park, New York, removed the tails of a tailcoat.

1892 Jacky Howe sheared 321 sheep in 8 hours and 40 minutes, a regular Australian shearer's workday. This was before electric shears.

1930 Harold Pinter, English playwright, director and screenwriter was born in London. He wrote *The Birthday Party* and *The Room*.

1970 The island nation of Fiji gained its independence from Great Britain in 1970. It is a national holiday.

Fiji celebrates its independence from Great Britain.

11 OCTOBER

2004: Nugget

Keith Ross Miller, the leading all-round cricketer, died age 84 in his birthplace, Melbourne. In 1945, Miller was the standout player in a game that featured the world's best players and sports writers wrote they ran out of adjectives to describe Miller's batting. One ball went over the top of the grandstand and another into the press box. Some spectators said they had to retreat to the bar for safety! Miller played in 55 Tests and was one of Bradman's elite 'Invincibles' team members. Miller's highest runs score was 147 and he claimed 170 wickets with 7 for 60 his best bowling score. He spent several years in the Royal Air Force as a bomber pilot. He resumed cricket aged 36, despite a bad back from a plane crash. Miller's charisma, movie-star looks and superb cricketing made him a hero and helped Australia shake off its postwar anguish. Miller was described as 'the greatest non-captain to ever captain Australia.'He later became a journalist and was honoured with a portrait at the MCG, UK.

1963: Piaf

Edith Piaf, the part Moroccan and French singer, died in the south of France aged 47. She was born to street entertainers, The Gassions. A promoter discovered her and renamed her 'la môme Piaf' (the waif sparrow.) Although tiny like a sparrow, she belted out her songs, with a unique, rich voice. Piaf became a vaudeville and cabaret star, especially popular during the 1940s and 1950s, singing of love and anguish, which reflected her life. Two of her best-known songs are 'Je ne Regrette Rien' and 'La Vie en Rose'.

1935: Steele Rudd

Arthur Davis, better known to Australians as 'Steele Rudd', died age 66 in Brisbane. He was born near Toowoomba, Queensland the eighth of 13 children. He remains popular today for his comic portrayals of the hardships the pioneering families endured trying to make a better life for themselves on their selections (farms). Rudd's books include *On Our Selection, From Selection to City, Grandpa's Selection* and *Dad in Politics*.

1887 Willie Hoppe who dominated billiards and won his first world championship at age 18, was born in Cornwall, New York.

1969 Cowboy Ty Murray, the Rodeo World Champion from 1989-94, was born in Arizona. He became the youngest cowboy millionaire.

1976 Mao Zedong's widow, Jiang Qing, was arrested with three others (The Gang of Four) and charged with plotting a coup against the Chinese government. She was sentenced to death, but it was commuted to life imprisonment. She later committed suicide.

1982 King Henry V111's flagship *The Mary Rose*, which was sunk in 1545, was successfully brought to the surface for salvage and possible restoration.

1993 England's Richard Roberts, age 50, co-shared the Nobel Prize in Medicine or Physiology, for his work in molecular biology and the discovery of 'split genes.'

Edith Piaf: built like a sparrow but sang like an eagle.

12 OCTOBER

1957: Lester Pearson

The Liberal Member of Canada's Parliament was notified that he had won the Nobel Peace Prize but the official telegram from Oslo had been delivered to a neighbour's house. When the press telephoned to interview Pearson, he thought it was it was a practical joker. He was awarded the prize for his creation of a United Nations Emergency Force to resolve the 1956 Suez Crisis. Pearson was also one of the founders of the United Nations and former president of its General Assembly. He wrote the framework for NATO. He was elected Canada's 14th Prime Minister in 1963. He died in 1972, aged 75.

1960: Nikita's Shoe

Nikita Krushchev, USSR President, shocked everyone when he banged his shoe on the table at the United Nations. He had become First Secretary of the Communist Party following Stalin's death in 1953 and boldly denounced Stalin in 1956. Although he apparently wanted peaceful relations with the West, his behaviour was often confusing. In a major confrontation at the UN over who was responsible for Cold War tension, Krushchev surprised everyone with his tantrum, but he knew it would achieve what his words had not—attention. The Cold War would drag on, reaching its worst point when the USSR and America locked horns over the Cuban missile crisis of 1961. Krushchev died in 1971.

1998: Agnes Grossmann

The pianist-turned-conductor led the Wiener Sangerknaben (Vienna Choir Boys) in Montreal. The concert was part of the choir's 500th anniversary tour. Grossmann, born in Vienna, was a touring concert pianist until she injured her hand. She then studied conducting from 1974-78. She spent many years alternating between Vienna and Canada. In 1996 she was appointed the Artistic Director of the Choir and guided it through its successful anniversary international tour.

2002: Bali Bombing

Eighty-eight Australians were killed when a nightclub was bombed in Kuta, on the Indonesian island of Bali. A bomb was detonated inside Paddy's Bar and when patrons fled outside, a car bomb was detonated outside The Sari Club. In all, 202 people died, mostly from severe burns, including 38 Indonesian bar workers and people from 22 different countries. Hundreds more were injured. Several religious extremists were arrested and charged.

1872 Ralph Vaughan Williams, English composer and conductor, was born at Down Ampney, Gloucestershire. He wrote symphonies, operas and music for stage and screen. His major work includes *Pilgrim's Progress*. He died in 1958.

1967 Zoologist Desmond Morris' new book *The Naked Ape* was published. It became an immediate bestseller. His book looked at humans as 'hairless mammals.' It was translated into 23 languages and is a now a classic.

1969 Sonja Henie the ten-time world figure skating champion died of leukemia age 57. By then she was one of the world's wealthiest women.

1997 Folksinger John Denver died in an airplane he was piloting at Monterey, California. He was an environmental and anti-nuclear activist. His songs include, 'Take Me Home Country Road'.

1999 The United Nations announced that the world's population had reached six billion people. One-third lived in China and India. A billion people are added every 12 years.

The carnage outside The Sari Club where 202 people were killed by bombs.

13 OCTOBER

1886: Dame Nellie Melba

The Australian opera singer and 'Queen of Covent Garden' made her debut in Brussels, in Rigoletto. Melba was born Helen Mitchell in 1861 in Melbourne, Victoria. She derived her stage name 'Melba' from her hometown's name. A flamboyant woman, she was the leading singer of her generation. She was admired by Australians for her glamourous lifestyle with royalty and international society and even for her many scandalous affairs. Her popularity may have been because, as one writer described her, 'Unlike so many who find success, she remained a 'dinkum hard-swearing Aussie' to the end'. She was the inspiration for the dessert Peche Melba and for Melba toast. Melba made four return tours home including visits to isolated country towns in 1902, 1907, 1909 and 1911. Audiences especially loved her duets with tenor Enrico Caruso. She was one of the first singers to record, from 1904 and her records show her exceptional voice. Her farewell concert was in her favourite role as Mimi in *La Boheme* in 1926. She died five years later at 69.

1979: The Sugarhill Gang

'Rapper's Delight' by The Sugarhill Gang was one of the first rap tracks to hit the charts. It went multi-platinum, selling over eight million copies. Hip-hop was born in the early 1970s, morphing beats and baselines from various musical styles and sound recordings. Flourishing at block parties in the New York City streets, the new genre was thought to be a novelty and stayed underground for many years before becoming the billion-dollar industry it is today. 'Rapper's Delight' was sixteen minutes long and was later cut for radio. Label owner Sylvia Robinson heard performer Big Bank Hank rapping outside a pizza cafe and asked him and Master Gee and Wonder Mike to record a single. It became the first hip hop single to take over the airwaves exposing this new form of music to soon-to-be fans everywhere.

1821 Rudolf Virchow, the father of cellular pathology, was born in Schivelbein, Pomerania. He was also a politician and writer. He died in 1902.

1862 Adventurer and writer Mary Kingsley was born. She spent her lonely younger years caring for her mother and reading books. In 1892, aged 30, she set off for West Africa to see the world, going places few, if any, Europeans had ever been. She died in 1900.

1921 Yves Montand, actor and movie star, was born in Monsummano Alto, Italy. He made more than 50 movies.

1947 Baron Sidney Webb died in Hampshire, England, age 88. He and his wife Beatrice were innovative social economists. They co-founded the London School of Economics and Political Science.

1995 Microsoft consolidated its domination of personal computing with the release of its long-awaited Windows 95.

Dame Nellie Melba: one of Australia's most famous voices and inspiration for several recipes.

14 OCTOBER

1888: Katherine Mansfield

One of New Zealand's finest writers was born in Wellington. She began writing as a child. Much of her writing was thinly veiled autobiography. Some scholars suggest her writing was also solace for having a miscarriage and her inability to have another child. She was bisexual and lived most of her adult life in England. After her brother was killed in a freak accident, Mansfield wrote about their childhood in New Zealand as a way of honouring him. Prelude published by Leonard and Virginia Woolf's press is considered one of her most technically fine pieces. Virginia wrote in her diary that Mansfield was the only writer she was jealous of. Mansfield's exquisite short story *The Garden Party* finally brought her renown. She died of tuberculosis in 1923.

1958: Sir Douglas Mawson

Australia's foremost Antarctic explorer died on this day aged 76 in Adelaide. Born in Bradford, England, his family immigrated to Australia, where he became fascinated by geology. When he was 26, he joined Sir Ernest Shackleton's Antarctic Expedition to climb Mount Erebus, an active volcano. He was also the first to reach the magnetic South Pole. Mawson led the first Australasian expedition in 1911 to explore and map Antarctica's coastline. With two others, he headed overland, covering 1000 km in five weeks. Mawson was the only survivor in one of the most enthralling stories of determination. He headed two more Antarctic expeditions, undertaking oceanographic and geological work. Later, famed alpinist Sir Edmund Hillary said that Mawson was his childhood hero.

1959: Errol Flynn

Fans mourned when the good looking actor died. Born in Hobart, Tasmania 1909, son of a marine biologist, Flynn's good looks led to a stage career in London, where he was spotted by a talent scout and signed up for Warner Brothers in Hollywood. His first movie was *The Case of the Curious Bride* in 1935. After appearing as a swashbuckling, athletic, charming rogue, like Douglas Fairbanks, in *Captain Blood*, he could not shake off his typecasting. During the next six years he appeared in *The Charge of the Light Brigade* and *The Adventures of Robin Hood*. Flynn's career had peaked and he became known for his hedonistic lifestyle.

1893 Lillian Gish was born in Springfield, Ohio. She appeared in more than 100 movies over 85 years. She appeared in her last movie, aged 94. She died in 1993.

1905 Eugene Fodor was born in Leva, Hungary. He wrote his first Fodor travel guide in 1936.

1942 A German submarine torpedoed a Canadian steamship in Cabot Strait, killing 137 people. In all, Germans sank 23 Canadian ships with a loss of 700 lives

1947 Chuck Yeager first broke the sound barrier in a Bell X1 plane. This ushered in supersonic flight.

1980 The dying Bob Marley performed his last concert.

Swashbuckling rogue Errol Flynn stole the hearts of many in his movies.

15 OCTOBER

1844: Johann Strauss Jr

The nineteen-year-old composer and conductor performed nineteen encores for his enthusiastic Viennese audience in his first concert. His last encore was one of Johann 'The Elder' Strauss Senior's famous waltzes. Strauss Jr was the world's first superstar musician. He travelled throughout Europe and performed for Queen Victoria, who waltzed with Albert, her husband. Later, Strauss was paid $100 000 to perform in the America. Eventually Strauss Jr exceeded his famous father in popularity and fame. The Vienna Philharmonic plays the Elder's masterpiece, *The Radetsky March* and his son's *Blue Danube Waltz*, every New Year's Eve. The *Blue Danube Waltz* is Vienna's unofficial anthem. Strauss Jr. wrote more than 170 waltzes; he died in 1899.

1903: Pixie O'Harris

The illustrator and author was born on this day in Cardiff, Wales. Her father was an artist and she was the fifth of nine children. The family immigrated to Western Australia when she was a teenager and then moved to Sydney by ship. During the voyage, she decided to change her name from Rhona to Pixie after someone called her a Welsh pixie. She wrote poems and illustrated books for some of Australia's leading children's authors. After she married and had her three daughters, she decided that hospitals needed some murals. She began painting whimsical fairy style paintings with little people. She decorated over fifty ward walls with her beautiful, gentle work. She received many honours, including the Queen's Coronation Medal. She died in 1991.

1997: Supersonic Thrust

Craig Breedlove set a world land speed record in his *Spirit of America* of 846.97 km/h (526.28 mph) in 1964. On this same day in 1997, Andy Green, a Royal Air Force fighter pilot, set a new land speed record when he achieved a speed of 1227.98 km/h (763.03 mph.) He drove the supersonic *Thrust SSC*. Going at high speed on land seriously challenges the human body's ability to withstand acceleration and also challenges the strength of the materials used in the vehicle. The vehicle repeated the mile in order to set the official record. Both times it created a shock wave in front of the car and a resounding sonic boom.

Supersonic boom: Andy Green breaks the land speed record in his Thrust SSC.

1844 Friedrich Wilhelm Nietzsche was born at Rocken, Germany. He changed the way philosophers looked at the world. He said, 'My ambition is to say in ten sentences what everyone else says in a book.' He died in 1900.

1917 The spy Mata Hari was executed by a French firing squad. She was born in the Netherlands and became a dancer. From romantic liaisons with Allied officers in World War 1 she learned information about tank construction, which she passed on to the Germans.

1976 Mystery: A cargo ship with fifteen aboard disappeared without trace in the Atlantic Ocean's so-called 'Bermuda Triangle.'

2004 Australian cricketer Shane Warne broke Sri Lankan bowler Muttiah Muralitharan's Test wicket-taking record of 532, by reaching a career total of 533 wickets.

18 OCTOBER

1922: Melina Mercouri

The Greek actress and politician, was born in Athens. She came to international attention in *Never On Sunday*; in all she starred in more than seventy movies. In 1977 she was elected a Member of Parliament and became the first woman appointed to the Cabinet, by Premier Andreas Papandreou as Minister of Culture in 1981. She died in New York in 1994.

1968: Drug Difficulties

John Lennon and Yoko Ono were arrested and charged with possession of marijuana when Ringo Starr's apartment was raided by police in London. Lennon claimed they were set up and tried to get a royal pardon for his subsequent conviction. Ringo had to sell the lease for his apartment because of an injunction by his estate managers. 'The whole thing was set-up. The *Daily Express* was there before the cops came' said Lennon. The next day John and Yoko appeared in Marylebone Magistrates' Court, where they were remanded on bail for the following month. John's lawyer tried to elicit a little sympathy by claiming that the stress of the arrest led to Yoko's subsequent miscarriage. John was reportedly worried that she'd get deported because she wasn't a British citizen. The conviction meant difficulty for John every time he tried to re-enter America, especially when he was coming to protest against the Vietnam war.

1975: Breaking Up and Getting Together

The famous folk rock duo reunited and create another top ten single, 'My Little Town'. When they broke up in 1970, they weren't on the best of terms. But 33 years spent mostly apart with only occasional reunion tours healed wounds. The duo grew up together as friends in Forest Hills, New York and started recording together in 1957 as Tom and Jerry. After breaking up, they discovered the reflective ring and lilting harmonies of folk music and re-formed as Simon & Garfunkel. The group recorded five albums and tracks for film scores. The track for *The Graduate* won a Grammy Award for Record of the Year in 1969 and Simon was honoured with a Grammy for Best Original Score for a Motion Picture. *Bridge Over Troubled Water* received several Grammys, including one for Album of the Year. Plans to record a new album were thwarted because of their inability to get along.

Paul Simon and Art Garfunkel performing together in 1970.

1877 The world's first residential phone service started with four customers in Hamilton, Ontario, Canada who had telephones installed by the Bell Company.

1883 The Ben Nevis weather station was opened to assist with weather forecasting on Britain's highest mountain in Scotland.

1921 Bang: Germany announced it had perfected an electric triple barrelled gun that could shoot 2000 bullets per minute.

1933 Merton Hodge's *The Wind and The Rain* opened in London. It ran for a record-breaking 1000 performances, before moving to Europe, then New York. The play had its origin in the playwright's days at university in Dunedin, New Zealand.

1968 American Bob Beamon made a world and Olympic long jump record of 29 feet 2 in. (8.9 m) His record stood for 23 years.

19 OCTOBER

1850: Annie S Peck

The pioneering female Alpinist was born in Providence, Rhode Island, America. She gained an international reputation when, as a middle-aged woman, she climbed Switzerland's Matterhorn in 1895. Her climb to Mount Huascaran's summit of 22 000 feet (7300m) was a world record for either a man or a woman in the western hemisphere. At 61, Peck summitted Peru's Mount Coropuna. She placed a 'Votes for Women' banner at its 21 500 foot (7160m) summit. She died in New York City in 1935.

1931: John Le Carre

The author was born in Poole, Dorset, England. His birth name was David Cornwell. He worked for the British Foreign Office and had to write under a pseudonym. He is known for his rivetting psychological and philosophical espionage thrillers, such as the 1963 *The Spy Who Came in From the Cold*. The book became a best-seller, winning the British Crime Novel and Somerset Maugham Award. Its success allowed Le Carre to resign from the Foreign Office to write full-time. He has declined to reveal his role at the Foreign Office. His books give hints of his knowledge of the espionage bureaucracy and of agent rivalry. His *Tinker, Tailor, Soldier, Spy* was based on the real life of double agent Kim Philby. Le Carre has written over 24 books, many of which have been made into movies.

2004: Margaret Hassan

The 59-year-old director of the humanitarian group, CARE International, was kidnapped on this day in Iraq. She was presumed murdered after a gruesome videotape was released of an execution. Iraqi police detained four men and recovered some of Hassan's personal effects, but her body was not found. She worked for CARE for thirteen years. The British-Irish civilian was married to an Iraqi and had lived in Iraq for 30 years. She learned Arabic and converted to Islam. She was opposed to the American occupation of Iraq. She is one of 200 people in the past decade who have been killed in 45 countries while trying to help civilians. The International Red Cross alone has lost 40 employees.

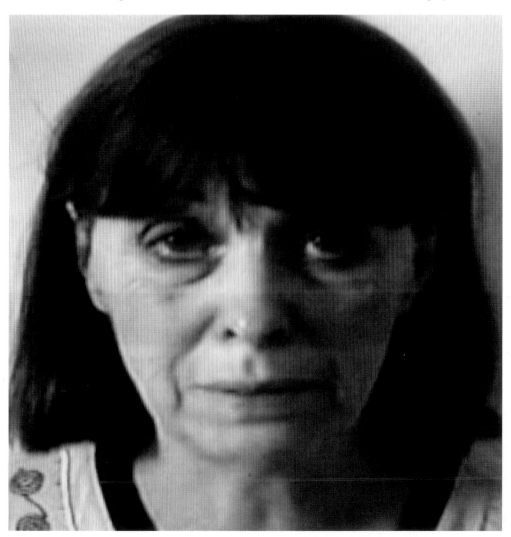

1856 Australia's longest bare-knuckle boxing match took place between James Kelly and Jack Smith, near Melbourne. It lasted 186 rounds, over six hours and 15 minutes.

1862 Auguste Lumiere was born. He was a photography and movie pioneer, with his brother Louis. Their factory made a variety of photographic products, and the brothers made the first film eve—of their employees leaving work.

1946 With wartime rationing easing, American women were allowed to wear longer skirts and dresses.

1970 British Petroleum announced the discovery of major oilfields under the North Sea in the British sector.

1987 British cellist Jacqueline Du Pre died of multiple sclerosis. Considered one of the most accomplished cellists of her time, the movie *Hilary and Jackie* was based on her and her sister's lives.

Humanitarian director Margaret Hassan appears in a terrorist video before being executed by them, despite being married to an Iraqi and converting to Islam.

20 OCTOBER

1873: Nellie McClung

The Canadian feminist, author, teacher and social reformer was born near Owen Sound, Ontario. McClung had women recognised as 'people' in the landmark 1929 'Persons Case' before the British Privy Council. When she toured sweatshops with the Manitoba Conservative Premier, Rodmond Roblin and he told her 'nice women did not want to vote,' McClung was incensed. She wrote and staged a popular satire, *The Women's Parliament,* to mock the politicians. Roblin was soon voted out of office and replaced by a Liberal. Women won the right to vote in Manitoba, where McClung was then living, in 1916, followed by all the other provinces. McClung next addressed the question of whether women could be appointed to the Canadian Senate. The Supreme Court ruled that when the Constitution was written in 1867 'persons' in the document referred to voters and because women could not vote, women were not persons. McClung took the case to the British Court, which ruled that women were indeed 'persons'. She died in Victoria, British Columbia, in 1951.

2003: Niagara Plunge

Kirk Jones went over the 175-foot Niagara Falls. He was the only person who to do this intentionally and survive. Although the Niagara River rushes at 570 000 litres a second, he bruised his ribs but was otherwise unhurt. Witnesses reported seeing him jump into the water, but Jones denied that he was attempting suicide. He was fined and barred from entering Canada for life. Jones was hired by a circus to groom elephants and talk to reporters about his wild ride.

1975: Diego Maradona

The Argentinian football legend played his first league game, aged 15. He started playing street soccer in the Buenos Aires slums, where he was born. His dexterity was quickly recognised and he performed at half-time soccer matches. In 1982 Maradona played for Barcelona, Spain and probably at this time became a heavy cocaine and ephedrine user. In 1986 he was at his peak and captained the Argentinian team for their World Cup victory. Drug abuse led to his ban from playing. He retired in 1997.

1616 Thomas Bartholin, Danish anatomist, was the first to chart the human lymphatic system. He published information to help people stay healthy during the plague. He died in 1680.

1671 Jean Talon, the Intendant of New France, as Canada was called, ordered the Quebec colony's bachelors to marry the French women brought over for them, or they would lose their hunting, fishing and fur-trading rights.

1882 Bela Lugosi was born in Lugos Hungary. He changed his birth name to reflect that of his birthplace. He was the iconic vampire in *Dracula*. He died in 1956.

1891 The first six-day international bicycling race began on high-wheelers at Madison Square Garden in New York City. Riders could stop for a rest. It was won by 'Rugger Bill' Martin.

1982 The world's worst soccer tragedy occurred in Moscow when 340 fans were killed during a USSR-Dutch game due to a crush on a staircase.

Argentine soccer legend Diego Maradona trips during training, in Sydney, Australia, for the World Cup qualifying match against the Socceroos in October 1993.

21 OCTOBER

1858: Can Can

The Can-Can Dance was first performed in Paris, part of Jacques Offenbach's *Orpheus in the Underworld*, in a theatre that Offenbach owned. Nobody was very interested in the musical satire of Orpheus and Eurydice and it received a lukewarm reception, until critic Jules Janin wrote, that it 'was a profanation of holy and glorious antiquity in a spirit of irreverence that bordered on blasphemy.' The public rushed to be scandalised. Offenbach was born in Cologne, but preferred living in Paris. He wrote 95 operettas and became very wealthy. His only serious opera was his *Les Contes d'Hoffmann* (Tales of Hoffmann), which remains popular.

1879: Let there be Light ... bulbs

Thomas Edison demonstrated his incandescent lamp, one of the most important inventions of the modern era. This prototype could burn for over thirteen hours and was suitable for domestic use. Soon candles and lanterns would be a thing of the past, to be replaced by electric lighting. The lamp consisted of a wire inside a glass bulb, from which all the air had been removed to create a vacuum inside. When an electric current was sent through the wire it heated up and the glow gave out light. People often called Edison, rightfully, a genius and he was fond of saying, 'genius is one per cent inspiration and ninety-nine per cent perspiration.' Edison also invented the phonograph, which led to today's recording industry. He held more than 1093 patents. He had set up his first laboratory at the age of ten and was home-schooled by his mother. Edison died in 1931, age 84.

1921: Sir Malcolm Arnold

The British composer was born in Northampton, England. He started as London Philharmonic Orchestra's principal trumpeter, but soon turned solely to composition. His musical inspiration is dance, song and serenades. He wrote nine symphonies, seven ballets, two operas, over 20 concertos and over 130 musical scores for movies, including *The Bridge on the River Kwai* and *Inn of the Sixth Happiness*. Arnold is a humanitarian who sees music as a communication among people and a gesture of friendship.

1922 New Yorker Marjorie Howarth became the first western woman to cross the third range of the South American Andes.

1966 A generation of a town's children was lost when 116 children and fourteen adults were buried in a coal slagheap at Aberfan, Wales. The coal heap became unstable from rain, and buried a nearby school.

1978 Frederick Valentich disappeared while flying his Cessna from Melbourne to Tasmania. Some speculated his plane was taken by a UFO. Others think he staged a suicide.

1982 Sinn Fein, the political arm of the Provisional Irish Republican Army, won its first seats in an election.

1984 'New wave' movie director Francois Truffaut died in Paris, age 52 from cancer. Two of his acclaimed movies are *Jules and Jim* and *Day for Night*.

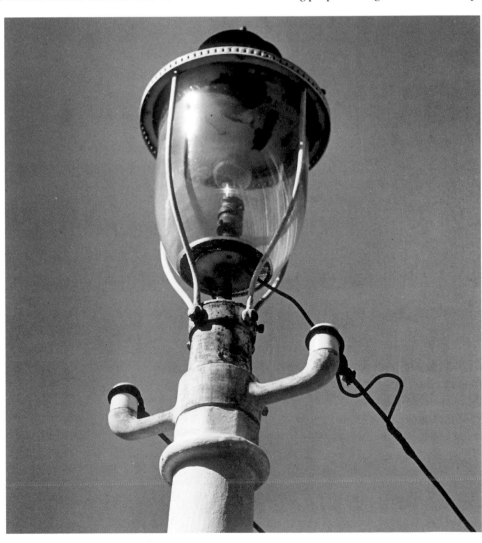

The lantern invented by Thomas Edison is now displayed at his laboratory.

22 OCTOBER

1943: Catherine Deneuve

The French movie actress was born in Paris. Her parents were both actors, as was one of her three sisters. Deneuve prefers to work in Europe rather than in Hollywood and has worked with some of Europe's best directors, such as Luis Bunuel, Francois Truffaut and actors such as Roger Vadim, Marcello Mastroianni and Gerard Depardieu. Her acclaimed movies include *Les Parapluies de Cherbourg* (which won three Oscars) and *Indochine* about French colonial Vietnam.

1962: Cuban Missile Crisis

When American President Kennedy denounced Soviet actions in Cuba on this day, it was the closest that the world has come to nuclear devastation. Now known as the 'Cuban Missile Crisis,' Kennedy appeared on national television and radio and demanded that President Nikita Krushchev of the Soviet Union remove missiles that had been installed in Cuba. Kennedy announced a shipping blockade to Cuba, to prevent more cargo ships that were transporting fighter planes, equipment and weaponry from arriving. Before his speech no one really knew what was happening in Washington DC, except that the President had stopped his congressional campaigning and that lights burned round the clock at his key advisers' offices. Both the USSR and American militaries mobilised. The United Nations tried a peaceful resolution. The world breathed a sigh of relief, a week later, when Krushchev announced that if the Americans removed missiles, aimed at the USSR from Turkey, he would remove the USSR missiles from Cuba. Kennedy agreed not to invade Cuba and to lift the blockade. The crisis ended as suddenly as it had begun.

1999: White Lightning

A revolutionary electric car set a new land speed record at Bonneville Flats, Utah. The car was a long, sleek machine measuring 25-feet (7.62 m) that hardly resembled a car, but looked more like a futuristic rocket. It reached a speed of 245.951 mph/395.821 km/h. It can accelerate to 100-mph/161 km/h in just eight seconds. It was driven by American Patrick Rummerfield.

A P2V Neptune US patrol plane flies over a Soviet freighter during the Cuban missile crisis in this 1962 photograph.

1925 American abstract expressionist painter Robert Rauschenberg was born in Port Arthur, Texas. He started painting as a US Marine age 47.

1973 Spanish cellist Pablo Casals died in Puerto Rico age 74. From age ten, he took a daily walk to observe nature and to reflect. He refused to play in any country that supported Franco's dictatorship in Spain.

1973 A ceasefire began in the Yom Kippur War. Egyptians and Syrians had launched a surprise attack on Israel with a massive tank invasion, taking Israel by surprise during the most religious of holy holidays. Israeli jets retaliated.

1988 Fifty-nine QANTAS employees pulled a Boeing 747 jet airplane 100-metres in 62.1 seconds at Perth Airport.

1989 Experimental playwright Ewan MacColl died aged 74. GB Shaw once quipped that other than himself, MacColl was 'the best living playwright in Britain.' He was also a political activist and a songwriter.

23 OCTOBER

Swallow Day

On this day the swallows 'officially' leave the Mission of San Juan Capistrano, heading for the Southern Hemisphere for warmth and abundant food. In reality, it is sometimes a day or two before or after 23 October. With a few scouts leading, the flock departs in a huge swirl for Southern Argentina, where they stay until about 19 March, when they return to the Mission. The Mission dates from 1776 and is the oldest building in California. Named for Italy's Saint John of Capistrano, the swallows live in mud nests in the side of the Mission. Legend has it that townspeople had evicted the swallows from the eaves of their homes, using broomhandles to dismantle their mud nests and so the priests invited the swallows to nest with them.

1925: Johnny Carson

The American TV presenter was born in Corning Iowa and grew up in Norfolk, Nebraska. Carson achieved iconic status as a talk show host on **The Tonight Show** from 1962-92. His co-host was the former American Marine Ed McMahon, a perfect foil for Carson's comic monologues. Carson's first guest was Groucho Marx and his last was Bette Midler. Carson had the uncanny ability to make his guests 'shine'. He launched the careers of countless comedians and actors. Although he was very wealthy, he never lost his Mid-western roots and drove himself to and from work, carrying a packed lunch. He had many hobbies, including celestial navigation. He spoke Swahili and was a serious astronomer. After retirement, he became more reclusive. Carson was awarded America's highest civilian award, the American Presidential Medal of Freedom in 1992. He died from emphysema in 2005.

1996: Gro Harlem Brundtland

Norway and Scandinavia's first female Prime Minister resigned. She was a physician who then became leader of the Labour Party and Norwegian Prime Minister in 1981. At 41-years-old she was also the youngest prime minister. She was re-elected in 1986-89 and 1990-96. Brundtland was the first woman to head the United Nations World Health Organization in 1998-2003. She had previously chaired the World Commission on Environment and Development, which produced the report 'Our Common Future'. An ardent global environmentalist, she was awarded the Third World Foundation Prize for leadership in Environmental Causes in 1998.

1752 French chemist and chef Nicolas Appert was born. He invented a way of hygienically heating foods and sealing them in airtight containers so that the contents could be eaten later, revolutionising the food industry and earning him a prize from the French government. He died in 1841.

1920 Japanese-American Tetsuya 'Ted' Fujita was born in 1920. A meteorologist, known as 'Mr Tornado', he and his wife Sumiko created a system for measuring tornado power.

1956 The USSR invaded Hungary. Hungarians fought back but were defeated. Their leader, Imre Nagy, was hung on a balcony on June 16, 1958. On the same day, on the same balcony 33 years later, Hungary declared its freedom.

1974 Greece's ex-Premier Papadopoulos and four other leaders of the 1967 military coup were exiled. An attempt to overthrow Archibishop Makarios in Cyprus in July 1974 backfired when Turkey invaded the island, which is still partitioned. The war in Cyprus led to the overthrow of the 'Colonel's Junta' on the Greek mainland.

1977 One-celled fossils, the earth's oldest life forms yet discovered were found in South Africa. They are around 3.4 billion years old and similar to blue-green algae.

Relatives of those killed defending the Cypriot president, Archbishop Makarios, during the 1974 coup, during a memorial service in Nicosia, Cyprus. The coup, engineered by the American-backed military junta running Greece, prompted the Turkish invasion and occupation of Cyprus. Northern Cyprus, including half of the capital Nicosia, is still under Turkish occupation.

24 OCTOBER

1868: Alexandra David-Neel

The female adventurer was born in Paris. At 56-years-old, when her peers were enjoying Parisian cafes, she accomplished what few men and no European woman, had ever done. She reached Lhasa, Tibet in midwinter. David-Neel had travelled through blizzards and over high mountain passes, disguised as a beggar to reach the 'Forbidden City.' She explained, 'a powerful attraction drew me to this strange and beautiful country.' Financed by her understanding husband, she spent 20 years exploring the Himalaya including India, Sikkim and Nepal. She learned Tibetan, became a Buddhist and learned about the mystical rites of yogis. David-Neel was one of history's most fascinating adventurers, yet she is little known outside Europe. In her later years, homesick for Tibet, she wrote several books, including *My Journey to Lhasa, Initiations and Initiates in Tibet* and *The Secret Oral Teachings in Tibetan Buddhist Sects*. She died in Digne in 1969, aged 101.

1945: United Nations Day

The UN officially came into existence when its Charter was ratified by signatories including China, France, the Soviet Union, the United Kingdom and the United States. There are now 191 member states. For nine weeks in 1945 the United Nations conference worked on its Charter. Its preamble is considered by many to be one of the finest expressions of purpose set forth in any language. Although the delegates came from nations, 'small, weak and strong and in different stages of political and social development,' these earnest individuals were 'determined to set up an organization which would preserve peace, advance justice and constitute a permanent structure for international cooperation.' This day is celebrated every year.

1969: Concorde Flies

The supersonic passenger Concorde prototype was first flown. A joint United Kingdom-France venture, the supersonic aircraft was built in Toulouse, France. Concorde went into commercial service in 1976. It cruised at a maximum speed of 2330 km/h, halving the flying time between London and New York City to just 3 and a half hours. The company was unprofitable and the Concorde was taken out of service on its anniversary day, 24 October 2003. With a spectacular finale, three Concordes landed at London's Heathrow Airport from Edinburgh, New York and France, just two minutes apart

1922: Cadbury chocolate company's George Cadbury died. With his brother Richard, George had expanded his father's cocoa and chocolate business. Cadbury's became the world's fourth largest chocolate company.

1947 American movie actor Kevin Kline was born in St Louis, Missouri. He won an Oscar for *A Fish Called Wanda*. He also appeared in *Sophie's Choice*, *The Big Chill*, and *De-Lovely*.

1960 The worst spacecraft disaster occurred, killing 91 people, when an R-16 rocket exploded at the Baikonur Space Center in the then-USSR.

1973 Votes: Australia granted the right to vote to its Aboriginal people.

1976 Hua Kuo-feng: More than one million people rallied to hear the proclamation that he was now Chairman of the Chinese Communist Party. He was also the Premier, and the head of the Military Affairs Commission, the first person to hold all three high spots.

American actor, Kevin Kline, (right) with British actors Michael Palin (left) and John Cleese (centre) posing behind America's Jamie Lee Curtis in 1988 in a promotional portrait for the film, *A Fish Called Wanda*, directed by Charles Chichton.

25 OCTOBER

1854: The Charge of the Light Brigade

The famous charge by British cavalry at the Battle of Balaklava during the Crimean War took place. The Light Brigade thought it was attacking an isolated Russian fort, but in fact the horsemen rode into heavy artillery. The Russians immediately fired cannon at them and slaughtered 478 of the 673 British soldiers. Britain and France were both allies of the collapsing Ottoman Empire, trying to prevent Russia from gaining a foothold in the Balkans and an increased presence in the Black Sea. The Crimean War, which lasted from 1853-56, cost 4600 British lives and an additional 17 500 died from disease. Because of political incompetence in the war, the British government fell in 1855, although the Allies went on to victory. It was the first war with war correspondents. Florence Nightingale's ministering to the Crimean wounded led to her founding of the first nursing school in London in 1860. It gave us the balaclava (a knitted head and neck helmet) and the poem 'The Charge of the Light Brigade', by Alfred, Lord Tennyson, which made him famous:

Someone had blunder'd;
Theirs not to make reply,
Theirs not to reason why,
Theirs but to do or die:
Into the valley of Death
Rode the six hundred.

1962: John Steinbeck

The American author was awarded a Nobel Prize for Literature. He published several books and stories about his native California, before his first really successful novel, *Tortilla Flat*. This was followed by *Of Mice and Men*. His work explores the relationship of people to the soil and in *The Grapes of Wrath* he brought the public's attention to the plight of impoverished farm workers in California: 'Man … grows beyond his work, walks up the stairs of his concepts, emerges ahead of his accomplishments.' He died in 1968.

1920 Greek King Alexander 1 died from a pet monkey bite, age 27.

1920 The Lord Mayor of Cork, Terence MacSwiney was also an Irish Republican Army leader. He died in prison after a 74-day hunger strike. He was serving a two-year prison sentence for possessing seditious documents.

1926 Galina Vishnevskaya a leading Moscow Opera soprano was born. She married Mstislav Rostropovich and was forced into exile with him in the USA for their support of dissident Soviet writer Alexander Solyzhenitsyn.

1991 Kazakhstan became independent from the USSR. It is a national holiday.

American novelist John Steinbeck (1902 - 1968) in portrait from 1930.

26 OCTOBER

1685: Domenico Scarlatti

The operatic composer was born in Naples, Italy. He was the sixth of ten children of the famous musician Alessandro Scarlatti. His father taught him and helped his son seek patronage and commissions from courts, such as the Medicis. Scarlatti wrote his first operas at the age of 17. He moved frequently for his work, to Rome, Venice, Palermo and the Vatican. In 1717 Scarlatti resorted to legal action against his domineering father to allow him to be independent. His work was both sacred and secular. He wrote over 500 sonatas (mainly for the harpsichord), oratorios and cantatas, mainly for the gifted Princess Maria Barbara of the Spanish court, where he lived for 28 years. He later wove Spanish dance, gypsy and folk rhythms into his music. He died in 1757 in Madrid.

1938: Last Cab

The last functioning Hansom cab was taken out of service in Dunedin, New Zealand. Before automobiles and taxicabs, people travelled by horse and carriage and usually in a Hansom cab. Its inventor Joseph Hansom had first patented his two-wheeled, one-horse, enclosed cab in the 1800s. The carriage was two-wheeled, with one horse and had an enclosed cab. The driver, brandishing a whip, was seated above and behind the passengers. It became popular worldwide.

1985: Uluru Returned

The freehold title to the ancestral lands around Uluru (formerly Ayer's Rock) in Central Australia, passed back to its Aboriginal owners, the Anangu. The tribe then leased it back to the National Parks and Wildlife Service. It is an Australian icon. It looks like a giant sandstone 'iceberg,' looming out of the never-ending sand plains of southwest Northern Territory. It is 70 million years old and is sacred to Aborigines. It is the world's second largest monolith, rising 862.5m above sea level. Its base circumference is 9.4 km. It has smooth sloping sides from weather and water erosion. It attracts 600 000 visitors per year and although to climb to the top of Uluru is akin to climbing a sacred church like Westminster Abbey or Notre Dame, nearly half of all visitors do so. It was listed as a site of World Heritage in 1987.

1825 American canal: the 350-mile Erie Canal was opened. It took eight years to construct. It provided water transportation between the East Coast and the Great Lakes.

1919 Tractors began replacing farm labour in the USA.

1994 Jordan and Israel made peace after 46 years of fighting over an area known as Wadi Araba on their border.

2000 Mad cow: When the long-awaited inquiry into 'Mad Cow Disease' was released in Great Britain, it criticized bureaucrats for having withheld information from the public about risks to humans.

A butcher in London's Smithfield meat market places a notice informing customers of the ban on sales of beef on the bone, including popular t-bone steaks and roast ribs, imposed to counter the threat of 'mad cow' disease spreading to humans. Agriculture Minister Jack Cunningham imposed the ban, because of fears that bovine spongiform encephalopathy (BSE) can be transmitted through the bone and marrow of cattle.

27 OCTOBER

1914: Dylan Thomas

The Welsh poet was born in Swansea. He published 18 poems when he was 19-years-old. He had a special affinity for his birth-place, its people and the countryside. In 1954, he wrote the radio play *Under Milk Wood* which celebrates the characters and the language of the seaside town. He wrote, 'Now as I was young and easy under the apple boughs/About the lilting house and happy as the grass was green.' His short story collections were *Portrait of the Artist as a Young Dog* and *Adventures in the Skin Trade*. Thomas died in New York while on a speaking tour of America aged 39 in 1953. Much of his work was released posthumously, such as 'Quite Early One Morning' and 'A Child's Christmas in Wales'.

1939: Albert Wendt

The Pacific region's leading writer was born in Western Samoa. He attended school in New Zealand and launched a teaching career, first in Samoa and then in Fiji. He identifies three 'homes' in Samoa, Fiji and New Zealand and has been influenced by the ethnicities of each, especially by their language and mythology. His first novel, *Sons of the Return Home*, has never been out of print. Wendt writes short stories, plays and poetry and is also an artist.

1962: Dawn Fraser

The Australian Olympian was the first woman to swim 100m freestyle in under one minute. She held the 100m freestyle world record for 16 years. She also held 39 world records and was the first swimmer to win the same event in three consecutive Olympics. 'Our Dawn' was born into a poor family in Sydney, the youngest of eight children. She won enthusiastic public sup-port for her anti-authoritarian behaviour. However, when she tried to steal an official flag at the Tokyo Olympics she was banned from swimming for ten years. Fraser served in the NSW Parliament from 1988-91. She was selected as Australia's greatest female athlete in 1988 and was the first female inducted into the Australian Sports Hall of Fame.

1925 James Buchanan Duke died aged 68. He was born in extreme poverty, but became one of the world's richest men through tobacco.

1939 English comedian John Cleese was born in Weston-Super-Mare. He appeared in *Monty Python's Flying Circus*, *Fawlty Towers* and *A Fish Called Wanda*.

1972 The National Black Theatre debuted in Sydney with *Basically Black*.

1991 Turkmenistan became independent from the USSR. It is a national holiday.

South Australian Dawn Fraser, the 1956 world record holder for the women's 110 yards (100m) freestyle (1min 4.5 seconds) and the women's 220 yards (200m) freestyle (2 min 21.2 secs).

28 OCTOBER

1955: Bill Gates

The world's richest man was born in Seattle. Gates had boasted that he would be a millionaire by the age of 25. He was raised strictly and was encouraged to read, with no television on school nights. When he was 13, the Teletype company connected his school to a mainframe computer. He soon learned the programming language BASIC. He loved computers and wrote game programs. With his fellow classmate, Paul Allen, later co-founder of Microsoft and the third wealthiest man in the world, they sometimes hacked into the system. They began doing computer work for hire and Gates imagined a world where everyone had their own personal computer. They wrote the first operating system for a PC, Microsoft, when he was 19. With his parents' permission, he dropped out of Harvard to pursue his dream. He convinced IBM to install Microsoft on their PCs and by 1987 he was a billionaire. Microsoft is installed on 75 per cent of all personal computers.

2003: Little Macca

The *Daily Mirror* newspaper ran a front-page banner, 'It's a boy! Exclusive-Macca baby a month early.' Macca, as Sir Paul McCartney is known in the press and his wife Heather, actually had a baby girl, named Beatrice Milly. The **Daily Mirror** hazarded a guess in their 'exclusive' that the baby boy might be named Joseph after Macca's uncle. The *Mirror's* sister paper, the *Scottish Daily Record*, provided the scoop. The editor said that they got their information from a 'very good source.' This was the second baby gender media case. When David and Victoria Beckham were having their second child, the international press decided that Victoria would be having a girl. She gave birth to their son, Romeo.

2004: Socrates

Brazil's famed soccer player, aged 50, came out of retirement to play for a tiny amateur team at Garforth, West Yorkshire. Socrates was a midfielder who captained Brazil in 1982 and 1986. He agreed to play for free. He expected to be joined by other retired leading players, Careca, Zico and Juninho. The coach said Socrates was in great shape and while smoking was not permitted 'on his time', he would probably make an exception for the world-famous player.

1927 Dame Cleo Laine, singer and actress, was born in Middlesex. She is the only singer nominated for a Grammy in jazz, pop, and classical. She is married to her bandmaster John Dankworth.

1960 Great Britain's first urban motorway, the M62 opened in Manchester.

1967 Actress Julia Roberts was born in Smyrna, Georgia. She won an Oscar for *Erin Brockovich*, and also appeared in *Mystic Pizza* and *Pretty Woman*.

1969 The Aga Khan, the spiritual head of the Moslems, married England's Sarah Crocker Poole. Poole took the name Begum Salima, and converted to Islam.

Microsoft Chairman Bill Gates speaks to government officials and business leaders from Canada, United States and Latin America in 2005. Gates announced that Microsoft has signed a partnership agreement with the Trust for the Americas, a non-profit affiliate of the Organization of American States (OAS), to provide technology and workforce skills training to youth and adults with disabilities in Latin America.

29 OCTOBER

1929: Black Tuesday

The Great Depression started in America, caused by too much price speculation on Wall Street. Analysts saw the ominous signs and warned that the buying sprees could not be sustained. There was simply too much credit and too little equity and real money. Some prices were as high as 150 times above earnings during the carefree, roaring twenties. On 26 October, just four days before investors were telling their brokers to 'sell at any price,' President Herbert Hoover said America 'was on a sound and prosperous foundation'. The economy collapsed. Businesses and life savings disappeared. Thirty million people worldwide lost their jobs. When Hoover ran for re-election, saying that the economy would right itself, Franklin D Roosevelt, won. FDR saw the need for government intervention. His programs put people to work, on the hydroelectric Tennessee Valley Authority and the Works Progress Administration.

1982: A Dingo Stole My Baby

Lindy Chamberlain's trial for her nine-week-old baby Azaria's 1980 death ended, with a sentence of life imprisonment with hard labour. It had attracted worldwide attention and was described as Australia's 'trial of the century'. Chamberlain was accused of slitting her baby's throat in her family car at an Uluru (Ayer's Rock) campsite. An original inquest supported Chamberlain's claim that a dingo snatched Azaria from their tent after Azaria's jumpsuit was found near a dingo's lair a week later. Analysts were puzzled by a lack of dingo saliva on the suit and the lack of blood in the tent, so she was tried. The press slanted their coverage. Chamberlain and her husband, the Reverend Michael Chamberlain, were described as not 'showing the expected emotions' grieving parents 'should.' Reporters wrote it was peculiar to take a baby camping. No motive was given for the 'murder.' Chamberlain's sentence tore Australia apart. She twice appealed her conviction and lost. Four years into her prison sentence, her baby's jacket was found in an isolated area near Uluru. Chamberlain was released. In 1995 another inquest returned an open verdict. In July 2004, a man said he shot the dingo carrying Azaria's body but did not tell police because he was afraid. The story has inspired an opera and movies, including one starring Meryl Streep and Sam Neill, *A Cry in the Dark* (1988).

1618 Sir Walter Raleigh was executed for disobeying orders. He explored both American continents.

1923 Turkey celebrates the founding of its Republic with a national holiday.

1923 The Charleston show *Runnin' Wild*, which introduced the dance, opened on Broadway.

1926 Canadian operatic tenor Jon Vickers was born at Prince Albert, Saskatchewan. He was highly acclaimed worldwide. He retired in 1988.

1971 American actress Winona Ryder was born in Winona, Minnesota. She has appeared in *Little Women, Girl, Interrupted* and *Beetlejuice*.

Members of the American section of the Salvation Army operate a soup kitchen outdoors in a vacant lot during the Great Depression in 1931.

30 OCTOBER

1948: Garry McDonald

One of Australia's favourite personalities, honoured as a Living National Treasure, was born. He hosted the Rip Snorters Show and the hilarious *Norman Gunston Show*, in which the 'Little Aussie Bleeder' interviewed celebrities and superstars alike, with toilet paper stuck to his 'shaving cuts'. Never stepping out of character, he once flustered the 'Iron Lady' Margaret Thatcher by asking if she had a drinking problem, when she refused to answer his questions about Ireland. He was perfectly cast as Arthur Beare in the ABC sitcom *Mother and Son*, opposite Ruth Cracknell. After her death in 2002, he suffered a serious breakdown and was hospitalised for depression and anxiety, which he talked about openly. He is also a stage actor and movie star. His performance in *Struck by Lightning* won him the 1990 Sydney Film Critics' Award for Best Actor.

1938: War of the Worlds

An American radio station, entertaining listeners with a program on classic books, was interrupted by 'news flashes' as Orson Welles and the Mercury Players read HG Wells' *War of the Worlds*. Some listeners thought that Martians really had invaded! The book, written in 1898, was a rivetting science fiction account of a Martian invasion of New Jersey. Welles, known as The Shadow's Voice, introduced the story and three announcements during program tried to ensure the public knew it was 'just a story.' When Welles read that the Martians 'landed' in Princeton, New Jersey, people 'saw' Martians everywhere. New Yorkers fled from highrises with handkerchiefs over their noses against 'Martian gas.' Hospitals were overwhelmed with traumatised patients.

1995: Quebec Stays Canadian

The citizens of Quebec voted on a secession referendum. A strong Separatist movement wanted Quebec to secede from Canada, to preserve its French identity. The vote was 50.6 per cent to 49.4 per cent to stay within the Federation. Today Canada is a bilingual nation, with English and French as official languages.

1786 Philippe de Gaspe, who wrote the first most important French-Canadian book *Les Anciens Canadien*, was born at Quebec City. He died in 1871.

1820 Canadian geologist Sir John William Dawson was born in Pictou, Nova Scotia. He worked mainly with fossils, of all sizes and species. He also promoted the expansion of Canada's scientific institutions. He died in 1899.

1925 Scottish inventor John L Baird performed the first wireless broadcast of moving objects. It used a cathode ray tube. Baird called his invention 'television.'

1957 The British House of Lords unveiled plans to admit women peers.

1997 Bill Berry shocked his fans when he left the enormously successful band REM. A drum machine replaced him.

The irrepressible Norman Gunstan, aka Garry McDonald, interviews a slightly flustered Zsa Zsa Gabor for the *Norman Gunstan Show* in 1978.

31 OCTOBER

1926: Harry Houdini

The legendary magician, illusionist and escape artist died, aged 52. A Hungarian, whose birth name was Ehrich Weiss, he was an unrivalled showman. He was an athlete, expert on the history of magic, a lecturer and he also liked to expose frauds. Houdini would have himself handcuffed and locked inside coffins or boxes and even lowered underwater and to the public's astonishment, he would free himself. His acts had dramatic names, such as The Upside Down Water Torture. He died in a freak accident in 1926, after boasting to some Montreal students that his stomach muscles could withstand heavy blows. However, he did not have a chance to ready himself before a student hit him without warning, rupturing his appendix. Despite his pain, he performed in Detroit that night. He was hospitalised after the show and died from peritonitis.

1950: John Candy

The roly-poly Canadian movie star was born in Toronto, Canada. His first big break was as a member of the famed Second City comedy troupe. He starred in a wide variety of movies that the public loved—from *Cool Runnings*, to *Spaceballs*, *Uncle Buck* and *The Blues Brothers*. He owned a chain of blues bars with fellow actors Dan Aykroyd and Jim Belushi. He had a serious weight problem, which may have contributed to his sudden death in 1994.

1961: Peter Jackson

The self-taught movie director was born in Pukerua Bay, New Zealand. He is best known for his adaptation of JR Tolkien's classic books, *The Lord of the Rings*. Filmed in New Zealand, the third installment, *Fellowship of the Ring*, won three Oscars, for Best Picture, Art Direction and Writing. His wife, Fran Walsh, is the screenwriter. She calls him a hobbit, because he is short, stocky and shaggy. His success was the first time a director had won three Oscars since James L Brooks. Jackson's first foray into movies was into horror. His homemade *Bad Taste* is a cult classic. He is remaking *King Kong*. Other successes are *Heavenly Creatures*, *Meet the Feebles* and *Dead Alive*.

1895 The great Australian boxer James Leslie 'Les' Darcy was born. He became a legend when he won both middleweight and heavyweight titles. He sought fame and fortune in the USA but died from an infection from dental problems, aged 22.

1896 William Virgin arrived in Brisbane after bicycling from Perth, Western Australia. It took him 60 days.

1899 Australian troops left for the Boer War in South Africa. It had broken out between Britain and the Transvaal on 11 October.

2003 Malaysian Prime Minister Mahathir Mohamad, who oversaw his country's emergence from an impoverished nation to a high-tech country, stepped down. He had led his country for half its history since independence in 1957.

Hungarian-born magician Harry Houdini (1874 - 1926), aka Ehrich Weiss, is strapped into a leather straight jacket by three men in 1915.

1 NOVEMBER

1 NOVEMBER

1935: Gary Player

The pro golfer was born in Johannesburg, South Africa, the son of a miner. Ranking first in total professional wins, Player is one of the most successful golfers of all time. Player began his golf career at age 17, winning the Grand Slam about a decade later. One of only five golfers to win the Grand Slam, Player is the only person in the 20th century to win the British Open in three different decades. Among his many victories are winning the British and US Open along with the Professional Golfers' Association title. He became the first non-American citizen to win the Masters in 1961 and went on to win twice more. Player is also an entrepreneur and businessman, designing golf courses and marketing apparel. The Player Foundation promotes education in South Africa and abroad.

1970: Nightclub Inferno 'Wipes Out a Generation'

A nightclub fire in France killed 142 people, most of them teenagers. The club was packed with revellers, almost all of them were from the close-knit town of St Laurent du Pont, near Grenoble. Nearly every family suffered a loss.

2003: Sulky Veteran

Herve Filion was the first North American to reach 15 000 harness (sulky) wins. He set his record with Seagrove at Dover Downs and in the next race guided Anaheim to his 15 001 win. Filion led his closest rival by almost 4 000 wins. He became a member of the Canadian Sports Hall of Fame at just 29 years old and six years later he was the youngest person ever inducted into the American Harness Racing Hall of Fame. Filion was the first French–Canadian named French Athlete of the World. He learned to ride as a child on an Angers, Quebec farm and won his first harness race at age 13. Filion was forced to sit out seven seasons from 1995 to 2002 after allegations of race fixing, a charge he adamantly denied. He had racked up over 14 000 purses and US$85-million in prize money. In 2003, aged 62, he was fit and back in the saddle again, winning races and adding to his record of more races than any other person in history. He said that his secret was to just to 'follow the horse.'

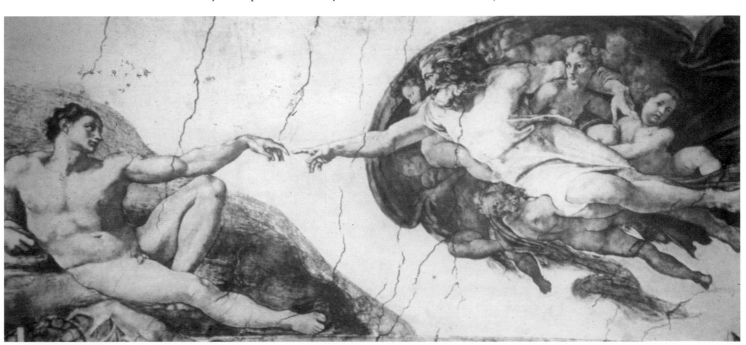

1512 Sistine Chapel opens. Michelangelo's ceiling in the Sistine Chapel, Rome, one of his finest works, is exhibited to the public for the first time.
1870 Christopher Brennan, the Australian poet and critic, was born in Sydney. He was a classical scholar whose work such as *XX1 Poems: Towards The Source* was loved by critics, but never found public popularity.
1884 Prime Meridian was set to create world time zones at Greenwich, England
1925 Harold S Vanderbilt and his friends invented the game of contract bridge, while they were waiting to transit the Panama Canal.
1951 Jacques Plante, Montreal goalie, invented the hockey mask, which has saved many players' teeth.
1981 Antigua and Barbuda celebrate independence from Great Britain. It is a national holiday.

Detail of the ceiling of the Sistine Chapel shows the *Creation of Adam*, a panel in the massive narrative work by Italian artist Michelangelo Buonarroti, completed between 1508 and 1512, in the Vatican City.

2 NOVEMBER

1922: QANTAS Flies

The first regular air service was established by the tiny Queensland and Northern Territory Aerial Service (QANTAS) between two remote Queensland towns, Charleville and Cloncurry. Flight was very important to Australians because of the extreme distances and isolation. The routes expanded to the Northern Territory and to other states. QANTAS grew from these humble origins into a major international airline. QANTAS began its international service from Australia to England in 1934.

1961: kd lang

The singer was born in Consort, Alberta, Canada. Kathryn Dawn Lang became interested in music from an early age and played the piano and the guitar while growing up. She played in The Reclines in the 1980s, before moving to New York City to pursue a recording album. Lang's staunch stand, for gay rights and vegetarianism, with her androgynous style, spiky hair and alternative lifestyle made her the antithesis of country music. Many country radio stations refused to play her music. However, in 1988 she won a Grammy award for her country vocals and won again the following year. By 1992, Lang's style shifted and she won another Grammy for pop vocals. Her Grammy award winning single 'Constant Craving' became her most popular song, selling millions and winning new fans. In 1996, Lang received her nation's highest honour for lifetime achievement when she became an Officer of the Order of Canada.

2000: International Space Station

The first resident crew of the orbiting *International Space Station* (ISS) arrived. The crew of two Russian cosmonauts and one American astronaut was launched from the Kazakhstan site that had launched *Sputnik 1* in 1957. They stayed for four months conducting experiments. Since then, crews have lived aboard the ISS almost continuously, learning how humans adapt to space. More international projects are planned. *Jules Verne*, the European Space Agency's automated supply ship, will dock at the ISS in late 2005. The Japanese Aerospace Exploration Agency is also developing an unmanned supply ship, which ISS's robotic arm will capture and connect to Node 2.

1885 Harlow Shapley, astronomer, 'The Modern Copernicus' was born. He discovered the Sun's position in the galaxy. He predicted that our Milky Way's galaxy's size was far larger than astronomers believed.

1913 Burt Lancaster, distinguished actor, was born in New York City. He began his career as an acrobat. He starred in more than eighty movies, including *From Here to Eternity* and received an Oscar for his role in *Elmer Gantry*. He died in 1994.

1947 Aviator Howard Hughes set a record with his world's largest plane, the 200-ton plywood flying *Spruce Goose* airplane. It flew just once.

1957 A titanium mill opened in Toronto, Ohio, the first in America to roll and forge titanium. Titanium is used extensively in hip, knee and other body implants.

Canadian musician kd lang performs at the 'Never Follow' bash in June 2003 at Gotham Hall in New York City.

3 NOVEMBER

1920: Oodgeroo Noonuccal

The Indigenous author was born on ancestral land at North Stradbroke Island, Queensland. She worked as a child-domestic. Under her Anglo name, Kath Walker, she published her first poetry book, *We Are Going*, in 1964. It was the first published writing by an Aboriginal woman and sold out in three days. Noonuccal received many awards for her activism and was made a Member of the British Empire (MBE). In 1988 she returned her MBE before the Australian Bicentenary, saying that she could not accept it with a clear conscience. 'The forbidding of tribal language, murders, poisoning, scalping, denial of land custodianship, destruction of sacred places ... 1988 marks 200 years of rape and carnage, all these terrible things that the Aboriginal tribes of Australia have suffered without any recognition even of admitted guilt from the Parliaments of England ... from the Aboriginal point of view, what is there to celebrate?' She published about 13 books of poetry and legends before her death in 1993.

1943: John Newfong

One of the first Aboriginal journalists was born near Brisbane. He wrote for newspapers such as *The Australian*, *The Bulletin*, *The Guardian* and the *South China Post*. In the 1970s, he edited *Identity*, a magazine for Indigenous Australians. An activist, he was considered both a brilliant writer and a mellifluous orator. He was one of the key figures to set up an Aboriginal Tent Embassy in Canberra to protest about Aboriginal rights. He died in 1999.

1967 Alexander Aitken

The famed New Zealand mathematician died. He spent most of his career at Edinburgh University. Aitken was born in Dunedin and did poorly in arithmetic until he was a teenager. He suddenly 'saw' numbers from a different viewpoint. He trained his memory 'like a Brahmin Yoga' practices meditation. He could multiply two nine digit numbers in his head and recite Pi to 707 decimals places. He could also render fractions to 26 decimal places in less than five seconds, for example 4/47 as a decimal was point 08510638297872340425531914. Aitken paid a price for his extraordinary memory, as he constantly and vividly relived the horrors of the WWI battlefields he had fought on.

1843 Lord Nelson's 5m high statue was manoeuvred in two sections to the top of its Trafalgar Square column for assembly.

1903 William Einthoven, Dutch scientist, publicly discussed his new electrocardiograph, a device to monitor blood flow in the heart.

1912 Ponche and Prinard, French inventors, flew the first all-metal plane.

1992 William Jefferson Clinton won the 1992 American Presidential election, achieving his boyhood dream.

Arkansas Governor Bill Clinton comforts Hillary Rodham Clinton on the set of the news program *60 Minutes* after a stage light unexpectedly broke loose from the ceiling and knocked her down in January 1992. Within a year he was President Clinton.

4 NOVEMBER

1922: King Tut

One of the most important archaeological discoveries of all time was made in Luxor, Egypt, when British archaeologist Howard Carter discovered the tomb and mummified body of the child-king Tutankhamen. Tut ruled from age ten to his death at 18. Tut's 3500 year-old tomb was discovered nearly intact, in contrast to the other Pharaoh's tombs which had been plundered.

1941: Charles Upham

The gallant New Zealander was presented with his first Victoria Cross for his exploits in Crete, in World War II. The Victoria Cross is the British Commonwealth's highest award for exceptional bravery. Born in 1908 in Christchurch, he worked as a farm valuer until 1939, when he enlisted in the 2nd New Zealand Expeditionary Force. His leadership and bravery under fire gained Upham his first Cross. He won it again in 1942 when, after leading his company into a major attack, Upham was shot through the elbow. He refused to quit. Alone, he detonated a German tank and killed several soldiers, while shepherding his men to safety. Upham was captured and held in the infamous Colditz fortress. After his release, the modest hero returned home where awed citizens had raised £10 000 for him. He refused the money, suggesting it be used for scholarships for children of deceased soldiers. He was the only combat soldier to win the Victoria Cross and one of the only three people to receive the Victoria Cross twice. Some say he deserved ten Victoria Crosses. Upham died in 1994.

2004: Arundhati Roy

The Indian author and activist received the Sydney Peace Prize for her dedication to advancing social equality, anti-nuclear activism and advocacy of non-violence. She donated the $50 000 prize to Indigenous Australians. Roy was born to a Hindu father and Christian mother in 1959 in Assam India. Roy's mother was a prominent social activist. Roy moved to Delhi at 16 and lived in a small hut, surrounded by poverty and illiteracy, which made a deep impact. She studied architecture, then film-making, before becoming a writer. Her first novel, *The God of Small Things,* won the 1997 Man Booker Prize. Translated into more than 30 languages, it was on the *New York Times* bestseller list for a year. She also writes essays and political works, such as *Power Politics* and *An Ordinary Person's Guide to Empire*.

1862 Eden Philpotts, prolific English poet, playwright and novelist was born in Rajasthan, India. He wrote more than 100 novels, including *The Farmer's Wife.*

1909 Sergei Rachmaninoff, the composer and pianist, made his American debut, choosing a university, Smith College, as his venue.

1946 The United Nations Educational, Scientific and Cultural Organization (UNESCO) was founded.

1970 Rapper Puff Daddy (Sean Combs) was born in New York City. His titles include *No Way Out* and *Back for Good Now.*

1996 The Spice Girls' debut album *Spice* was released. It sold 28 million copies.

Indian author Arundhati Roy is presented with the 29th Booker Prize for Fiction for her book *The God of Small Things* in London in October 1997.

5 NOVEMBER

1879: James Clerk Maxwell

The Scottish physicist died, aged 47. He was born in Edinburgh in 1831 and was known for his pioneering work in electricity, optics, astronomy and magnetism. Maxwell published his first paper at age 14. One of Maxwell's first achievements was showing Saturn's rings were made of a series of small solid particles. Studying colour, he showed that colour photographs could be made with filters of red, green and blue. He also described the behaviour of electric and magnetic fields. He calculated that the speed of propagation of an electromagnetic field is approximately that of the speed of light. He demonstrated that light is an electromagnetic wave, which paved the way for quantum mechanics. Albert Einstein called Maxwell the 'most profound and the most fruitful (physicist) since the time of Newton'. The world's largest telescope, in Hawaii, is named after him.

1913: Vivien Leigh

The actress was born near Darjeeling, India. Her pregnant mother spent 15 minutes every day gazing at the Himalayas so their beauty would be passed to her baby. Her family moved to England and at seven years old, Vivian went to the theatre for the first time. She insisted on seeing the same play sixteen times and decided she wanted to be an actress. Her first casting was in a small role opposite Laurence Olivier. They married and for twenty years performed on stage and screen together. At age 26 she won an Oscar for Best Actress in *Gone With The Wind*. She won again for *A Streetcar Named Desire*. Her life unravelled in her thirties, when she had two miscarriages, was divorced and was diagnosed with tuberculosis and manic depression. She died from tuberculosis in 1967 at the age of 53.

1991: Robert Maxwell

The media magnate died in mysterious circumstances when he disappeared from his yacht near the Canary Islands. There was speculation he committed suicide. Maxwell was born into extreme poverty in Czechoslovakia. His parents were Orthodox Jews who were Nazi victims. After World War II, he moved to Berlin and published scientific journals. His meteoric rise in the media industry led to him eventually becoming a billionaire. Owner of *The Mirror*, Maxwell served in Parliament from 1964–70. After his disappearance, it was discovered that he had misappropriated millions of pounds from company pension plans, leaving thousands of retirees penniless.

1893 Raymond Loewy, French industrial designer, was born in Paris. He said, 'Between two products equal in price, function and quality, the better looking product will outsell the other.' He had enormous influence on product and logo design. He died in 1986.

1906 At 1.30 pm physicist Marie Curie made history when she gave her inaugural lecture at the Sorbonne University. She was its first female lecturer.

1977 Guy Lombardo, Canadian bandleader, died aged 75. He was born in London, Ontario. With his Royal Canadians, his rendition of 'Auld Lang Syne 'is a New Year's Eve staple. He sold over 100 million records.

1992 *Nature* magazine reported that traces of 5000 year old beer in a pottery vessel were found at an Iranian Sumerian archeological site.

2003 The final episode of the movie *The Matrix (The Matrix Revolutions)* was released in theatres worldwide at 9 am.

British actress Vivien Leigh (1913–1967) as the tempestuous Scarlett O'Hara, the Academy-award-winning part she played in *Gone With the Wind*, directed by Victor Fleming in 1939.

6 NOVEMBER

1810: Rum Hospital

How many cities can boast owning a hospital paid for by alcohol? Sydney's Rum Hospital was built from rum revenues. The Governor, Lachlan Macquarie, signed a contract on this day with Alexander Riley and Garnham Blaxcel, giving the partners a monopoly on rum importation into the New South Wales Colony, as long as the two used some of the proceeds to build a hospital. The monopoly was for four years and for 205 000 litres. After 1814, rum was taxed with an import duty. Rum was a staple for the military and for visiting sailors. The Rum Hospital, a beautiful sandstone building, was completed in 1816. Two wings survive, housing the State Parliament and the Mint Museum.

1860: Ignace Jan Paderewski

The brilliant composer, pianist and Poland's third Polish Prime Minister was born in Kurylowka, Poland. Every major Polish city has a street named after him. His life alternated between phases of political activity, outspoken nationalism and his musical career. He began his musical education at the Warsaw Conservatory at the age of 12, becoming one of the most popular concert pianists and gifted composers of his era. In 1913 he settled in America and raised money for Polish victims of World War I through concerts. He represented Poland at the League of Nations and was elected Prime Minister of the newly independent Poland in 1919. After four years, Paderewski returned to concert life. During World War II he became head of the Polish National Council, Poland's Government-in-Exile in London. While Paderewski was touring to raise money, he died suddenly in America in 1941. He was buried at Arlington National Cemetery, but once Poland became a free country, his remains were reburied there in 1992.

1908: Final Spike

Premier Sir Joseph Ward drove the last spike of the main railroad between Wellington and Auckland, linking the two major cities of the North Island of New Zealand. Service began three days later. It had taken twenty-three years to build the 685.5km line. It was constructed primarily by hand, with dynamite, picks, shovels, horses and oxen. Construction was extremely difficult, because of the rough mountainous terrain and deep ravines. The line contributed significantly to the development of the Central North Island.

1938 Italy, under fascist rule, instituted race laws against Jews. All students were expelled from school and from public office.

1949 English actor Nigel Havers was born in London. He appeared in *Chariots of Fire* and *Empire of the Sun.*

1999 Australia's referendum to replace the monarchy with a republic was defeated by 54.87 per cent to 45.13 per cent.

2004 Johnny Warren, Australia's beloved 'Captain Socceroo', died. He was part of the only Australian team to play in a World Cup, in 1974, and captained the team from 1967–70. He was given a state funeral in Sydney.

Blockade ships, sunk by the Egyptians during the battle for the Suez Canal, lying at the canal entrance in Port Said, originally published in *Picture Post* in 1956.

7 NOVEMBER

1917: October Revolution

The Bolsheviks installed Vladimir Lenin as Russia's first Premier. Russia used the Julian calendar and historians still call Lenin's installation the 'October Revolution'. The Bolsheviks seized power from a provisional government in a carefully planned coup. The provisional government had forcefully replaced Tsar Nicholas II. Along with Nicholas's autocratic government, Russia had suffered terribly in World War II. There was widespread corruption and massive food shortages, which led to peasants seizing land igniting the Revolution. The young revolutionary implemented sweeping Communist reforms based on Karl Marx's theories. Lenin, however, could not prevent the civil war, which broke out in 1918 killing millions. Lenin's goal was to spread socialism worldwide, but he died in 1924. One of the most ruthless dictators in history, Joseph Stalin, gained control.

1926: Dame Joan Sutherland

The celebrated soprano was born in Sydney. Her mother taught her voice and piano as a child. Sutherland won a top Australian vocal competition and moved to London to study. She debuted at the Royal Opera House in 1952 in *Die Zauberflote*. She married conductor Richard Bonynge. Sutherland's repertoire of roles and powerful voice made her the leading coloratura soprano in 20th century opera. Her career took her around the world, where she sang at leading opera houses. Her signature role is probably Lucia, in *Lucia di Lammemoor*. Her last performance was at Covent Garden in 1990 in *Die Fledermaus*.

1943: Joni Mitchell

The Canadian singer, songwriter and guitarist was born in McLeod, Alberta, Canada. Her birth name was Roberta Joan Anderson. Mitchell began her career singing in coffeehouses. When she became pregnant in 1965, she gave up her daughter for adoption. Her first major album, *Joni Mitchell*, resonated with the times, launching Mitchell into her long career as a rock performer. Her poetic lyrics and wide-ranging voice, covering more than four octaves, produced an unforgettable sound. Mitchell was reunited with her daughter in 1997. She was inducted into the Rock and Roll Hall of Fame in 1997. In 2002 Mitchell won a lifetime achievement Grammy as 'one of the most important female recording artists of the rock era'.

1861 The Melbourne Cup, one of the world's most famous horse races, was run for the first time. Archer, ridden by J Cutts, won.

1863 The first indoor athletic meet was held in Ashburnham Hall, London, featuring four running events.

1885 The last spike was driven at Craigellachie, British Columbia, for the Canadian Pacific Railroad.

1910 Irishman Victor Herbert, one of the world's greatest operetta composers, premiered his *Naughty Marietta*, his sixth. It is still very popular.

1918 Evangelist Billy Graham was born in Charlotte, North Carolina.

Canadian musician Joni Mitchell in an image shot for the fashion magazine *Vogue* in November 1968.

8 NOVEMBER

1895: X-Ray Roentgen

Wilhelm Roentgen discovered x-rays. While working in his University of Wurzburg laboratory, he detected radiation being emitted by cathode ray tubes. He called them x-rays because 'x' is the mathematical symbol for the unknown. A few weeks later, the first X-ray photograph was made of a woman's hand. Physicians quickly realised that x-rays could detect broken bones and foreign objects in the bodies, such as bullets or coins. Roentgen won the first Nobel Prize for Physics. He was born at Lennep, Prussia, in 1845 and died Munich in 1923.

1922: New Heart Doctor

Christiaan N Barnard, the pioneering heart surgeon, was born in Beaufort West, South Africa. After receiving his medical degree from the University of Cape Town, he studied for a doctorate at the University of Minnesota Medical School. He was appointed director of surgical research at the Groote Schuur Hospital, South Africa. After spending years experimenting with animal heart transplants, Barnard performed the world's first human heart transplant operation in 1967. Grocer Louis Washkansky, age 55, was dying after a series of heart attacks and took two minutes to make up his mind to be experimented on. The donor was a car accident victim. The nine-hour operation was successful but Washkansky died eighteen days later due to unexpected immuno-suppressant drug complications. The heart continued to beat strongly. Barnard's second patient survived for 19 months.

1958: The Hope Diamond

The valuable gem from India, which had become a symbol of bad luck, was donated to the Smithsonian Institution in Washington DC. Originally, it was a magnificent 112-carat steel-blue diamond, embedded in a statue of a Hindu god. It was stolen in 1642 by a thief who was mauled to death by wild dogs. French Queen Marie Antoinette acquired it and was sent to the guillotine in the French Revolution. The British banking firm that the jewel is named after purchased it and went bankrupt. The next owner, at the *Washington Post,* lost two adult children. Jeweller Harry Winston acquired it and donated it to the Smithsonian. By then it was only 44-carats and worth US$1.5 million.

1519 Hernan Cortes, Spanish Conquistador, arrived in Mexico's interior and took the Aztec emperor Montezuma prisoner.

1656 Edmund Halley, best known for the comet named after him, was born. He was the English Astronomer Royal and first observed the comet in 1682. He accurately predicted its return in 1758. It will return in 2061.

1942 Jockey Angel Cordero Jr was born in San Juan, Puerto Rico. On his retirement in 1992 he was placed second in career earnings, with over $164 million, and third in wins, 7076.

1975 The Comoro Islands became the 143rd member of the United Nations.

2003 Britain's Prince Edward, the Earl of Wessex and his wife, Countess Sophie, had a baby daughter. They named her Lady Louise Windsor.

Actress Michelle Pfeiffer wearing the legendary Hope Diamond.